THE INEVITABLE MILLIONAIRES

THE INEVITABLE MILLIONAIRES

By E. PHILLIPS OPPENHEIM

AUTHOR OF

"The Passionate Quest," "The Box with Broken Seals,"
"Curious Quest," "Michael's Evil Deeds," "The
Great Impersonation," "The Great Prince
Shan," "The Wrath to Come," etc.

A. L. BURT COMPANY

Publishers   New York

Published by arrangement with Little, Brown and Company

Printed in U. S. A.

Printed in the United States of America

THE INEVITABLE MILLIONAIRES

CHAPTER I

At precisely half-past eight o'clock, on a grey February morning, two amiable-looking, middle-aged gentlemen left a medium-sized house of comfortable appearance, in the neighbourhood of Hampstead, and commenced a walk undertaken by them daily, in the interests of health, with the exception of Sundays, public holidays and a fortnight in August. There was sufficient resemblance between the two to proclaim them brothers — at first sight, indeed, they might have been taken for twins. They were both about five feet five inches in height, they both had kindly, if somewhat insignificant faces, shrewd grey eyes, and tight, firm lips. Their names were Stephen and George Henry Underwood, and their ages respectively fifty-one and forty-eight. There were many who professed to be unable to tell them apart, and the differences between them were, in fact, scarcely noticeable. Stephen's brown moustache was, perhaps, a little scantier than his brother's and the obtruding note of grey was more obvious; the hair around his ears was a little more grizzled and there was a trifle less colour in his somewhat thinner cheeks. Otherwise the likeness between them was almost remarkable. They both wore broad-toed shoes, hand-sewn to order by a bootmaker in a remote alley situated in one of the backwaters of the City, dark business suits of unfashionable cut, differing only slightly in pattern and material, collars of antiquated shape, inoffensive ties and black bowler hats. They avoided in their attire both the flamboyant splendours of the professional City man and the sporting note affected by the stockbroker and his mate. They were City merchants, and they desired to dress as such.

They went through their usual little programme as they turned the corner of the street into the broader thoroughfare. George Henry looked up at the skies and down at his furled umbrella. They spoke always first of the weather.

" The rain will keep off, I think," George Henry remarked, glancing from his umbrella to the sky.

" I hope so," was the amiable reply. " There are plenty of clouds about, but they seem high."

" I wonder," George Henry surmised, " at what hour Mr. Duncan will send us the balance sheet."

" He promised it by midday," his brother reminded him. " If you have not returned from Mincing Lane, I shall not, of course, open it until you come."

" The result," George Henry observed a little nervously, " cannot fail to be satisfactory."

" There is no doubt whatever about that," Stephen agreed. " We have been very fortunate, George Henry."

" Very fortunate indeed, Stephen."

They walked steadily on until they reached the Park, which they crossed diagonally. They traversed Portland Place and the upper part of Regent Street. At Oxford Street they descended into the Tube and reached their offices in Basinghall Street as the clock was striking ten. The premises themselves were not imposing, but there was a suggestion of opulence in the spacious but murky warehouses behind. As they passed through the clerks' office they both raised their hats and said good morning, a greeting which was at once returned by three capable-looking clerks, a cashier, a manager and an office boy. Stephen glanced at one empty stool and frowned.

"Harold is late again, I see," he remarked as, arrived at their inner office, they divested themselves of their coats and hats.

George Henry sighed.

"I fear that his heart is not in the business," he said. "However, we must make allowances. He is young, very young."

"I am inclined to wish," Stephen continued, "that his father had chosen some other avocation for him. However, as it was his wish that he should enter this business, we must do our best, George Henry. If he does not settle down soon I should suggest that we send him out for a visit to one of our Burmese properties."

"He will probably find fewer distractions there," George Henry agreed.

Stephen was seated now before an immense pile of correspondence. His eyes glittered with anticipatory interest. He divided the pile neatly, and passed half across to his brother.

"It is hard to realize what distractions there can be to compare with those offered by the ramifications of a business such as ours," he observed.

"The boy is young," George Henry murmured tolerantly. "You must remember that we are getting to be old fogies, Stephen."

"Old fogies! Rubbish!" was the indignant denial. "You are only forty-eight, George Henry. You are a young man."

"And you," George Henry rejoined with spirit, "are only three years older. That is no difference at all. Three years do not count. We are practically of the same age. And as to being old fogies ——"

George Henry broke off in his speech and glanced for a moment out of the window. His thoughts travelled back along the course of his exceedingly well-ordered life, a life conducted with the utmost propriety, with the most rigorous monotony of good conduct. He had committed no foolish actions, he had never once been conscious of any desire to look into the land of adventure which lay somewhere on the westward side of that line drawn between Hampstead and the City. He was satisfied — perfectly satisfied — and yet, he was passing middle age, he was certainly becoming an old fogy. He suddenly recollected his task. Pencil in hand, he dealt with his pile of correspondence, making notes in the margin of each letter. As soon as they had finished their piles, they exchanged them. There was scarcely a comment made, each was always satisfied with his brother's decision. When they had come to an end, George Henry rose to his feet, took up his hat, put on his overcoat, drew on his gloves and departed for Mincing Lane. Stephen sent for his manager, his cashier, and his typist in turn. The business ran like a well-oiled machine.

At twelve o'clock, George Henry returned from Mincing Lane. Upon the desk in front of Stephen was a long legal envelope, inscribed with the name of the firm.

"The balance sheet has arrived from Mr. Duncan," Stephen announced. "Shall we examine it together?"

"It would be advisable to do so," George Henry agreed, taking off his coat and hat without undue haste.

It was Stephen who, by immemorial custom, cut open the sealed flap of the envelope and George Henry who stood by his side. They turned over the rustling pages and glanced at the figures announced as the final result with joint and breathless awe.

" We are millionaires," George Henry murmured.

" With a few thousands to the good. Our profits for last year, even after depreciating the Burmese properties, amount to one hundred and thirty thousand pounds."

" Incredible! "

" It is nevertheless true. The firm of Duncan and Company are the most careful accountants in the City. There is no possibility of any mistake."

The brothers looked at one another with the shame-faced air of schoolboys convicted of a misdemeanour. They were shrewd men of business and hard workers, but wealth such as this was almost beyond their desires.

" After all," George Henry, who was the optimist of the firm, pointed out hopefully, " we are only half a millionaire — I mean we are only a millionaire between us."

" It is impossible to escape from the fact," Stephen groaned, " that we are worth exactly five hundred and three thousand pounds each."

There was an awkward silence. The possession of such a sum was without doubt criminal. George Henry peered once more into the envelope.

" Here is a letter from Mr. Duncan," he announced.

" Read it," his brother begged.

George Henry adjusted with precision a pair of gold-rimmed eyeglasses upon his nose, cleared his throat and read:

17 Thrigmorton Street,
February 9.

DEAR SIRS,

    I enclose your annual balance sheet, upon which I will make no comment save to offer you — shall I say my wondering congratulations? Your stock in trade and securities have been depreciated to the fullest extent, and a sum of twenty thousand pounds for charities included in the profit and loss account.

I feel that the time has now arrived when it is my duty to forward to you the enclosed letter, left in my care by your late father, with instructions to pass it on to you under certain contingencies which have now arisen. I feel sure that you will do your best to realize your obligations in the matter.

Sincerely,
THEODORE DUNCAN.

"A letter from our father," Stephen murmured, gazing at the envelope.

"It is certainly his handwriting," George Henry declared.

They lingered for a moment over it, as one does over a communication from the dead. Then Stephen reverently cut the flap of the envelope and withdrew the enclosure. He read out its contents in a low tone:

MY DEAR SONS,

I am leaving you a business which, barring any great changes in the commercial world, seems to me likely to make you both, in a very short time, exceedingly rich men. I send you a few words of advice, begging you to avoid a certain mistake into which I feel that my perhaps too frugal habits have led me. You know the conditions under which you spent your boyhood — pleasant, I trust, but governed all the time by the most rigid economy. Up to these last days I believe I am correct in saying that I have never drawn from the business more than fifteen hundred pounds a year. I have had no expensive tastes to gratify, our charities are fixed by an ancient deed of partnership, and I have been happiest in the modest way of living to which I have been accustomed. Of late, however, I have seriously questioned the wisdom, the policy and the integrity of living upon the twentieth part of one's income. I have been convinced of a new truth. It is the duty of the man enjoying a large measure of prosperity to spend a reasonable proportion of his earnings.

I charge you, therefore, Stephen and George Henry, without waste or ostentation, yet with a certain lavishness, to disseminate amongst your fellow creatures a considerable portion of the income which I feel will accrue to you. Avoid the Stock Exchange or gambling upon horses. Do not speculate in any way unless the result of such speculation is likely to bring definite good to a deserving fellow creature. Without undue extravagance, try to find pleasures the gratification of which demands the spending of money. The art of spending is as difficult as the art of saving. I beg you both to cultivate it, so that, if your wealth should at any time become known to the world, you will avoid the, to me, entirely opprobrious epithet of " miser."

These are my last words to you, my sons, and I conclude with all love.

Your affectionate father,
STEPHEN UNDERWOOD.

Stephen laid down the letter.

" This is most disconcerting," he declared.

" A thunderbolt! " George Henry faltered.

" Our dear father must have arrived at these views quite late in life," Stephen ruminated. " I see that the letter is dated only a week or two before his death. It is a very serious charge that he lays upon us."

" Very serious indeed," George Henry assented in a tone of abject misery.

As men confronted with an unexpected crisis, they stood looking at each other helplessly. George Henry waited, as was his custom, for his brother's initiative.

"The charge upon us is one that we must accept," the latter declared firmly. "We must spend more money."

"A great deal more," George Henry echoed.

"We must change the whole routine of our life and our habits," Stephen continued dolefully.

"Entirely," his brother acquiesced with kindred dejection.

The senior partner in the firm of Underwood Brothers took down a small bowler hat from its peg and handed a similar article of apparel to his brother.

"We will begin with luncheon," he declared firmly.

The healthy colour faded from George Henry's cheeks. He was momentarily aghast.

"You mean that we are not to lunch at Prosser's?" he exclaimed.

"Certainly not," was the firm reply. "We will lunch —at the 'Milan'."

CHAPTER II

It is probable that George Henry had never admired his brother more than at the moment when he made this bold pronouncement. The " Milan " was known by name to both of them and represented all the things which they had hitherto studiously avoided in life. Needless to say, neither of them had ever crossed its portals.

" We shall need money," he observed in an awed tone.

" That we must at once arrange," was the firm reply. " We must make it a habit now to carry money with us. One can never tell when the opportunity for expenditure may arise."

They left their place of business, George Henry collecting himself sufficiently to observe, with a sigh, that Harold's stool, which had been temporarily occupied during the morning, was again vacant. A few minutes later the swing doors of a neighbouring bank were pushed open, and the brothers entered. They were neither of them of commanding presence, their attire was ordinary, their bearing unassuming. Nevertheless, the atmosphere of the bank for the next few minutes can only be described as resembling one velvety purr. A cashier hurried from the back regions to greet them with a welcoming smile. The commissionaire raised his hat a whole foot away from his head. The manager himself waved his hand from behind the curtains of his private office and embarked upon a desperate struggle to get rid of an importunate client, who desired to increase his overdraft. Meanwhile, Stephen produced a

cheque book from his pocket, carefully filled in the
counterfoil first, and, in a reasonable space of time,
handed across the counter a cheque for a thousand
pounds.

" In tens and twenties, if you please," he directed.

The cashier received the cheque with an unctuous
smile, drew a glass receptacle filled with water to his
side, wetted his forefinger, and commenced the business
of counting.

" Five hundred pounds in tens, Mr. Underwood, and
five hundred in twenties," he remarked urbanely a few
minutes later, as he pushed the two little piles of notes
across the counter.   " Wonderfully mild weather we
are having."

" Extraordinary for the time of the year," Stephen
agreed.

" Quite remarkable," George Henry echoed.

Then there was a brief silence.   The brothers had
produced very similar brown morocco pocketbooks and
were absorbed in the task of dividing the money.
Finally this was accomplished and they turned to leave
the bank, after a further exchange of civilities.   Before
they reached the door, however, they were overtaken by
the bank manager, who had got rid of his client.

" Good morning, gentlemen! " he exclaimed cheerfully.   " I'll walk along with you to Prosser's.   You've
left us a little money to be going on with, I hope."

Neither brother replied to the time-honoured joke.
They exchanged glances, and George Henry nodded
slightly.   It was Stephen who accepted the onus of disclosure.

" We are not going to Prosser's this morning, Mr.
Lawford," he announced deliberately.

" Not this morning," George Henry echoed.

Mr. Lawford stopped short upon the pavement. His appearance indicated shock.

" Not going — to Prosser's? " he faltered. " God bless my soul! "

He glanced feverishly at the date upon the newspaper which he was carrying. It was Tuesday, beyond a doubt — a common, ordinary week-day. Reassured, he sought for enlightenment.

" You are both all right, eh? " he asked anxiously.

" Perfectly," George Henry assured him.

" The fact is," Stephen announced, with an elaborate air of unconcern, " we are lunching in the West End."

" Having just a snack at the ' Milan '," George Henry put in airily.

" God bless my soul! " Mr. Lawford murmured again, thereby displaying a pitiful lack of originality in his emotional outlets. " Ah! — a customer, perhaps? " he added, seizing eagerly upon a possible explanation. " I thought you always left that sort of thing to Mr. Hanworth? "

" We do," Stephen acquiesced. " If you are going to Prosser's, perhaps you will be good enough to tell William not to reserve our places to-day."

Mr. Lawford had found himself. He understood that any further expression of astonishment would be out of place.

" Certainly! Certainly! " he agreed. " You haven't forgotten that this is boiled beef and dumplings day? " he added jocularly. " Well, well, good morning! Prosser's won't seem itself, without you."

The brothers hailed a taxicab, and Stephen gave the address. There was a brief silence after they had started on their pilgrimage westwards.

" Mr. Lawford seemed quite surprised," George Henry observed presently.

" Unreasonably so, I thought," Stephen assented severely. " Mr. Lawford is a man of the world. He should realize that one's movements are subject to — er — derangement."

George Henry coughed.

" Except on holidays," he ventured, " and the week when you had a bilious attack, we have lunched at Prosser's, at the same table, every day for eleven years."

Stephen frowned.

" It is too long," he declared. " I am very glad that Mr. Duncan thought the time had arrived to send on our dear father's letter. If we are not careful, we shall get groovey. We must make changes — in other directions as well, perhaps. We must not get into a rut."

George Henry shivered a little with excitement as he listened to his brother's bold words. The taxicab driver leaned backwards and addressed them through the window.

" Café Parisien or restaurant? " he inquired.

George Henry was, by accident of places, the recipient of this inquiry. Vaguely excited by his brother's words, he was all for adventure. The Café Parisien sounded foreign and mysterious. His voice almost shook as he replied:

" The Café, driver."

He leaned back in his seat with the air of one who has performed a great deed. Stephen smiled approvingly.

" The Café Parisien sounds most attractive," he admitted. " This, I suppose, is it."

The taxicab had turned into the " Milan " courtyard, and pulled up outside the glass-covered portico on the left-hand side. A liveried servant opened the door. Gorgeous persons in silk coats and knee breeches relieved them of their hats and umbrellas in a little lobby crowded with a most distinctly cosmopolitan throng. It was, perhaps, not altogether to be wondered at that, when the brothers pushed open the swing doors and stood upon the threshold of the restaurant, they were conscious of a certain sense of confusion. The room was full, and there was no one to recognize in them new and important patrons. They missed the obsequious approach of the head waiter at Prosser's, the respectful greetings of City men to whom their name was holy, the urbane smile of the frock-coated manager himself. At Prosser's, too, the feminine element was entirely absent — here it was insistent and amazing. A dark-eyed Frenchwoman, wearing a military widow's veil, carrying a small dog under her arm, and displaying more ankle and leg than either Stephen or George Henry had seen for a great many years, enveloped them in a little cloud of perfume and pushed past with a muttered — " Pardon, messieurs ! " And at every table. The brothers exchanged doubtful glances. George Henry coughed.

" These young ladies seem rather young to be lunching in a public restaurant," he murmured.

" They are, perhaps, older than they seem," Stephen replied, with an air of wisdom.

It was at this precise moment that Providence intervened on behalf of the newcomers. The High Priest of the Café, gazing around him for a means of escape from an undesirable but persistent client, saw them blocking the way. His necessity invested their presence with a new significance. He bore down upon them like a whirlwind. His bow and smile were such as were usually reserved for patrons of the highest distinction.

" We should like some luncheon," Stephen confided. " We have been recommended here by a friend."

Monsieur Louis, recovering from the shock of this somewhat quaint introduction, looked around the place long and searchingly. He would have been glad to have found a retired table for these unusual but opportune patrons. The place, however, was packed.

" If you could wait for a quarter of an hour, gentlemen," he ventured.

The faces of the two brothers fell simultaneously. It was obvious that the suggestion was unwelcome.

" We are used to lunching punctually at a quarter-past one," George Henry explained. " My brother's digestion ——"

" There is a table here," Stephen interrupted, pointing to one just inside the door.

The *maître d'hôtel* hesitated. It was true that he had the table in question at his disposal, for it had only that morning been given up by a regular patron who had returned to America. It was one of the most desirable in the room, and he had been reserving it as a *bon bouche* for some especial client. Like all great men, however, confronted with a crisis, he made up his mind quickly. With a shrug of the shoulders he withdrew the " Reserved " card from its place, and invited his new patrons to be seated.

" It was reserved," he explained, " but no matter. And for lunch? "

Stephen took up the menu and George Henry looked over his shoulder. The result was chaos and distress. Once again, however, the pioneer of this enterprise was equal to the occasion.

"We do not understand the French language," Stephen observed simply, laying down the *carte*. "What joints have you ready? — or we should be glad to try the dish of the house."

The lips of Monsieur Louis twitched. It was the affair of a moment, however.

"Allow me to serve the *table d'hôte* luncheon," he suggested. "And to drink?"

"A little Perrier water with lemon in it," Stephen replied. "Afterwards, two glasses of port."

Monsieur Louis made his escape, and paused for a moment by his desk to recover himself before he plunged once more into the fray. The brothers were served with their luncheon and enjoyed it. They vied with one another in their praise of everything that was set before them. Each was anxious to proclaim the experiment a success.

"A most delicious omelette," Stephen declared.

"Those little things in small dishes were most savoury," George Henry proclaimed.

"And the thin steak — *entrecôte minute,* they called it," his brother continued, "had a most agreeable flavour. I sometimes wonder ——"

Stephen paused to take another sip of his port, and proceeded with vinous confidence.

"I sometimes wonder whether Mrs. Hassall is quite as good a cook as she used to be."

"It is melancholy to have to contemplate a change," George Henry sighed, "but her cutlets last night were floating in grease."

"We will give her a fair chance," Stephen decided Jesuitically. "We will dine here one night and compare the result."

George Henry shook with excitement.

"We should have to wear evening dress," he murmured.

"We are provided in that respect," Stephen reminded him, with dignity. "I remember thinking last year, at the dinner to Mr. Ferguson, how well your dress coat looked."

"It is eighteen years old!"

"I see no reason why a dress coat should not last for a lifetime. It is a garment for use on rare occasions. George Henry!"

"What is it, Stephen?"

"The youth at the table opposite, with the exceedingly well-favoured young lady. It seems to me — yes, it is Harold!"

The recognition appeared to be mutual. The fashionably dressed young man indicated arose, muttered something to his companion, and somewhat sheepishly approached the table at which his uncles were seated. He wore a black lounge suit with a thin white stripe running through it, a white flannel collar with a long, carefully arranged tie. His hair was brushed sleekly back, and a monocle dangled from a cord around his neck. His coat curved in at the waist exactly as the coats of all the other young men. The sight of him, and the consciousness of their relationship, seemed to bring the brothers into more definite touch with their surroundings. They welcomed their nephew, therefore, with unexpected cordiality.

"This is indeed a surprise, Harold," Stephen declared.

"Mutual, what?" the young man rejoined nervously. "What price Prosser's, eh?"

"We are seeking a change," George Henry remarked. "It is our first visit here."

"Tophole grub," the young man murmured, with a sidelong glance back towards his table.

"We have lunched excellently," Stephen admitted. "We are pleased with the place. How is your mother, Harold?"

"A1. She is down at Bournemouth for a few days."

The uncles tactfully avoided any reference to a possible connection between that fact and Harold's luncheon companion. Stephen became suddenly inspired.

"Since you appear to be accustomed to the ways of this place, Harold," he said, "you can possibly advise us upon the subject of the remuneration ordinarily tendered to the waiter. At Prosser's ——"

"Ten per cent. of the bill," Harold interrupted. "Same everywhere at these places."

Stephen smiled a well-pleased smile and nodded understandingly at George Henry.

"That is easy to calculate," he remarked. "And, Harold?"

The young man, who was becoming more at his ease under the influence of this unexpected geniality, assumed an air of interest.

"The head waiter with the dark moustache, coming up the room now, was very civil to us on our arrival. Would it be in order if we were to tender him also some recognition — say, a shilling?"

Harold glanced behind and his face was transformed by a beatific grin.

"Monsieur Louis?" he exclaimed. "Lord love us, Uncle Stephen! A shilling! My hat!"

Stephen's forehead was puckered and he became instantly contrite. Obviously he had been on the point of a *faux pas*.

"Advise us, if you please, Harold," he begged simply. "We wish to do the correct thing."

"Monsieur Louis," Harold explained, with bated breath, "is a pedagogue, a mandarin, a — er — the big bug of the place. He gets about two thousand a year salary, and commission. You could send him a cheque for fifty pounds at Christmas time, perhaps, or give him a sure Stock Exchange tip, or make him a present of that pearl pin you are wearing. But to offer him money — a shilling! Phew!"

The young man seemed suddenly wordless. His uncles were both humble and penitent.

"We are very much obliged to you, Harold," Stephen acknowledged. "You have probably saved us from committing a grave mistake."

"One moment," George Henry intervened, as Harold showed signs of backing away. "Our curiosity has been somewhat excited by the — er — dissimilarity between the faces of the young ladies who seem present here in such large numbers and their attire. They seem mostly to be still in short skirts, but to have an older appearance, so far as regards their features and deportment. One hears that at boarding-school nowadays ——"

"Fluff," the young man interrupted laconically. "It's a great place for it."

"Fluff," George Henry repeated gravely.

"I am afraid," Stephen admitted with amiable candour, as he toyed with his last drop of port, "that the phrase conveys nothing to us."

"Chorus girls," Harold explained patiently — "young actresses and cinema débutantes, what? Those short skirts are all the go now. Fetching, too, ain't they, with white silk stockings and black patent shoes?"

"And the young lady who is your companion?"
George Henry inquired diffidently.

"Oh, she is on the musical comedy stage. Jolly nice
girl and clever, too. Blanche Whitney, her name is.
She's looking out for some guy to finance her. So
long!"

The young man departed, and his uncles exchanged
somewhat furtive glances. Stephen cleared his throat.

"It is very good-natured of Harold, no doubt," he
declared. "The lives of these poor girls who are forced
to work for their living are doubtless dull and strenuous,
and a little change may be desirable. But I cannot
think that he is quite wise in entertaining this young
lady for luncheon in the middle of a business day. I
am afraid that Amelia would disapprove."

George Henry coughed. He had the air, somehow,
of sympathizing with his recalcitrant nephew.

"We must remember," he said, "that we are, to a
certain extent, in what is termed Bohemia. Until we
appreciate the conditions a little better, perhaps, we
had — er — we should be wiser not to worry Amelia."

"I quite agree," his brother assented, unfolding the
bill which had just been brought to him. "Amelia would
doubtless wonder at our own presence here."

Stephen with great care added up the items of his
bill, calculated the ten per cent., and received the waiter's bow and thanks.

"I think, George Henry," he declared, with an air of
satisfaction, "that we have made a move in the right
direction. The cost of our luncheon was enormous —
fully three times as much as the charges at Prosser's."

"Capital!" was his brother's cheerful comment.

"At the same time," Stephen reminded him, "it will

take a great many lunches to help us to any real extent towards our object."

" I fear," George Henry sighed, a little hypocritically, " that we must look upon this change in the whereabouts of our midday meal as the first step towards changes all round."

" You are right," Stephen agreed. " You are very right indeed."

The room now was overhung with a faint cloud of cigarette smoke. The hum of conversation had grown louder, a general air of relaxation prevailed. George Henry found himself glancing often at a couple of fair-haired young ladies who were lunching at an adjacent table. He was conscious of a peculiar elevation of spirits, a sense of suppressed excitement, pleasurable but most unusual. He found himself suddenly interested in his age. After all, he was still on the right side of fifty.

" One misses, perhaps, the exchange of a few remarks with Mr. Ferguson and our other friends," Stephen reflected, a little wistfully.

" In time," George Henry surmised, looking innocently up at the ceiling, " we may perhaps make acquaintances here."

" Quite possible, quite possible," his brother assented. " I think, if you are ready, we might now take our departure. We have the export accounts to go through this afternoon, you know."

They rose, George Henry with much reluctance. It was absurd, of course, but the nearer of the two fair young ladies had certainly glanced more than once lately in his direction. He straightened his tie, stood up and wished that he were a little taller. Monsieur Louis, passing down the room, paused before their table.

" The luncheon all right, I hope, gentlemen? " he inquired, with one of his famous bows.

A cold shiver passed down Stephen's spine at the reflection that a short time ago he had actually contemplated offering this august being a shilling. He remembered that it was his nephew who had saved him — the boy should never lose by it! Then inspiration came. He would atone for the unoffered insult.

" The luncheon was excellent," he replied. " My brother and I would like you to accept this little offering," he added, drawing his pearl pin from his tie. " We should like this table reserved for us every morning, except on Saturdays and Sundays, at one-fifteen, and for dinner to-night at eight o'clock. Our name is Underwood. Good morning! "

However timid their entrance to the hallowed precincts of the Café had been, the honours certainly remained with the brothers on their departure. Monsieur Louis, with the pin in the palm of his hand, was speechless. His bow was automatic, and his murmured word of thanks inaudible. He drew a little breath and straightened himself.

" Charles," he directed an adjacent *maître d'hôtel*, " that table is reserved for dinner to-night at eight o'clock, and every day except Saturdays and Sundays for luncheon, for those two gentlemen. Their name is Underwood."

The waiter hesitated.

" There have been a great many inquiries for it, sir," he reminded his chief.

Monsieur Louis waved him away.

" We have here," he announced, " a new order of patron. Where they come from or what they may be I do not know, but the table is theirs."

Monsieur Louis' stately progress down the room was checked by a summons from Harold Margetson. He stopped short.

" Know those two old buffers? " his young client inquired.

" Except that their name is Underwood," Louis replied, " I know nothing of them."

Harold grinned.

" They are my uncles," he declared. " And they are rolling in it. No one knows what their income is. Millionaires, I should say, both of them."

" Dollars or pounds? " the young lady by his side asked quickly.

" Pounds — good English pounds," her escort assured her. " They've got it to burn."

Miss Whitney's very beautiful eyes glistened. She became thoughtful.

" The gentlemen will lunch here every day," Louis announced. " I have promised them Mr. Higgins' table."

" By Jove, Louis! " the young man exclaimed, with a faint whistle. " They've got round you all right! "

" Your uncle is very generous," the *maître d'hôtel* murmured, opening his palm. " He has just given me this."

The two young people stared at the pin.

" It's worth a cool fifty," Harold muttered.

Miss Whitney's manner was no longer abstracted. She laid her hand upon her companion's.

" I must know your uncles," she declared firmly. " When did you say that they were coming again, Louis? "

" They dine to-night at eight o'clock, madam."

" So, then, shall we," she insisted. " Not a word, Harold, or we shall quarrel."

The young man grinned.

" You're as clever as paint, Blanche," he declared, " but — I don't know what they would say if they saw me here with you again."

" I'll make that all right for you," she promised. " You leave everything in my hands. All you have to do is to be here on time."

" I'm agreeable," the young man assented. " We'll dine all right, but if you think there's anything doing with those old curmudgeons of uncles of mine you're on a dead wrong 'un. Don't say I didn't warn you."

The young lady smiled.

" Nice boy," she murmured tolerantly. " You don't need to worry, anyway."

CHAPTER III

THERE was no obvious change that afternoon in the routine of business at number 140B, Basinghall Street, where the offices of Messrs. Underwood and Sons were situated. Both Stephen and George Henry, however, were conscious of a subtle change in their attitude towards the various tasks which they essayed and accomplished. They seemed imbued with an altogether unusual spirit of latitudinarianism. Harold's late return passed unnoticed. The delinquencies of one of their continental travellers in the matter of expenses was dealt with from an unprecedentedly liberal point of view. The salary list was scanned and several advances decided upon. When, after having arrived back from lunch at least a quarter of an hour later than usual, the heads of the firm took their departure at a quarter to six instead of six o'clock, comment was rife. The senior members of the staff were discreet enough to hold their peace. Their juniors, however, did not hesitate to express the general feeling, handicapped as they were by the presence of Mr. Harold Margetson.

"Are the walls of Jericho about to fall?" an invoice clerk demanded.

There was a little buzz of comment. Information was sought from Harold, who was hastily divesting himself of his office coat.

"Can't imagine what's up," he confided. "All I know is that this quarter of an hour is a godsend to me. But I'll tell you fellows one thing, if you want to know," he added, pausing, entirely against the regulations, to light a cigarette. " They're breaking out. I've seen 'em."

For the first time in their lives the much-discussed principals of the firm took a taxi from the Bank to Hampstead. Stephen smiled complacently as he saw the fare registered upon the dial.

" Taxicabs will help us, George Henry," he said, as he alighted. " I am about to pay this man eight shillings. Any other form of conveyance would have brought us here for a shilling. We have certainly something to hope for from taxicabs."

" We might have one down to the ' Milan,' " George Henry suggested, as they walked up the flagged path. " As the evening seems stormy and we shall be in evening clothes, I think it would be advisable."

" I am quite of your opinion," Stephen agreed. " These minor efforts at expenditure are worth consideration. They mount up — beyond a doubt they mount up."

The house, which they entered by means of a latch-key, was a semi-detached edifice, fairly spacious, and furnished with sober Victorian utilitarianism. A trim little maid helped to divest them of their coats and hats. A strong smell of cooking pervaded the place.

" Dear me! " Stephen exclaimed. " We have omitted to let Mrs. Hassall know that we are not dining at home."

" Mrs. Hassall," George Henry remarked, " will probably be annoyed. Would it be as well, Stephen, if you were to step down and explain the matter? "

" There is no necessity," was the hasty reply. " Ellen here will deliver our message. Give our compliments to Mrs. Hassall," he added, turning to the little maid,

" and say that dinner will not be required this evening. My brother and I are dining out."

The maid was aghast. There was no precedent for anything of this sort.

" I don't know what Mrs. Hassall will say, sir," she protested. " There's a joint in the oven and the fish ready to go into the frying pan. Would you like to have a word with her yourself, sir? "

" Certainly not," Stephen declined. " You can deliver our message, Ellen, and say that the dinner can be disposed of in any way Mrs. Hassall thinks fit. We are going upstairs to dress."

Ellen retired to the lower regions. The brothers ascended with dignity to their apartments. Each brought out his carefully wrapped-up dress suit, selected a suitable shirt, and adorned it with the plain gold studs that they used on special occasions.

" Shall you shave, Stephen? " George Henry called out across the landing.

" I think it would be advisable," was the firm reply. " We have, I fear, become a little slack in our home life. There is a button off my patent boot, and I am not satisfied with the condition of my white tie."

There was the sound of heavy footsteps upon the stairs. George Henry retired precipitately into his room, leaving his brother to bear the brunt of the forthcoming attack. Mrs. Hassall, stout, breathing heavily, red faced, beady eyed and angry, knocked at his door with her knuckles.

" Can I have a word with you, sir? " she demanded.

" Certainly not at present, Mrs. Hassall," Stephen answered, with great courage. " I am changing my clothes."

" I'm a married woman," Mrs. Hassall persisted.

" And we've got to decide about the shoulder of mutton one way or the other."

Stephen slipped the bolt noiselessly into its place and breathed more freely.

" We have already sent word, Mrs. Hassall, that we shall not be dining at home," he said. " My brother and I will see you in the dining room when we descend. Kindly put the bottle of sherry and two glasses upon the table," he added, in a spirit of bravado.

Mrs. Hassall withdrew, making inarticulate sounds. The brothers continued their toilet. They issued from their rooms almost at the same moment. They were dressed exactly alike, and each had had the same inspiration with regard to headgear. The trouble about Stephen's silk hat, however, was that it bore a deep crape band, the last time he had worn it having been at the funeral of a friendly rubber merchant, some year or so ago.

" Mrs. Hassall desires a word with us, George Henry," Stephen announced.

" I heard her. I fear, Stephen, that we shall have trouble with Mrs. Hassall."

" She must be taught her place," Stephen declared valiantly. " I have ordered the sherry to be placed upon the table, George Henry. I thought that a glass before we started might be refreshing."

" An excellent idea! "

They descended to the dining room, where the table was laid for two. Upon the sideboard were the sherry and two glasses. They helped themselves and took up positions upon the hearthrug. Mrs. Hassall lumbered into the room a few minutes later.

" I should like you to understand, sir," she said, addressing Stephen, " that your dinner for to-night is cooked and, if you're not home to eat it, it's wasted. I've been here all day. I've had no message. It's a good joint — one I chose myself. And mutton at one and elevenpence a pound!"

"The fault is entirely ours," Stephen acknowledged. "Pray eat the dinner yourself, Mrs. Hassall — you and Ellen."

"And what should we be doing, I'd like to know, with fillets of sole, a shoulder of mutton and an apple pie?" Mrs. Hassall demanded angrily. "There's enough of the cold braised beef from yesterday for our supper. When I cook a dinner I like it eaten, and I hate waste."

Stephen sipped his sherry, set down the glass, and straightened his tie.

"Mrs. Hassall," he said, "it is unfortunate that we had no opportunity of letting you know, but the fact remains that my brother and I are dining out. You may do precisely what you choose with the dinner you have provided. The responsibility is ours, not yours. Be so good as to ask Ellen to call a taxicab."

"A taxicab!" Mrs. Hassall exclaimed. "Why, there's the bus at the corner."

It occurred to George Henry that it was time that he asserted himself.

"Come, come, my good woman!" he protested. "Surely my brother and I may indulge in a taxicab if we think fit!"

Mrs. Hassall stared at him disparagingly.

"And in them clothes, too," she observed. "And no chance to air them nor nothing. Do you know you haven't worn them for a year, Mr. Stephen? No, nor not you, Mr. George Henry."

"The clothes have been properly taken care of," Stephen replied. "Ellen," he added, raising his voice

a little, " be so good as to call a taxi. Mrs. Hassall,
if you have anything more to say, please say it
quickly."

" I've a great deal more to say," she declared. " A
great deal more than you'd like to hear, I'm thinking.
Such goings on! "

" Then please don't say it," Stephen enjoined.
" You're a little angry, Mrs. Hassall. Wait until to-
morrow morning. It is possible, by that time, we may
have something to say to you. My brother and I are
contemplating changes in our domestic arrangements."

Thenceforward Mrs. Hassall was a broken woman.

" Changes," she faltered, " after eighteen years.
Changes indeed! And, unless I make a hash of that
shoulder of mutton for to-morrow night's dinner ——"

Stephen ruthlessly interrupted her. The taxicab was
outside. He finished his sherry and bravely led the way
to the door.

" Mrs. Hassall," he said, " good night. Take my
advice and serve the dinner for yourself and Ellen. Do
not be alarmed about to-morrow; we shall have nothing
to say that will not be agreeable to you. Do not sit
up. We have our latchkeys. Good night. Good
night, Ellen."

They took their places in the taxicab. George Henry
looked at his brother with admiration.

" I congratulate you, Stephen. You were firm but
diplomatic. I sometimes think that Mrs. Hassall has
been with us too long."

" We must not forget," Stephen said judicially,
" that, during the whole of the period of her service
with us, we have taken every opportunity of impressing
upon her our desire for the strictest and most absolute
economy. In her ignorance of the changed circum-

stances she would, no doubt, look upon a wasted dinner as a tragedy. She is what we have made her, George Henry. She is too old to change. We must pension her. A substantial pension, I think."

" Capital! " his brother assented. " Considering the length of time that she has been with us, we must be liberal. I do not think that three hundred a year will be a penny too much."

" Not a penny," Stephen agreed. " We are making a very good start indeed. Three hundred a year is capital."

CHAPTER IV

THE brothers arrived at the "Milan" punctually, left their coats and hats with the vestiaire, and, entering the restaurant, took their places at the table which had been reserved for them. Monsieur Louis himself hurried forward to greet them. His bow was magnificent. He laid before them a bill of fare which comprised most of the known edibles of the world. They gazed at it in some perplexity. George Henry was fascinated by the picture on the cover, which represented two very *décolletée* ladies being entertained by a male being who seemed to be a sort of Bacchanalian tailor's dummy.

" You will leave the dinner in my hands, perhaps? " Louis suggested.

" We will do so with pleasure," they both assented, with a joint air of relief.

" Have you any suggestions to make, gentlemen? "

" None whatever," Stephen answered firmly. " We leave the matter entirely in your hands. We are accustomed to plain food and we appreciate good cooking. My brother has a weakness for a sweet dish."

" And to drink? " the immutable Louis inquired, making rapid notes with his pencil.

George Henry took the bit between his teeth.

" A pint bottle of champagne," he suggested boldly.

" A very good choice," Stephen acquiesced. " We will leave the brand to Monsieur Louis."

The head waiter bowed and retreated. The brothers exchanged congratulatory glances. They felt that they had made a good start, and they began an interested study of their surroundings.

"It appears to me, Stephen," George Henry remarked, in a somewhat disquieted tone, "that the fashions in evening dress have changed during the last ten years. Most of the men seem to be wearing short coats and black ties."

"Our own attire," Stephen pronounced, with bland confidence, "is perfectly in order. Nevertheless, if you would feel more comfortable — as this sort of thing is likely to be an everyday affair with us — we will call at Mr. Hogge's to-morrow and discuss the matter with him."

George Henry stroked his moustache a little nervously.

"I am wondering," he confessed, "whether these City tailors are quite the people."

"We have dealt with Hogge for twenty-five years," Stephen reminded him.

"An excellent man, no doubt," was the hasty admission, "but perhaps not quite used to clients who visit these fashionable places."

"You are doubtless right," Stephen decided, after a moment's reflection. "We must consult one of our friends with reference to a West End tailor. Perhaps Harold might be able to advise us."

At that precise moment Harold and Miss Whitney made their appearance. They had, as a matter of fact, been having a cocktail in the lounge outside, until they were quite sure that their prospective victims had arrived. Harold was wearing one of the short coats to which his uncle had alluded, and a black bow, tied in the orthodox manner. He paused before his uncles' table. His companion paused too.

"What ho!" he exclaimed cheerfully, having completely forgotten the little speech which he had rehearsed outside. "Here again, eh? Seeing life some, what?"

Stephen, whose manners were of the old school, rose to his feet, displaying an unexpected length of tail coat. George Henry followed his example.

"The dears!" Miss Whitney, who was standing modestly in the background, murmured under her breath. "Harold, won't you introduce me to your uncles?" she asked, taking a tentative step forward and laying her hand upon his arm.

The introduction was duly performed. Miss Whitney smiled very sweetly and was almost shy. She was wearing a black gown, and the absence of any colour upon her cheeks — a source of much comment amongst her acquaintances — accentuated the somewhat pathetic expression which was part of her pose.

"Kind of trouble here to-night," Harold declared jerkily, remembering, at last, his cue. "Louis has forgotten to keep my table. Never knew him make such a bloomer before."

"We've been waiting outside quite a quarter of an hour," Miss Whitney sighed, "and I am so hungry. How clever of you to get the best table in the room, without any trouble!"

"Perhaps," Stephen suggested, after barely a moment's hesitation, "you would care to join us?"

"Are you sure we shouldn't be disturbing you?" Miss Whitney asked, with a bewildering smile. "It would be simply sweet. I am dying to sit down. Every one has been so trying this afternoon."

Miss Whitney was, apparently, dying for other things, which Louis, who had been watching the little pantomime with immovable face, immediately on its termination promptly produced. Very soon the brothers were drinking their first cocktail, and Stephen's whispered admonition to his nephew to order anything the young lady would like resulted in the appearance of a gold-foiled bottle of superior size to their own, which was now reposing in an ice-pail. Miss Whitney took the conversation into her own hands. There was no doubt that she was a young lady of remarkable tact.

" It's so dear of you," she declared, " both of you," she added, with a wonderful glance at Stephen — " to leave that grubby old City and come up here to see life. And so sensible, too. There are other things in the world, aren't there, Mr. Underwood, besides making money? "

" I suppose there are," Stephen admitted doubtfully, " but I am bound to confess that, so far as my brother and I are concerned, we have somewhat neglected them. The conduct of a large business is very engrossing."

" You should take an interest in the theatre," she suggested.

" Neither my brother nor I," he replied, " have witnessed a theatrical performance since Sir Henry Irving last played in ' The Bells.' "

" You don't object to the stage? " she asked anxiously.

" Not in the least," Stephen assured her.

" Nor to any one connected with it," George Henry echoed, with a little bow.

" You dear! " Miss Whitney exclaimed, patting his hand.

George Henry glanced at the table on his right, which was, unfortunately, this evening occupied only by a prosperous-looking American and his wife. To be patted on the hand by a very attractive young lady was a new and extraordinarily pleasant situation. Somehow or other, though, he could not help thinking how much more thrilling it would have been if the donor of the caress had been the young lady with the wonderful smile, who had occupied that particular table at luncheon time.

"My brother and I," he announced boldly, "think of paying a visit to the theatre very shortly. Are you acting in anything at present, Miss Whitney?"

She sighed. The pathos now was unmistakable. She shook her head very sadly.

"I have had terribly bad luck, Mr. Underwood," she confided. "I have a wonderful musical comedy, with a delightful part for myself, and the man who was going to produce it for me — died, only a few weeks ago."

"Pegged out without a moment's warning," Harold put in. "Filthy luck for Miss Whitney. She'd been counting on his putting up the stuff."

The brothers were puzzled but interested.

"It isn't an expensive production," Miss Whitney continued, feeling her way cautiously, "and the very theatre for it is in the market at the present moment."

"It's a corking good piece of work," Harold remarked. "A fortune in it, with Miss Whitney in the title rôle. The man who puts up the dibs is on a winner every time."

The faces of Stephen and his brother suddenly cleared. They exchanged surreptitious glances. What had before been mysterious to them was now becoming clear. There was a business side, of course, to all theatrical ventures.

"Pardon me," Stephen inquired, "but the person who advances the money to secure the production of

such a piece as you were speaking of, is usually, I believe, a loser?"

"Not in a case like this," Miss Whitney assured him
eagerly.

"Miss Whitney never loses any money for her backers," Harold declared. "They touch the oof every
time."

The brothers seemed unaccountably depressed, and
Miss Whitney was content to let the subject drop for
a time. Meanwhile, the service of dinner progressed.
It was a queer *partie carrée*, the conversation, clumsily
stage-managed by Harold, chiefly consisting of references to benevolent strangers who had befriended some
undiscovered genius, assisted them towards a stage
career and reaped princely rewards. For some reason,
however, the *morale* of the story generally fell flat. Towards the end of dinner, George Henry, who was half-
way through his second glass of champagne, snatched
at an opportunity when his brother and nephew were
engaged in conversation, to ask a question of Miss
Whitney.

"Did you happen to notice," he inquired, "a very
attractive young lady — there were two of them, in fact
— seated at this table on the right at luncheon time?"

Miss Whitney reflected.

"Why, of course!" she exclaimed. "That was
Peggy Robinson and little Julia Winch."

"Are they on the stage?" he asked timidly.

"When they get a chance," Miss Whitney replied.
"They were in the chorus at Daly's until a month ago.
Peggy isn't bad-looking. Better let me introduce you."

George Henry coloured up to the roots of his hair.

"I wasn't thinking of anything of that sort," he
stammered. "I am too — too ——"

" Too what? " she laughed.

" I shouldn't know what to say to young ladies who are on the stage."

Miss Whitney laughed again.

" Oh, Peggy would find plenty to talk about," she observed, a little dryly. " You might find her conversation a little monotonous, but you could have all of it you wanted. Mr. Underwood! "

George Henry leaned a little across the table, a proceeding which her gesture invited.

" Do you think there would be any chance of interesting your brother, or both of you, in a theatrical speculation? "

George Henry coughed. It was really very foolish of him, but his old habits of caution, engendered by a quarter of a century of commercial life, were too strong.

" I really could not say, Miss Whitney. We have neither of us been used to speculations of any sort."

The young lady sighed, and the conversation became general again. Miss Whitney had lost heart.

" Hopeless old dears! " she whispered to her escort.

" Sit tight," he replied, under his breath. " They're biting all right."

Stephen, in fact, presently reopened the subject himself.

" If it is not an impertinent question, Miss Whitney," he asked, " what amount would be necessary to ensure the production of your musical comedy? "

Miss Whitney was not one of those young ladies, flitting through Bohemia, to whom money counts as nothing. She came, on the contrary, from an exceedingly hard-headed stock of successful tradespeople, and she had learnt the art of caution. She leaned across

towards Stephen, her eyes bright with interest, and a
rather becoming little frown upon her forehead.

"It all depends, Mr. Underwood," she replied. "The
thing could be done, no doubt, including a short lease
of the theatre, for a matter of five thousand pounds.
On the other hand," she went on, "there are extras —
and perhaps super-extras — which might make the
amount up to seven or eight thousand. The person, or
syndicate, who found the money would be entitled to
five per cent. interest and half the profits, after paying
author's fees."

"That seems to me a perfectly reasonable arrangement," Stephen murmured, glancing tentatively at his
brother.

"Quite so," George Henry echoed.

Blanche Whitney's spirits revived. She talked gaily
until the end of the meal, a little surprised to find that
her glowing account of the fortunes realized by various
theatrical syndicates aroused so little enthusiasm in her
listeners. At a quarter to ten Stephen took out his
watch.

"It is our custom," he said, "my brother's custom
and mine, to retire at half-past ten. We have just
time to reach home pleasantly and read the papers for
a few minutes."

"You are not going already?" she exclaimed.

"With your permission, Miss Whitney."

"My brother and I," George Henry intervened, "are
most punctual in our habits."

The little party broke up. Blanche attached herself
to Stephen and, with a pretty little gesture, detained
him after the others had passed out.

"Mr. Underwood," she begged, "do tell me. Do you
think this idea appeals to you at all? I can't tell you

how happy it would make me," she went on, " to feel that I was going to owe this success — and I am going to have a big success — to you."

" If I were to entertain the suggestion, it would be upon one condition," Stephen said slowly.

" Please tell it me? " she insisted.

" My nephew Harold is very young and his mother is anxious about him. He is only just of age, and he has yet his way to make in the world. I hope you will not misunderstand ——"

" I understand exactly," Blanche Whitney interrupted. " Harold is only one of a crowd of nice boys I go about with sometimes. My friendship with him amounts to nothing. You believe that, don't you? "

" I believe anything that you choose to tell me," he assured her courteously.

" Do this for me, Mr. Underwood," she whispered, " and I will see just as much or as little of Harold as you tell me. You shall decide all those things. One only makes use of children like that. I have always much preferred older men."

Stephen, for a moment, felt vaguely uncomfortable. He glanced towards the door, and was exceedingly relieved to see that George Henry was approaching.

" My brother and I will think over this matter of business," he told her.

" To-morrow I shall come and see you in the City," she announced firmly.

CHAPTER V

THE brothers left their abode at Hampstead within five minutes of their accustomed time on the following morning. They carried out their usual programme of progression, but it was obvious that their serenity had been disturbed. As they entered the Park, George Henry spoke the first word which had passed between them.

"Mrs. Hassall," he observed, taking off his hat for a moment as though to cool his forehead, "is a very unreasonable woman."

"Singularly so," Stephen agreed. "I really never suspected that she was possessed of so violent a temper."

"Your reference to the pension was opportune," George Henry continued.

"Opportune but tardy," Stephen assented. "Perhaps if I had commenced with a reference to the pension, the interview would have been less stormy."

George Henry was swinging his umbrella a little as he walked. Somehow or other, even the Park seemed different this morning. Perhaps his share in the encounter with Mrs. Hassall had stimulated him. At any rate, he was filled with a sense of adventure. It was as though a border of flowers had grown up in the night on either side of that straight black line that led from Hampstead to Basinghall Street, and from Basinghall Street to Hampstead.

"If Mrs. Hassall has made up her mind to leave this afternoon, Stephen," he said, "have you any suggestion to make as to our movements? We can scarcely trust ourselves alone in the house with such an inexperienced maid as Ellen."

Stephen shook his head.

" That is out of the question," he declared. " We must not forget that our chief concern now must be to arrange for a considerable increase of our daily expenditure. It is in my mind to inquire about furnished suites of rooms, including attendance, in the West End."

George Henry moistened his lips and swung his umbrella once more.

" That sounds expensive," he remarked hopefully.

" I believe that such suites are very expensive indeed," Stephen assented. " We shall have to accustom ourselves, also, to the services of a manservant."

" And of whom do you propose to make these inquiries? " George Henry asked.

" Of Harold," Stephen said firmly. " There is no need to go outside the family. Harold, as you know, has been brought up in a world which is entirely strange to us. Our sister Amelia has lived amongst fashionable people ever since her marriage. Harold was sent to Eton, and there is no doubt that he shares his mother's tastes. You see, for instance, how naturally he fits into his surroundings at such a place as the ' Milan.' He wears the right sort of clothes and seems entirely at home there. I think that he will be able to give us all the information that we desire."

The brothers completed their journey without further reference to the absorbing subject of the moment. For an hour after they arrived at the office, they proceeded through the usual routine of dealing with their correspondence and with pressing matters on which their decision was necessary for the wheels of this money-making firm to run smoothly. As soon, however, as they reached a pause, Stephen turned to the clerk who had been taking his instructions.

"Will you send Mr. Harold in, if you please," he directed.

The message reached Harold in a moment of gloom. His own correspondence had been unsatisfactory in the extreme — and monotonous. There seemed to exist, on the part of certain tradespeople in the West End, a unanimous and poignant desire for some sort of settlement, on his part, of their accounts. His tailor, in particular, seemed both hurt and aggrieved by Harold's indifference to his continual applications. Then Miss Whitney had telephoned, announcing herself engaged for luncheon and, in reply to his complaints, had told him to run away and play. It was altogether a rotten world. He followed the clerk into the private office, full of forebodings, but adopting, for the moment, an attitude of cynical depression. After all, perhaps something might be done in the way of blackmail.

"Harold," his Uncle Stephen began, "there are a couple of matters concerning which we should like to consult you."

Harold was startled out of his assumed composure.

"Consult me," he repeated a little feebly.

"Take a chair," Stephen enjoined.

Harold's spirits commenced to rise. He had never before been invited to sit down in his uncles' presence.

"In the first place," Stephen continued, "we desire the address and an introduction to a firm of first-class London tailors."

Harold pinched his leg violently and swallowed. He said nothing.

"We also desire a similar introduction to a hosier, accustomed to supply fashionable details of men's clothing," Stephen proceeded. "And, finally, your Uncle George Henry and I have decided to leave Hampstead and come to live in the West End. We thought of taking a furnished suite or flat with attendance. You could, perhaps, suggest a desirable locality."

Both these martinets, of whom he had always stood in secret awe, were waiting upon his words, almost deferentially. Harold, who had entered the room in fear and trembling, felt his hands creeping towards his trouser pockets. A new vista of prosperity, including the termination of all his financial troubles, was dawning upon him.

"My tailors are the people for you," he declared almost eagerly. "Hyslop and Hyslop, in Savile Row. Absolutely *the* cut. No one else in it. I'll take you there. And, as for the hosier," he added, remembering another offensive document in his pocket, " there is only one place — Borrodaile's in Bond Street. Better let me run you round there."

" We will visit these establishments with you this afternoon," Stephen decided.

It was almost too good to be true!

" Look here," Harold warned them, " you understand, of course, that you won't be able to buy clothes at the prices you pay to that man Hogge, in Cheapside, or collars and shirts at Hope Brothers' prices."

" We understand that perfectly," Stephen assented. " There is no harm in telling you, Harold, that it is our intention, your Uncle George Henry's intention and my own, to increase our yearly expenditure. We are leaving Hampstead at once. In fact, I may say that we have already left it."

" Ye gods!" Harold gasped. " What about Mrs. Hassall? "

" We have pensioned her," was the amazing reply.

" Your Uncle Stephen and I have decided," George Henry explained, " that we have developed a certain tendency towards living in what one might call a rut."

" A rut! Precisely! A rut!" Stephen echoed.

" We are, accordingly," George Henry continued, " about to alter our method of living."

" Capital!" Harold exclaimed. " If you want showing round a bit on the Q.T.," he added confidentially, this vision of a new Eldorado expanding before his eyes, " I can arrange it for you. There isn't much goes on in town I don't know something about."

" It would be more becoming at your age, Harold," Stephen intervened coldly, " if you thought a little more about your work here and a little less about such matters. With your uncle and myself it is different. We are in a position to retire at any moment, should we care to do so. You still have your way to make in the world."

" Quite so," the young man assented, his hopes a little dashed.

" I mentioned a service flat a moment ago," Stephen proceeded.

" Why not the ' Milan '? " Harold suggested. " You seem to have taken a fancy to the place. You can move into a little suite there this afternoon, if you want to. All slap up-to-date and everything. And you can have your meals served in your private apartments, or visit the restaurant when you like."

Stephen and George Henry exchanged glances.

" The idea appears to me to be excellent," George Henry pronounced. " The place is bright and cheerful, and I have no doubt that the prices will be satisfactory."

"We shall be lunching there to-day, and will take the opportunity of interviewing the manager," Stephen assented. "That will do, Harold. We will make an appointment with you later on."

Harold left the office a little dazed but feeling, somehow, that there was some hope left in the world. George Henry at once took down his bowler hat from the peg, glanced at his watch, and turned to his brother.

"It is time for me to go to Mincing Lane, Stephen," he announced. "I shall be back at half-past twelve. You have not forgotten, I suppose, that Miss Whitney spoke of calling to see you this morning."

Stephen moved a little uneasily in his chair.

"No, I had not forgotten, George Henry," he replied. "I suppose ——"

His brother waited patiently. Stephen, however, was momentarily dumb.

"You were thinking of Hepplethwaite's indigo?"

Stephen stroked his chin thoughtfully. His forehead was slightly puckered and his eyes seemed more than ordinarily blue. His fingers were playing a tattoo upon the blotting-pad. There were certain rare indications of self-consciousness about his demeanour.

"To tell you the truth," he explained, a little lamely, "I was wondering whether, if Miss Whitney should happen to call, it would not be as well if you were here."

George Henry shook his head. There had already been visions in his mind of the sensation which such a visit would cause in the office.

"Nothing," he pointed out, "must interfere with my visit to the Mincing Lane warehouses this morning. There are several matters of importance awaiting my arrival."

"You are quite right," Stephen agreed resignedly.

"If it is possible, however, for you to return a little earlier than usual, I should be glad."

"I will certainly do so," George Henry promised, with the ghost of a smile upon his lips.

Stephen's mingled fears and hopes were soon realized. Watched across the strip of dusty floor which lay between the outer swing doors and the office by a score of gaping young men, ushered into the sanctum of the partners by a dumb-stricken clerk, diffusing about her, in that stern commercial atmosphere, little wafts of delicate and voluptuous femininity, Miss Whitney made her appearance, scarcely a quarter of an hour after George Henry's departure. Stephen, studiously avoiding his subordinate's almost agonized stare, bowed and motioned his visitor into a vacant easy chair.

"What a dear, ducky place!" the young lady exclaimed, as she threw herself back into its depths, crossing her legs and displaying a quality and quantity of silk-clad limb which sent the middle-aged cashier, gasping, from the room. "So this is where you sit and make all that money! Where is the other Mr. Underwood?"

"My brother," Stephen explained, "has gone to pay his usual morning visit to our warehouses in Mincing Lane. He will be back before long."

"I'm not missing him," Miss Whitney declared cheerfully, drawing up her chair and leaning across the desk. "We can manage without him, can't we, Mr. Stephen?"

"Up to a certain point, yes," was the somewhat awkward rejoinder.

She laughed at him softly and leaned a little nearer. A gleam of sunlight beautified the really rich gold of her hair. A little waft of most unusual and very seductive perfume floated across the dust-hung atmosphere.

"You are so queer, you two," she murmured. "Do you do nothing apart? Have you no separate lives at all?"

"None," Stephen answered simply. "You see, we were at school together, we came into business together, and, since my father's death, we have kept house together."

She was a little puzzled at his complete unself-consciousness.

"You have neither of you ever been married?"

"Certainly not," Stephen replied. "And we are much too old now," he added, "to contemplate such a thing."

"Men are never old," she whispered.

Stephen looked around. The room seemed to be getting closer and closer, and he decided that he must consult George Henry about a new ventilator.

"You have brought some papers with you," he inquired, "referring to the matter we were discussing yesterday?"

Miss Whitney opened her bag and drew out a type-written agreement.

"I thought it simplest to put it in this form," she said, a little apologetically. "It is, of course, only for your consideration."

Stephen adjusted his gold eyeglass, and, with his forefinger following the lines, read it through word by word. Then he touched the bell and gave a message to the elderly clerk who answered it.

"The agreement seems to me to be in order," he said, "but it is our custom, my brother's and mine, never to sign anything in the shape of a legal document without legal advice. Our solicitor is in the outer office, going through an account with the cashier."

"You mean that you are going to advance the money?" she exclaimed, a little breathlessly.

"We have decided," Stephen replied, "provided no unexpected difficulties arise, to make the investment."

She looked at him with a faintly puzzled air in her warm brown eyes, as though wondering at his self-containment. Then the door opened, and exactly the type of lawyer whom the brothers Underwood might have been expected to employ made his appearance. Stephen rose to his feet.

"Mr. Jardine," he said, "allow me to present you to Miss Whitney."

Mr. Jardine bowed. It was one of the weak moments of a starch-fed life. He was unable to conceal his surprise. He was even a little confused.

"Be so good," Stephen continued, "as to look through this document and tell me whether, from a legal point of view, it is in order. Pray be seated."

The lawyer read the document through from beginning to end. When he had finished, he held it before his face for a moment. Afterwards he was able to meet his client's inquiring gaze with a moderate amount of composure.

"Legally speaking," he pronounced, in melancholy tones, "the document is in order."

"Be so good as to take it, then," Stephen directed. "Prepare a copy for Miss Whitney and one for myself. You will wait upon Miss Whitney according to her convenience, with a cheque for six thousand pounds, and obtain her signature."

"The matter shall be attended to," the lawyer promised, making vague bows and leaving the room like a man in a trance.

Miss Whitney leaned across the table and laid her fingers upon Stephen's hand.

" How can I thank you! " she whispered, with a world of appeal and promise in her grateful glance.

" On the contrary," he replied, " it is we who owe you thanks — my brother and I. We were, in fact, looking for an investment of the sort which I feel sure this will turn out to be."

She was a little puzzled at his demeanour. In the whole of her experience, which had been considerable, she had never met anything like it before.

" You will take me out to lunch, won't you? " she begged. " We must have a little celebration — just we two."

There was one strange moment, during which Stephen found himself thinking that it would be very pleasant indeed to take Miss Whitney out to a *tête-à-tête* lunch. And then he was himself again.

" My brother will return in a few minutes," he said. " We always lunch together. It will give us great pleasure to have you as our guest."

Blanche Whitney threw herself back in her chair and laughed. She laughed so naturally and so easily that the tears came into her eyes. Then she rose to her feet, came round to his side and looked down at him.

" Mayn't I give you a kiss? " she asked.

" For God's sake, no! " he stammered in terror. " Forgive me, my dear Miss Whitney, do you realize where we are — and — and ——"

" Oh, I forgot we were in your stuffy old office! " she exclaimed. " Never mind, it will keep."

Stephen produced a carefully marked cambric handkerchief, on which ten drops of lavender water had been sprinkled, and dabbed his forehead.

"What will keep?" he gasped.

"The kiss, of course," she answered. "Do you know, I believe you are shy."

He turned towards the door with the air of one prepared to welcome a deliverer. George Henry, after a careful knock, which his brother much resented, entered. The latter coughed.

"Miss Whitney and I have arranged that little matter, George Henry," he announced. "If you are agreeable, she has been kind enough to promise us the pleasure of her company at luncheon."

"That will be very pleasant," George Henry declared brightly. "I will send for a taxicab."

"Miss Whitney, then, will excuse us for a moment," Stephen said, rising to his feet.

They both left the room; they both returned in about five minutes, with their hands spotless, their hair neatly brushed, their faces shining.

"The taxicab is at the door," Stephen announced.

Miss Whitney rose to her feet. She was feeling a little hysterical.

"I think," she said, "that I should like to be a partner in your firm."

CHAPTER VI

THE luncheon party at the "Milan" had its surprises. Stephen and George Henry, with their guests, had scarcely seated themselves when the fair-haired young lady who had occupied the table on their right the day before strolled in alone and gazed around the room in a disappointed manner. Miss Whitney stretched out her hand and the two embraced affectionately. There was not the slightest suggestion of conspiracy in their greeting.

"You dear thing!" Miss Peggy gushed. "How sweet you're looking!"

"I am so happy!" her friend exclaimed, with much excitement. "Let me introduce you to the two dearest men in the world. They are my new syndicate. We are really going to do 'The Singing Bird.'"

Miss Peggy was loud in her congratulations. She gave both her hands to the two men and promptly took George Henry's seat.

"We must talk about this," she declared. "I am so happy for Blanche's sake. She is such a dear."

"Your friend Miss Robinson will, perhaps, do us the honour of lunching with us?" Stephen suggested.

"I am so glad you've asked me," that vivacious young lady confessed. "It makes things more comfortable, you know, and I hadn't the least idea of going away. How are you two ever known apart?" she went on. "Because I want to talk to this Mr. Underwood" — laying her hand on George Henry's arm. "I am sure your brother and Miss Whitney have ever so much to say to each other."

A strand of golden hair brushed George Henry's cheek. A strange and wonderful confusion swept through his senses. He felt himself very hot and exceedingly nervous. He gripped the menu firmly in his hand.

"My name is George Henry, and my brother's Stephen. Supposing," he suggested, "we order luncheon."

The two young ladies took that task in hand and managed it very well. Miss Peggy, it appeared, drank milk when in public, at her mother's request, but on this special occasion of rejoicing was content to waive her usual abstinence, and cocktails, with Chablis to follow, were served for every one. She confided presently to George Henry that she was troubled so often with a cough — waiting about to get engagements was hard, and there were so many girls ready to make use of any means whatever to snap up any vacant post. Did he think there would be room for her in the chorus of "The Singing Bird?" He appealed to Miss Whitney. In a few seconds the matter was arranged. Luncheon became more and more cheery. One or two strange individuals, immaculately dressed, and all possessing a class of features well known in the City, were introduced by their Christian names at various times to the brothers Underwood — "my new syndicate" — by Miss Whitney. At the end of the meal the hosts of the little luncheon party were possessed of a very considerable theatrical acquaintance. Notwithstanding the glamour of their surroundings, however, at a quarter-past two, George Henry and Stephen exchanged a covert glance, and a moment or two later both rose to their feet.

"You will excuse us," Stephen said, after having paid the bill. "My brother and I have appointments."

The young ladies parted from them with immense regret. There was to be another meeting later in the week, and Miss Peggy whispered in George Henry's ear something about ringing him up. The girls watched their hosts depart in absolute silence.

"Can you beat them?" Miss Whitney murmured at last, turning to her friend.

"I don't believe they are real," the latter declared. "I had to pinch George Henry's arm to feel sure that he was alive. Tell me about ——"

The heads of the girls drew closer together and their conversation became mysterious. Meanwhile the brothers were on their way to interview the manager. They were ushered, after a few minutes' delay, into his private office. Amenities were exchanged.

"What can I do for you, gentlemen?" the manager inquired.

"We have called to know whether you have a furnished suite to let in the best part of the hotel," Stephen explained.

The manager dotted down a few numbers, rang the bell, and handed them over to a reception clerk.

"Mr. Jonas will show you what we have," he said. "I trust that he will be able to suit you."

He dismissed them with a formal bow. "Unlikely clients," he had decided at once, from their appearance. The reception clerk agreed with his chief, but he did his duty. Several of the suites which he showed them were fairly attractive, but Stephen shook his head to all of them.

"These are too small," he said. "We require some

thing with a little more space. Two sitting-rooms, two bedrooms and two bathrooms."

" A suite of that size will be expensive," the reception clerk ventured to remind his prospective clients.

" We are prepared to pay a reasonable figure," Stephen replied.

The young man showed them two suites in the Court. He considered it a waste of time, but he carried out his instructions with parrot-like politeness.

" These suites are better," Stephen acknowledged. " What is the price? "

" Number eighty-nine is thirty guineas a week. Number one hundred and nine is forty."

" Inclusive of what? " Stephen inquired.

" Inclusive of attendance, lighting and heating," was the polite reply.

The prospective tenants stepped on one side.

" The prices are most satisfactory," Stephen declared. " Do you realize, George Henry, that forty guineas a week is over two thousand pounds a year."

" Quite so, but that has to be divided between the two of us," George Henry reminded his brother.

" True, but even then the increase is enormous. I think that we might live quite comfortably here," Stephen ventured.

" I prefer it to Hampstead," George Henry acknowledged, in a tone of awed enthusiasm. " Life will seem strange at first, but we shall soon get used to it. There is an air of comfort about the place which appeals to me."

" I agree," Stephen acquiesced. " I agree entirely. There is no disguising the fact that Mrs. Hassall was beginning to assume a position of domination towards

us which was at times irritating. I look forward to our
residence here with pleasure — I could almost say, with
pleasure and relief."

"We will decide, then," George Henry said, "to take
one of the suites."

"Certainly," was the prompt assent. "The question
is, which shall it be?"

George Henry deliberated.

"Number eighty-nine seems to me to be cosier. If
anything, I rather prefer it. It is, however, unfortunately, ten guineas a week less."

"Of course," their cicerone remarked, beginning to
wake to the possibilities of business, "if you were taking
the suite for any length of time, it is possible that Mr.
Holman, our manager, might see his way clear to accepting a little less."

"No, no!" Stephen exclaimed hastily. "We should
not think of asking him. We find your price quite
reasonable. We have decided, in fact, to take number
one hundred and nine."

"By the week?" the young man inquired.

"By the quarter," Stephen replied. "If you will
show us the way back to the office, we will deposit a
cheque for the first quarter's rent. We shall be moving
in this afternoon."

Mr. Jonas led them downstairs and back to the office.
His demeanour was greatly altered. He talked at length
of the conveniences and resources of the establishment.
He predicted that the new tenants would find themselves, in every way, comfortable. He led them into
the office and made his announcement with a little air
of triumph.

"These gentlemen," he told the manager, "have decided upon suite one hundred and nine. I have agreed

to let it to them for three months at forty guineas a week."

Mr. Holman bowed.

"We desire," Stephen said, producing his cheque book, "to pay you the first quarter's rent in advance."

"Pray take a seat, Mr. Underwood," the manager begged.

"If any references are needed ——" George Henry began.

Mr. Holman shook his head and smiled as he watched Stephen write out the cheque.

"A cheque on the Bank of England," he said, "is quite satisfactory to us."

"We wish to move in to-day," George Henry announced.

"The rooms will be at your disposal in an hour," the manager replied. "I trust that you will be very comfortable. The head waiters of the restaurant and café will wait upon you during the evening."

The brothers left the hotel and took a taxicab to Savile Row. They were both a little nervous.

"It is a great change for us," Stephen meditated, "a great change in our daily lives."

"It has been forced upon us," George Henry pointed out. "No one could ignore such a solemn injunction as we have received. Our duty has been made perfectly plain, and I venture to think that we have made a good start."

"You are quite right," Stephen assented. "I think that we shall be very comfortable at the ' Milan.' For a place of that description, our rooms seem to me to be quiet and unostentatious. When we have brought a few of our personal trifles, such as our books and family portraits, it will, I am sure, seem quite homey."

They found Harold anxiously awaiting them when they reached their destination. He pounced upon them directly they left the taxicab and led the way inside a palatial establishment. Depositing his charges on two plush chairs, he departed in search of the principal of the establishment, whose name was Mr. Ernest Poulton. The latter welcomed him warmly.

"I felt quite sure, Mr. Margetson, that, after my letter, you would be bringing me in a cheque this morning," he declared. "How much shall I prepare a receipt for?"

"You can chuck that for the moment," Harold replied eagerly. "I've brought you in two of the best customers you could possibly have."

The principal looked disparagingly through the glass partition to where Stephen and George Henry were seated.

"Are you referring to the two hayseeds outside?" he asked.

"Yes, and don't be a fool," Harold enjoined. "Those are my uncles, Stephen and George Henry Underwood, of the firm of Underwood and Sons, in the City, where I shall be a partner some day. Worth a million, if they're worth a penny. Bank at the Bank of England. You've only got to make the simplest inquiry. Cash down for all they buy."

"This sounds most interesting," Mr. Poulton admitted. "They certainly look as though they needed to change their tailor."

"Come with me," Harold insisted. "You will find that I am not romancing. When you've taken their order and realized what it means to you, you'll be very sorry you ever wrote me that most uncalled-for epistle. However, ' Forgive and forget ' is my motto. Come along."

Mr. Poulton made his best bow to his new customers.

" You would like to be measured for some clothes, gentlemen, I understand," he said. " Of what description, may I ask? "

" You are the principal of the firm? " Stephen inquired.

" My name is Poulton. I am the only active partner," the other assented.

" Let me explain our position," Stephen continued. " My brother and I have been living very retired lives. We are City men, ànd two suits a year from a City tailor have been the extent of our purchases. We have decided to change our mode of life. We have taken a suite at the ' Milan.' We require you to furnish us with all the clothes necessary and suitable for two people of our age."

Mr. Poulton bowed.

" Lounge suits, I presume, morning suits and evening clothes? "

" All those," Stephen answered firmly.

" Especially the evening clothes," George Henry put in. " We should like those first."

" Certainly," Mr. Poulton agreed. " What about sport? "

" Sport! " Stephen repeated.

" Sport! " his brother echoed meditatively.

" At present," Stephen explained, " we have not decided to indulge in anything of that sort. My brother and I have it in our minds to ride in the Park a little later on, and to take up golf. Perhaps, after all, it would be as well for you to provide suitable attire for these diversions."

Mr. Poulton coughed and dropped his pencil hurriedly.

" Our prices ——" he began.

" We will leave the matter of prices to you," Stephen interrupted. " We do not expect to be overcharged, but we wish to pay such prices as are usual."

" And terms," Mr. Poulton ventured, feeling that there must be a catch somewhere.

" My brother and I have no running accounts," Stephen explained. " We will pay you cash for the clothes as you deliver them."

Mr. Poulton bowed low. Royalty itself could not have drawn from him a more respectful salute. He pointed to a little row of private rooms.

" If you will step this way, gentlemen," he said, " I will send a cutter to take your measurements. Afterwards we can discuss the matter of materials."

Harold lingered behind with Mr. Poulton. The latter's manner had become more genial.

" Well, what about it, old dear? " Harold demanded, buttonholing him forcibly.

" We shall much appreciate your uncles' custom," Mr. Poulton declared. " You can consider the letter, which you received this morning, unwritten."

" I should jolly well think so," Harold grumbled. " And what about that brown suit I mentioned? "

" You can place your order," Mr. Poulton conceded graciously. " The suit shall be proceeded with at once."

From Savile Row, Harold piloted his charges to Borrodaile's in Bond Street, where a somewhat similar programme was gone through. A plentiful stock of socks, shirts, ties and underclothes was conscientiously ordered. On the way back to the City, Stephen addressed a few words of mingled explanation and admonition to his nephew.

"Harold," he said, "I think it as well to take you into our confidence to a certain extent. Your Uncle George Henry and I have decided to entirely alter our course of life, in consequence of a letter written by your grandfather before he died, which he left with one of his executors to be delivered to us when our prosperity was assured. It appears to be the wish of your grandfather that we should endeavour to spend a reasonable portion of the profits we make in the business. We are endeavouring to conform to his wishes."

"Jolly old buffer he must have been," Harold murmured approvingly.

"We shall repeat this explanation to your mother on her return," Stephen went on. "In the meantime, you would be well advised to be discreet."

"Mum's the word, so far as I am concerned," Harold assured them. "Never was one to go blabbing things about."

"We are not altogether satisfied with your work," Stephen continued, "but we wish to encourage you. Your uncle and I have decided to start you now at a reasonable salary. You should have learnt enough of the business to earn it. We shall watch you closely, and if you show no signs of ability or desire to further the interests of the firm, we shall ask your mother to make other arrangements for you. In the meantime, we have opened a salary account for you at the rate of five hundred a year."

Harold was startled, elated and serious, within the next few seconds. He ended on the latter note.

"Now I know where I am," he promised, "I'll earn it. Best thing you could have possibly done for the firm. I am with you now, all the way through."

"We shall be glad to appreciate your more strenuous

efforts," Stephen said. "It is your Uncle George Henry's idea that a position of greater responsibility in the firm might induce you to take a serious interest in its affairs. I trust that neither he nor I will be disappointed. We will leave it at that, Harold."

"Certainly," George Henry echoed. "We will leave it at that."

That night the two tenants of number one hundred and nine, Milan Court, moved into their new quarters. They arrived with a moderate amount of luggage of a mediocre description, and dined downstairs in the grill-room in morning clothes, at Harold's suggestion. They spent the remainder of the evening in their sitting room, where they played a game of chess, read *The Times*, and were, generally speaking, extraordinarily content. At half-past ten the waiter came to pay his final call.

"Is there anything more I can get you, gentlemen?" he asked.

"Nothing, I think," Stephen replied.

The waiter glanced towards the sideboard.

"I could give you some Antiquary whisky, sir," he suggested. "A bottle, if you like, and some soda water."

The brothers exchanged glances.

"It is an excellent idea," Stephen assented. "Certainly, bring a bottle."

The man smiled and departed.

"We are not obliged to drink it, you know," Stephen continued apologetically. "It looks hospitable to have something of the sort on the sideboard."

"I once took some whisky for the toothache," George Henry observed. "I found it rather pleasant."

The waiter brought the bottle and glasses, accepted

with gratification a munificent tip, and wished his new patrons a warm good night.

"We will make the experiment," Stephen declared. "I have scarcely, if ever, tasted spirits, but a great deal of whisky seems to be drunk by people who exercise a reasonable care in life."

He mixed two whisky and sodas. They leaned back in their armchairs. In the far-away distance they could just hear the sound of violins from the orchestra, playing in a private supper room. George Henry sipped his whisky and soda — and liked it.

"This is a great change for us, Stephen," he said.

"A very desirable change," Stephen assented. "I have just been to look at our beds. The linen is beautiful. The mattresses are far better than our own. Whoever designed and furnished these rooms was imbued with a wonderful idea of comfort. I do not think that we shall regret Hampstead."

"Or Mrs. Hassall," George Henry murmured. "I do not know whether it has occurred to you, Stephen, but Mrs. Hassall used to treat us as though we were a couple of children. We were never allowed to give orders. We had what we were given, and wore the clothes that were put out for us."

"It was quite time," Stephen declared, with a sigh of content, "that we got rid of Mrs. Hassall."

CHAPTER VII

IT was a matter of surprised comment amongst their friends and of quiet congratulation between their two selves, that the complete change in their life and outlook made so little difference to the personality of the brothers. They simply exchanged one set of habits for another. They returned from the City with the same punctuality, ascended together to their rooms, read the evening paper, glanced through any private correspondence, took warm baths — Mrs. Hassall had always been very disagreeable about the geyser at Hampstead — changed into dinner clothes and descended to dine between half-past seven and eight o'clock, if they had no engagements, or earlier if, as had become their habit, they were visiting a theatre. They saw several plays, sitting always side by side in the middle of a row of stalls and, on the whole, they enjoyed these mild dissipations very much. They retired practically always at the same time, after a single whisky and soda, and they slept, as had always been their custom, soundly and well. At eight o'clock precisely their breakfast was served — very nicely served, too — in their sitting room. The papers were by the fire. They were surrounded all the time by perfect, almost obsequious service. At nine o'clock they left the " Milan " by the back entrance and walked along the Embankment the whole of the way to the office.

In the cut and style of their clothes their tailor had proved himself an artist. He had permitted himself a

little latitude, based upon his knowledge of their position and personality.   There was still just a suggestion
of the old-fashioned merchant of dignity and repute in
the clothes they wore in the City.   The entire absence
of self-consciousness made their transition, perhaps, into
the ranks of modernity almost unnoticeable.   Determined not to break off altogether with old associations,
they occasionally lunched at Prosser's.   The charm of
the place, however, had gone.   They were forced to
admit to themselves that, compared to their new home,
they found the food indigestible, the cutlery open to
criticism, and the service slow.   They came away always with the air of men who have performed a virtuous
action.

"We must not abandon old friends," Stephen used
to say.   "We must not altogether cast off old associations.   We must find our way gradually into the money-
spending world."

They found many people eager to be their pioneers,
but, notwithstanding their complete change of life and
ideas, they remained shrewd and cautious men of affairs, free from all manner of ambitions, conscientious
as to their desire to spend money, but without the least
intention of wasting it, and it was their business to
which they still devoted the greater part of their time
and the whole of their interest.

Meanwhile, the period of rehearsals which followed
the signing of the agreement for the production of
"The Singing Bird" occupied a great deal of the time
and attention of Miss Blanche Whitney, in particular,
and her friend, Miss Peggy Robinson, in a lesser degree.
As soon as the first excitement was over, however, these
two young ladies were conscious of a strong revival of
interest in their eccentric syndicate.   They strolled into

lunch at the " Milan " one morning at about a quarter
to one, and, by special permission, and with the proviso
that they must move should the gentlemen desire it, installed themselves at the round table just inside the
door.

" Tell me, Blanche dear," Peggy asked confidentially,
" how are you getting on with your old thing? "

Blanche laid down the roll of music which she was
carrying, and leaned across the table.

" I think you will agree, Peggy," she said, " that I
have had my fair experience of men."

" A very unfair experience, I call it," her friend assented heartily. " You've had all the luck."

" I used to fancy," Miss Whitney continued, " that
I was up to every move of the game — could see through
a man, however clever he was. Well, dear, I tell you
frankly I am up against it. I can no more understand
Mr. Stephen Underwood than I could the sphinx. I
don't know what he wants or what he doesn't want."

" And believe me," Miss Peggy confided, " George
Henry, as he calls himself, is exactly the same."

" It isn't fair upon a girl," Miss Whitney declared
thoughtfully.

" It's absolute idiocy," Peggy agreed. " It isn't as
though they were mean. I was a little hard up last
Thursday ——"

" I saw the bill tumble out of your pocket," her
friend interrupted. " Did it come off? "

" Come off! I should think it did! Made me feel
horribly ashamed of myself afterwards, it was so easy.
I simply daren't ask him to come to the flat, Blanche.
I believe he'd faint. I'm thinking of hiring a mother
and inviting him to tea."

" I have made up my mind," Miss Whitney pro-

nounced firmly, " to know once and for all where I
stand."

Punctually at a quarter-past one the brothers arrived. They greeted the young ladies cordially, but
with their usual precision of manner, took their places
at the table and ordered a simple but expensive lunch.
Towards its conclusion Blanche, who had been a little
distraite, leaned across towards Stephen.

" Can I have one moment with you on a matter of
business, Mr. Underwood? " she begged.

" Most certainly," he assented. " Please speak quite
openly. My brother, as you are aware, will be equally
interested in anything you may have to say."

" This matter concerns you only," the young lady
declared, a little impatiently. " Please be good-natured
and come along."

Stephen allowed himself to be led to an easy-chair in
the small lounge. His companion sat very close to him.

" Mr. Stephen," she began, " we have never discussed
the matter of the super-extras."

" Dear me! " he exclaimed. " You must tell me what
they are, Miss Whitney. I understood ——"

" Do you need me to tell you? " she asked quietly.

" I am sure you realize," he replied, in perfect inno-
cence, " how ignorant I am of all theatrical matters."

She took him by the arm and led him, much to his
discomposure, through the crowded café and into the
larger lounge. There she found a retired corner and
ordered coffee and liqueurs.

" My brother —— " he ventured.

" Oh, he saw you come through! " she interrupted.
" Peggy will bring him here. Please listen. You know,
don't you, that I am the principal lady in ' The Singing
Bird '? "

" Naturally."

" The principal lady in a musical comedy," she went on, " has a certain position to keep up. I haven't been like some girls. I have been careful. I don't care about having the usual class of young man hanging around me, trying to pay a dressmaker's or a bootmaker's bill. I have lived carefully and on my own. As the principal star in ' The Singing Bird ', I can't do that any longer."

" You require something for personal expenses? " Stephen suggested, a little timidly.

" I want a furnished flat, with telephone, heaps of flowers, a moderate amount of jewellery, and either an electric coupé or a small limousine motor car to take me back and forth to and from the theatre," she declared without hesitation.

" God bless my soul! " Stephen exclaimed. " Is this — necessary? "

" It would make me very happy," she whispered.

" What sum of money," he inquired, after a brief pause, " would put you in the position which you feel you ought to occupy? "

" A thousand pounds down, and a hundred and fifty pounds a month during the run of ' The Singing Bird '," she answered firmly. " The jewellery we might leave for a little time."

" If this is usual," Stephen said, " I will instruct my solicitor to add it to the agreement."

" Don't be an idiot," she admonished, squeezing his arm with tentative affection. " You must arrange this privately. Now here come your brother and Peggy. Please give me my answer."

" It shall be as you wish," he promised.

Miss Blanche Whitney went through the day with a superior smile upon her lips, and the air of one looking into a new and very desirable world. For about a week now she was more occupied than ever. Then one morning, just before the time appointed for the first production of " The Singing Bird ", she took a taxi and drove down to the City. She arrived precisely at twelve o'clock, created the usual sensation in the counting-house, and was ushered without delay into the private office, where she found Stephen alone. He rose at once to greet her.

" There is nothing wrong? " he asked.

" Nothing whatever," she answered. " I came to see you, and I knew that I should find you alone just now."

She seated herself opposite to him. An unexpected ray of sunshine seemed to find a home in her beautifully coiled hair, and Stephen was conscious of the fascination of that strange, unfamiliar atmosphere with which she surrounded him. She leaned across the table, opened her bag and took from it a little key.

" Mr. Stephen," she announced, " I have taken my flat and furnished it. I am moving in later in the day, and I have brought you this."

She held the key across towards him. Stephen took it mechanically into his hand, turned it over, and laid it down by his side.

" You see," she continued softly, " this couldn't go into the agreement, could it? There is only one spare key."

Miss Whitney was a young woman of the world, but the moment or two of silence which passed had for her, too, a certain indefinable poignancy. She looked into Stephen's eyes, and she knew that he understood at last.

" My dear young lady," he said, " it is very kind of you to pay me this visit. I am not, as I am sure you know, acquainted with much of the gossip which goes on in the theatrical world, but I should like to ask you a question. Is it not a fact that you have been engaged for some years to Mr. Allan Durward, the tenor in 'The Singing Bird'?"

"The engagement was broken off last week," she confided. "I broke it off the day after you and I sat in the lounge at the 'Milan.'"

"And just why?"

"Because he has no money," she answered stolidly; "because I have had enough of being poor; because, supposing 'The Singing Bird' isn't a success, I don't want to be driven back to the chorus."

He played with the key for a moment or two. His eyes seemed to be studying its pattern. Perhaps even Miss Whitney failed to follow his thoughts at that moment. When he looked up at her, his smile was very kindly.

"My dear young lady," he said, "'The Singing Bird' will not fail. If it does, there are other musical comedies, and a talented young couple like yourself and Mr. Durward, with a joint fortune of ten thousand pounds, will never know want."

"Ten thousand pounds!" she gasped. "What are you talking about? We haven't a penny between us."

Stephen, with some deliberation, withdrew a bunch of keys from his pocket, unlocked a drawer and produced a cheque book. After carefully testing his fountain pen to be sure that it was in order, he wrote out a cheque with great precision. When he had blotted it, he showed it to her.

"It is my intention," he said, "to commute those super-extras you spoke of and to place this money in trust for you and Mr. Durward on the day of your marriage, which I suggest should be the day of the first performance of ' The Singing Bird.' "

She sat looking at him for several moments. She had a queer feeling in her throat, a strange falling away of all the littleness and small schemings of her daily life. She was back again in her school days. Somehow, the atmosphere had changed. Stephen handed the key across to her, with a grave little bow.

" I am too old for marriage, dear Miss Whitney," he concluded. " I hope that you will be very happy."

George Henry came back from the Mincing Lane warehouse punctually at a quarter to one.

" I have engaged a taxicab, Stephen," he announced. " If you are ready, we will wash."

Stephen rose and reached down his hat.

" George Henry," he said, " it is never wise to become too much the creatures of habit, nor should one desert altogether old friends and associations. It is boiled beef day at Prosser's. Shall we lunch there? "

The suggestion made no appeal to George Henry. He was on the point of a mild protest, when something in his brother's appearance made its impression upon him.

" By all means," he assented. " I will dismiss the taxicab."

" And, George Henry," his brother continued, as they walked arm-in-arm along the narrow street, " I have been looking at our business engagements and I think that, if Mrs. Lomax could receive us, it would be a good plan to take our holiday a little earlier this year. I propose that we should go to Worthing on Thursday."

George Henry smiled.

" You forget, Stephen," he said, " that it is our duty

to abandon these inexpensive holidays. Mrs. Lomax's lodgings are quite comfortable in their way, but they are inexpensive."

" Quite right, quite right," Stephen agreed. " What do you suggest, then? "

" I have heard Folkestone spoken of as an expensive place," George Henry continued. " I propose that we write to the principal hotel there, engaging the best suite they have to offer, and arrange for a motor car for the whole period of our stay."

" Splendid! " Stephen agreed. " But I have a better idea still."

" Well? "

" I suggest that we purchase a motor car. I believe that a good one will cost us nearly two thousand pounds, and, without the most careful supervision, their upkeep also is expensive."

" Excellent! " George Henry assented with enthusiasm. " We will go and choose one on our way home. I saw some very handsome ones in a shop in Bond Street the other day."

" If our business engagements permit," Stephen proposed, as he pushed open the swing doors of Prosser's, " we will leave the office a quarter of an hour earlier this evening, in order to arrive at the establishment you speak of before closing time."

Prosser's had lost its charm, and it occurred to both the brothers in turn that boiled beef was a somewhat heavy dish for the middle of the day. Nevertheless, they exchanged civil greetings with their old acquaintances and did their best to enter into the spirit of the place. Mr. Lawford, the bank manager, arrived a few minutes after them, and invited himself to the vacant place at their table.

"I have good news for you, gentlemen," he exclaimed cheerfully.

"Good news?" they repeated.

"You remember — but of course you do — those South American bonds which I advised your auditors to write off at stock-taking?"

"I remember them quite well," Stephen acknowledged. "We decided that they were probably worthless."

The bank manager smiled.

"So far from being worthless," he announced, "there has been a great find of minerals on Government land, and the bonds have appreciated, on the news this morning, to their face value, and are still rising. You may count yourselves the richer, gentlemen, by twenty thousand pounds."

"Wonderful news!" Stephen sighed.

"Most unexpected!" George Henry echoed.

Mr. Lawford strolled across the room for a moment, to speak to an acquaintance. The brothers exchanged doleful glances.

"This just about reduces us to where we were, after all our extravagance," Stephen declared, with marked traces of irritation in his manner.

"It is most disappointing," George Henry commented. "After all our efforts!"

At a few minutes before six that evening the brothers descended from a taxicab and entered an imposing establishment with great plate-glass windows, in Bond Street. A tall young gentleman, dressed in the height of fashion, abandoned with reluctance a conversation with another of his own genus, and advanced a languid step or two towards them.

"What can I do for you, gentlemen?" he inquired.

"We are looking for a motor car," Stephen announced.

"One that opens and shuts," George Henry put in.

The young man recovered from his first shock, and pointed to three specimens of the combined automobile industry and coach-builder's art, which occupied the entire floor space.

"These," he said, "are our three models — coupé, touring and limousine."

"And the price of this one?" George Henry asked, patting the limousine.

"A little expensive, I am afraid," the young man confessed, with a patronizing smile. "Two thousand six hundred pounds, as it stands. Not dear, really, considering that it is our engine, and the finest coach-building work in the trade. But still, expensive."

George Henry opened the door and sat inside. Stephen followed his example. They handled the fittings with interest, punched the cushions and admired the ingenuity of the spare seats. The young man returned to his conversation with his friend. After the latter's departure he strolled back.

"I think this one will do," George Henry said, looking out of the window.

"Eh?" the young man exclaimed, losing his presence of mind.

"We will take this one," Stephen declared, opening the door and stepping out. "Kindly make out the bill."

The young man pulled himself together.

"I beg your pardon," he said. "We are really not used to quite such prompt business transactions. I am to take it, then, that you would like to purchase this car for two thousand six hundred pounds?"

" Precisely," Stephen assented. " Can it be sent home at once? "

" I don't imagine there will be any difficulty about that," the young man declared. " Just step into the office a minute, will you, while I make out the account. Is your chauffeur anywhere handy? "

" We have no chauffeur at present," Stephen admitted.

" Perhaps you can recommend one? " George Henry suggested.

" This is our first car," Stephen explained, accepting a chair and producing his cheque book.

" I congratulate you upon your choice," the young man said. " Ours are the best engines in the world."

" Expensive to run, aren't they? " Stephen asked hopefully.

The young man looked up reproachfully from the invoice which he was making out.

" We claim," he pronounced deliberately, " that, for what it represents, ours is the most economical running car on the market."

" That seems rather a drawback," George Henry murmured absently.

" I beg your pardon? " the young man demanded, knitting his brows.

George Henry corrected himself.

" I mean, of course," he said, " that it is very satisfactory."

" Notwithstanding our six cylinders," the salesman continued, " we claim our eighteen miles to the gallon."

" Dear me! " Stephen exclaimed.

" Capital! " George Henry echoed, without enthusiasm.

The young man handed the invoice to Stephen and

watched the writing of the cheque. He was all the time wondering what manner of men these were whom the Lord had delivered into his hand.

"If I might say so without presumption," he observed, "I should conclude that you neither of you know much about motor cars?"

"We know nothing at all," Stephen confessed.

"Absolutely nothing," George Henry agreed.

The young man studied the cheque. It was an open one upon the Bank of England.

"You are, of course, aware," he said, "that the car requires filling with petrol, oil and grease, and needs a little tuning up all round before she is ready for the road."

"No doubt, no doubt," Stephen agreed. "You will perhaps undertake this for us?"

"I will do so," the young man promised. "I can also, if you like, spare you a temporary man for a fortnight, until you are able to engage one. If you will tell me where to deliver it, I will bring the car round myself to-morrow evening."

"We live at the Milan Court," Stephen told him. "We return there each day from the City at about six o'clock."

"And where are you going to keep the car?" the young man inquired.

The brothers exchanged glances.

"There will probably be facilities at the hotel," Stephen suggested.

The young man shook his head.

"No garage there," he said. "I will arrange that, too, for you, if you like."

"We shall be much obliged," Stephen replied.

"The bill for the petrol and grease ——"

"Kindly bring that with you," Stephen interrupted. "We will pay for that to-morrow evening."

"You will allow me, I hope, to take you for a short run," the young man ventured. "I should like to show you what the car will do."

"It will give us great pleasure," Stephen assented.

They shook hands — the young man insisted upon that — and the brothers returned to their waiting taxi-cab.

"A very excellent idea of yours, Stephen," George Henry said cheerfully. "I have been thinking it over. There is the upkeep of the car, the garage, and the chauffeur's wages. It will entail weekly disbursements of a considerable amount."

"If it were not for those South American bonds," Stephen sighed, "we might consider that we had made an excellent start."

CHAPTER VIII

THE holiday at Folkestone was a success, absolute and complete. There was not a single moment when either of the brothers regretted the stuffy front room at Worthing, the morning perambulation to the beach, the conscientious inhalation of ozone, the evening stroll along the promenade, all the inevitable routine of former vacations. They enjoyed their palatial sitting room in the best hotel at Folkestone, they enjoyed watching the shipping day by day, and, more than anything, they enjoyed the long motor rides which they took upon every possible occasion. Their somewhat quaintly chosen car happened to be one of the best makes, and the chauffeur, whom they had borrowed, an excellent driver and, for his profession, almost honest. They found a new joy in life as they passed from county to county, ranging the coast or exploring the picturesque places inland. It was one of the sights of Folkestone to see the brothers — correctly attired, for they had informed their new tailor of their purchase — taking their morning or evening ride in their very handsome car, seated side by side, unostentatious but quietly happy. It was a complete change for both of them. Twice a week they received their manager, who came down by the morning train from London, gave their advice and directions upon the conduct of the business, and forgot it again until his next visit. Their weekly bills gave them moments of pleased surprise. The garage bill, produced a little apologetically by Brooks, their chauffeur, almost succeeded in imparting a thrill.

"Our holiday," Stephen announced, having spent a

portion of the evening with pencil and paper, " has cost us at least thirty times as much as any previous one. I consider that highly satisfactory."

" I quite agree," George Henry declared. " I hope that nothing else like those South American bonds occurs to spoil our efforts."

" We are doing our best," Stephen said simply. " We can't do more."

Early on the following day, unchanged, save for a deeper shade of bronze in their cheeks, and for the fact that they still wore the grey tweed suits prescribed by the autocrat of Savile Row for holiday wear, Stephen and George Henry returned to town. Their warning came as soon as they reached the remotest suburbs. They returned to a city which seemed to have adopted a single phrase, " The Singing Bird ", as its national motto. It was flashed at them from the busses, even in the purlieus of Croydon, blazoned out in the theatrical columns of the daily newspapers, and stared at them in flaming letters from every hoarding. It was the prominent placard outside every box office.

" I wonder," Stephen asked his brother a little nervously, " did you ever read any of the accounts of the production of ' The Singing Bird '? "

" I did not," George Henry confessed. " I seldom take any interest in that part of the newspapers which is devoted to theatrical news. I read, I think as you read, the markets, the Mincing Lane prices, and the leading articles."

" Precisely," Stephen agreed. " We have not been in a position to know, really, whether the play was a success or a failure. Miss Whitney would probably have written or wired to the Milan Court. As you know, we have had no private letters forwarded. I —

er — seem to have taken it for granted that the play would be a failure."

"I thought that it was an accepted fact," George Henry declared, in an aggrieved tone, "that all theatrical speculations were failures so far as regards the person who put the money in. In all our calculations we have reckoned upon that six thousand pounds as being lost. It will throw us out completely if, by any chance, the play should prove successful."

They soon found out the truth when they reached the office. Even there were stacks of telegrams and letters of congratulation. Mr. Jardine's manner as he greeted them — he had heard of their proposed return and was in attendance — was almost reverential.

"Mr. Stephen," he said, "and Mr. George Henry, I have always looked upon you both as astute business men with a great eye for profitable investments, but never in my life did I suppose that you had genius. To-day I am forced to acknowledge it. Your investment of six thousand pounds in 'The Singing Bird', and your insistence upon being the sole members of the proposed syndicate, seems likely, from all the figures I can procure, to pay you at the rate of — well — four to five hundred per cent."

It was a moment of bitterness, but the brothers conducted themselves with dignity. They got rid of Mr. Jardine as soon as possible. Stephen leaned over from his chair and held out his hand to his brother.

"George Henry," he said firmly, "we must not despair. One successful investment shall not break our purpose. There is money to be lost or spent in the world, and we will spend or lose it."

George Henry returned his brother's grip of the hand with much emotion.

"I envy you your courage, Stephen," he admitted. "I must confess that I am a little disheartened. What with the profits of 'The Singing Bird' and the new valuations of those South American bonds, we have really done very little good for ourselves so far."

"We must not despair," Stephen insisted firmly. "There are still possibilities before us. A supper, say, to the entire company of 'The Singing Bird', or, better still, a dinner on Sunday and a supper to follow. Articles of jewellery to every member of the cast — we can conceal their value. A diamond pendant, say, for Miss Whitney. Why not a small automobile for her husband? These things would be only gracious acts of expenditure. They will be entirely justified. Leave it to me, George Henry. Somehow or other we will make those profits shrink."

George Henry brightened up considerably. On their way back to the "Milan", Stephen made a further suggestion.

"I think," he said, "it would only be an act of courtesy on our part if we took the earliest possible opportunity of witnessing this production."

"I was about to suggest the same thing," his brother agreed.

"It would be more seemly, I think, considering the sums we are drawing from the production, if we took a box," Stephen said.

"A box by all means," George Henry assented. "We'll get one of those side ones where we can look down on the stage."

On their arrival at the "Milan" they made their way to Keith Prowse & Company's office. The man smiled at their artless inquiry.

"There isn't a seat to be had for a month," he an-

nounced, " and we are turning hundreds away every
night."

" That is most unfortunate," Stephen declared.
" We have particular reasons for wishing to see the
play."

The man looked at them for a moment, with interest.

" I beg your pardon," he said, " but are you by
chance the two gentlemen living in the Milan Court,
friends of Miss Whitney? Underwood, I think the name
was? "

" Underwood is our name," Stephen admitted.

" A box has been kept for you every night since the
show opened, until half-past eight," the man told them.
" Miss Whitney insisted upon it, so that the moment
you came back from the country you should be able
to see the show. You will find a note from us, advising
you of the fact, in your rooms."

" Very thoughtful of Miss Whitney," Stephen declared. " We will take it for to-night, if you please.
How much will it be? "

The man handed over a slip of paper.

" The box is free," he said.

" We should prefer to pay," George Henry ventured.

The young man shook his head.

" This is a special arrangement with Miss Whitney,"
he explained. " She would be very angry if I were to
take the money."

They dined early and occupied the box in solitary
splendour.

The house was packed from floor to ceiling. Miss
Whitney, on her first appearance, was received with
tumultuous applause. She recognized her syndicate at
once and kissed her hand to them. George Henry
fanned himself with his programme. Stephen returned

the salutation with a grave bow. The performance, which seemed to the brothers very much like the few other musical comedies they had seen, only, perhaps, a little better, continued, punctuated by rounds of applause, to the end of the first act. Soon after the curtain had fallen there was a ponderous knock upon the door. Stephen opened it, to find a commissionaire standing there.

"Miss Whitney has sent me to take you behind, sir," he announced respectfully.

"Both of us?" George Henry inquired, rising to his feet.

"Certainly, sir."

They found themselves in a confusing atmosphere of affection, congratulations, and make-up. Miss Whitney's welcome was almost overpowering. What it might have been, if it had not been for her make-up, Stephen shuddered to think. She made certain slight changes to her toilet, without the slightest hesitation, disappearing now and again behind a screen, but continuing the conversation without a break. Every one seemed to come in when he liked, and Mr. Allan Durward was handing whisky and sodas round freely. Everybody was very gay. Miss Whitney's business manager, summoned in haste, attached himself to Stephen, whom he seemed to consider as a sort of superior being.

"Finest coup, that of yours, I ever heard of, Mr. Underwood," he declared. "You put down the whole of the money and you take the whole of the profits, except, of course, Miss Whitney's share. A magnificent piece of speculation, I call it. Great piece of luck for Miss Whitney, too, to find a backer who has such confidence in her. You have watched her career closely, I suppose, Mr. Underwood?"

Stephen returned an evasive reply. A bell rang, and all desultory conversation was at an end. The brothers took their leave, George Henry a little disappointed at the absence of the young lady whom he most desired to see. On their way back, however, they came face to face with Miss Peggy Robinson, who, in an exceedingly diaphanous costume, was sitting about in the wings.

" I thought you'd never come," she exclaimed. " I've been waiting here to catch you on your way back."

" I hoped you'd be in Miss Whitney's room," George Henry replied.

She made a little grimace.

" Blanche is a dear, of course," she continued, " but, after all, she's a star and I'm only a chorus girl — can't go wandering in and out of her room just when I like. Are you going to wait and take me out to supper? "

George Henry shook his head.

" My brother and I do not take supper," he replied.

" It makes it very late for us," Stephen explained. " We have our work in the morning."

The young lady sighed.

" Lucky men! " she exclaimed. " I often wish I had something to do in the City instead of this wretched business every night. May I come and lunch with you to-morrow, Mr. George Henry? "

" With pleasure," the latter assented.

The commissionaire hurried them off. The curtain was just going up as they took their seats.

" Our new aims in life," Stephen remarked, as he drew his chair a little back behind the curtain, and rubbed his cheek with his handkerchief, " must necessarily, at times, take us into unfamiliar scenes. I am not sure, however, if I really appreciate this acquaintance with the more intimate life of the theatre."

George Henry was brushing the powder off his sleeve.

"It is a great pity," he said, "that a charming young lady like Miss Robinson should be compelled to earn her living in such a manner. Her father, I understand, was a country doctor, and she was brought up most strictly, in the country."

"That is curious," Stephen observed. "Miss Whitney's father was a professional man. She told me so on our first meeting. That reminds me," he went on, "her business manager, with whom I was talking this evening, must have made an absurd mistake. He spoke of her father as being connected, in the acrobatic way, I believe, with a famous circus."

"He was a man of most unreliable appearance," George Henry remarked. "I should place no confidence whatever in his statements."

"If I had seen him before the contract was signed," Stephen went on, "I should have considered that six thousand pounds most satisfactorily and completely disposed of. As it is, he tells me that the American rights in themselves will prove a fortune."

"Never mind," George Henry said consolingly. "Don't forget, Stephen, that we have an appointment to-morrow with a man who assures us that he can make rubber out of seaweed."

"Quite true," Stephen assented. "We have also answered the advertisement from the man who wants to turn a thousand divers loose to explore the bottom of the North Sea. There may be, as he says, hundreds of millions of pounds' worth of treasure there, but the collection of it will certainly prove difficult."

"We must not forget, either," George Henry continued, " the man who is coming to see us about extracting gold from distilled sea water."

" I remember the man," Stephen declared, his good spirits reasserting themselves. " He was very shabby."

" A hole in his boot," George Henry recalled. " Evidently in very low water."

Stephen nodded.

" He is coming on Thursday," he said, " to repay the five pounds he borrowed and to make a proposal with regard to the formula. I feel sure, George Henry, that any transactions with him would result in a complete and satisfactory loss of the sum involved."

" I quite agree," George Henry declared. " We must make a point of being in on Thursday morning."

CHAPTER IX

An air of subdued but gentle melancholy seemed to be depressing the spirits of both Stephen and George Henry as they partook of their midday meal at their accustomed table in the grill-room at the " Milan ", one morning a week or so later. Things were not going well with them.

" Have you, by chance," Stephen asked his brother, as he sipped his Perrier water, with its slice of lemon floating at the top, " glanced at our private drawings account this month? "

" I spent a few minutes looking it through this morning," was the dismal reply.

" You found the result, as I did, disappointing, I fear."

" Very disappointing, indeed."

" Ours," Stephen continued, leaning back in his place and gazing out of the plate-glass windows of the restaurant, " is a difficult position. We have the desire to spend money, George Henry, without a doubt. It is our lack of experience which is at fault, and certain original instincts which it is impossible to overcome. The idea of absolute waste is repugnant to both of us. We could not, for example, order a bottle of champagne which we had no intention of drinking, and see it wasted, to swell our daily expenditure. We are both handicapped by a strict sense of reasonableness. For instance, we found ourselves able to assist our friend Professor Hirschfelt in his scheme for extracting rubber from seaweed, because he is undoubtedly a scientific man and we know nothing against him. On the other hand, it was quite impossible for us to take shares in a diamond mine from a gentleman who was introduced to us as Mr. Douglas Fitzgerald, when we happened to know that his real name was Joseph Levenstein and that he was an undischarged bankrupt."

"Quite impossible," George Henry assented. "To throw money away is not to spend it."

"We have had our disappointments, too," Stephen mused. "Our rather dilapidated friend with his most intelligent scheme for producing gold from sea water never came near us again."

"And we had only advanced him a paltry five pounds," George Henry reflected bitterly. "He might at least have asked for twenty. Then, there is 'The Singing Bird', Stephen. All your calculations were at fault there."

"I admit it," Stephen agreed. "I take the blame willingly. At the same time, who ever heard of two ignoramuses like you and me making a small fortune out of their first theatrical speculation?"

"The fact of it is," George Henry pronounced, "we have the knack of attracting money, Stephen, and we haven't the knack of getting rid of it. It is a serious matter for us."

"And there seems to be no one to help us," Stephen continued. "Nearly all the propositions that are brought to us are either an insult to our intelligence or else are so good on the face of it that we dare not risk investing. Our principal hope, at present, is Professor Hirschfelt, but he would not accept more than five thousand pounds. Ah! here comes Monsieur Louis with our port."

The chief *maître d'hôtel* himself superintended the

filling of their glasses from the little dust-encrusted bottle, borne in a cradle. Amenities as to the weather were exchanged.

" Mr. Margetson was asking after you a few minutes ago, sir," Louis informed them. " He is seated behind the screen there."

" Alone? " Stephen inquired.

" I think not, sir," was the discreet reply.

Stephen sighed.

" If one of us only shared Harold's weakness for the other sex! " he regretted. " There is no doubt that, for constant and effective spending-power, we need their help. A really extravagant lady friend to whom one of us was devoted would be a godsend. Have you seen Miss Robinson lately, George Henry? "

" Not this week," was the somewhat depressed reply. " She declares that she cannot afford to lunch here alone, and that if she lunches every day at our table she will expose me to comment."

" Remarkably thoughtful, and in excellent taste," Stephen observed warmly.

" I can see Harold now," George Henry announced, a little abruptly. " He is seated with a young lady in deep mourning and a very fat man. They appear to be looking in this direction."

" I should think it very possible," Stephen observed, " that they are talking about us."

They were.

" What we want," Mr. Hiram B. Pluck of New York declared, " is a backer."

" A mug with money," Harold put in.

" Somebody with the artistic or historical sense," the young lady murmured.

Mr. Hiram B. Pluck beamed as he raised his huge tumbler of whisky and soda to his lips, and listened placidly to the chink of the ice as its contents glided down his capacious throat. He set the glass down empty and appeared refreshed.

"The right person," he declared, "must be in existence, and, if anywhere in the world, why not in London? You have brains in this City, sir," he went on, addressing Harold, "you have money, and you have imagination. You have also the artistic and the historical sense."

The young lady exchanged glances with Harold.

"Uncle," she said, "Mr. Margetson has an idea."

Mr. Hiram B. Pluck's smile was meant to be encouraging, but it was obvious that he was not an optimist as regards any idea which might proceed from their companion's brain. Nevertheless, he glanced towards him politely.

"I've got two uncles," Harold announced, "who are rolling in it — kind of hard nuts in a way, but they seem lately to have taken to looking around, as though they wanted to chuck a bit of the stuff about. Until this year they'd never invested a cent outside their business, and lived in a house at Hampstead at ninety pounds a year. Now they have blossomed out into an Embankment flat here, and they backed ' The Singing Bird.' "

Mr. Pluck was more interested.

"The backing of ' The Singing Bird '," he admitted, "is an encouraging feature. I should like to meet your uncles, sir. My niece would like to meet them."

"They are funny old Johnnies," Harold declared, "but as regards meeting them, there is no difficulty about that. See the table behind the door?"

"I see it," Mr. Pluck confessed. "I see also," he went on hopefully, "two healthy and simple-minded hayseeds, dressed by one of your West End tailors. Are those your uncles, boy? I like the material."

"Those are my uncles," Harold assented, "and they are sitting there waiting for it. And so far as regards an introduction ——"

"It's five per cent. on whatever we get out of them," Mr. Pluck promised.

"And my thanks," the pale young lady with the dark eyes and widow's weeds murmured.

Harold rose to his feet.

"It's worth a shot, anyway," he decided. "I'll introduce you as we go out."

Mr. Hiram Pluck signed the bill for the party, and the trio turned towards the exit, Harold slightly in front. The American disclosed a height of something over six feet, with a most immense girth. He wore a light grey suit, a beflowered tie, and the biggest smile upon one of the largest faces in Christendom. His hair was cut short and his eyes were blue. He wore a low collar of the disappearing type. His shoes were the hall-mark of his nationality. Harold paused as he reached his uncles' table, and exchanged cordial greetings with them.

"Uncle Stephen," the young man said, "I should like to introduce my friend, Mr. Hiram B. Pluck of New York. These are my uncles, Mr. Pluck — Mr. Stephen Underwood, Mr. George Henry Underwood."

Mr. Pluck gripped the hand of each in turn, looking them straight in the eyes as he made his little speech.

"Glad to meet you, Mr. Underwood. Glad to meet you, Mr. George Henry Underwood. I'd like to have you know my niece — the Countess of Cheshire."

The young lady smiled very sweetly, and there was more hand-shaking. The ever-attentive Monsieur Louis brought chairs.

" Come, this is very friendly," Mr. Pluck declared. " Gentlemen, you will pardon the liberty. The liqueurs are upon me."

Stephen Underwood hastened to explain their dietetic rules.

" My brother and I," he said, " take Perrier water with our lunch ——"

" With a slice of lemon," George Henry intervened.

" And a glass of port afterwards," Stephen confided. " We have no taste for anything beyond that. If, however, your niece," he added, with a stiff but very polite bow, " will honour us by taking a liqueur and some coffee here, my brother and I will join you in the latter beverage."

Mr. Pluck sat down, a little depressed. For a moment he permitted the burden of conversation to devolve upon his niece.

" I always envy you your table so, Mr. Underwood," she said, smiling across at them and wondering which was which. " My husband and I used to lunch here often — before his unfortunate accident."

Both Stephen and George Henry expressed their mute sympathy at the mention of the accident. They were neither of them students of the journalism of the moment, and they were consequently unaware of the fact that the late Earl of Cheshire had thrown himself from the top window of a lodging house in Bloomsbury, in a fit of delirium tremens.

" We find it very pleasant," Stephen admitted.

" It is also convenient," George Henry put in. " We live in the hotel."

" Oh, you lucky men! " the Countess sighed. " What wouldn't I give to be able to afford a flat here! "

The brothers Underwood, ignorant of the world in which countesses moved and had their being, maintained a discreet but sympathetic silence. Harold found an opportunity of cutting in.

" Nunks is going to see to that," he reminded her encouragingly. " What ho for the giddy pageant."

Mr. Pluck shot a grateful glance at his young companion. This was precisely the opening he desired. He pulled down his waistcoat and laid his hand upon the table in a portentous manner.

" I object to that word pageant," he declared. " Pageants cut no ice, nowadays. They have had their day. When my scheme is fairly launched I'll twist the neck of any one who murmurs the word."

" I once attended a pageant at Hampstead ——" George Henry began.

" On the Heath," Stephen interpolated. " The characters were historical, and if I remember rightly ——"

" It came on to rain," George Henry proceeded reminiscently.

Mr. Pluck was wound up, and the fate of that pageant at Hampstead remained untold.

" I shall, with your permission, gentlemen," he said, " take you into my confidence. I shall disclose my scheme."

" I am afraid Mr. Underwood will not be interested," the young Countess protested, with a languishing glance at George Henry, whom she had decided was the more susceptible of the two. " You see, it is really only an idea of my uncle's for my benefit."

" We should be very interested to hear about it," Stephen declared. " We have extended our luncheon interval lately, and we do not leave here until half-past two."

Mr. Pluck looked a little puzzled, but he went ahead.

" You two gentlemen," he began, " may or may not have heard of my nephew-in-law, the Earl of Cheshire. He cut no ice in this world, and I'm laying odds he'll find none where he's gone to, however badly he may want it. In plain words, he was a bad lot, and he died leaving my niece here penniless."

The young lady's beautiful eyes showed signs of moisture. Stephen and George Henry gave vent to brief murmurs of sympathy.

" My niece," Mr. Pluck continued, " appeals to me. I am a practical man of business, and I cast around for means to help her. I pay her a visit at her country estate, and the means are disclosed to me. Imagine, gentlemen, if you will, a miniature castle, set in the midst of a forest, with sloping terraces, a semicircle of park, and more forest. The moment I stood upon those terraces an idea — the idea of my life — swept in upon me. I stood upon the stage. The amphitheatre before me would hold five thousand people, all comfortably seated. Here was the grandest open-air theatre the world had ever seen! I wired for Harrison Kinmo. You know Harrison Kinmo? "

Neither of his two principal auditors appeared to have that pleasure. Mr. Pluck was surprised and a little shocked.

" Mr. Harrison Kinmo," he said, " is the greatest writer of historical, romantic and picturesque plays whom the world has ever seen. That man is a poet, sir, an artist, a genius. He stood by my side on the lawn and he burst into tears."

Mr. Pluck drew back to observe the effect of his words.

"Dear me!" Stephen murmured, with an effort at sympathy which was palpably strained.

"How extraordinary!" George Henry echoed, in a dazed manner.

"He was overcome," Mr. Pluck explained. "He saw here the ideal setting for the great work of his life. He wired to town that morning for the manuscript, and believe me, gentlemen, he spent the whole of the time until it came in walking up and down that lawn, issuing from the castle each time as a different character, and reciting as much as he could remember of his remarkable play. When the manuscript arrived, he read it. My niece and I were thunderstruck. Helen?"

The young lady appealed to looked earnestly at Stephen.

"Mr. Underwood," she assured him, "nothing so wonderful, so poetical, so romantic has ever been written."

"There's a million dollars in it," Mr. Pluck declared, with bated breath.

"Your scheme, I presume, is," Stephen ventured, "to construct an open-air theatre in the park and produce this play. Where will you draw your audiences from?"

"Special trains from London, sir," was the prompt reply. "Forty minutes' run without a stop. Saloons, if we can work it, with refreshments on board. We'll build a wooden hotel out of sight amongst the trees. Dinner out of doors before the performances, drinks whenever they like — at a price."

"Our climate," George Henry pointed out, "is not entirely propitious for such schemes."

"That's the worst of you Britishers," Mr. Pluck complained. "You've no faith in your own climate. It's no worse than any other. If this thing were got through quickly, we'd be ready to produce in August and get two of your finest months in. Then we'd close down and start next year with the first day of spring."

"How much money would you consent to receive from outsiders towards the flotation of this scheme?" Stephen inquired.

"Ten thousand pounds," was the firm but modest reply. "That would pay for the seating of five thousand people, the erection of a temporary hotel, and a moderate sum down, on account of fees, to the author of the play."

"My brother and I," Stephen admitted, "are interested. We will discuss this matter together and, if convenient to you, meet here at the same time to-morrow. At the present moment you must excuse us."

"It is within two minutes of half-past two," George Henry explained.

The brothers made their adieux and departed. Mr. Pluck gazed doubtfully after their retreating forms. He felt a little nonplussed.

"How do we stand?" he asked Harold. "Have they bitten?"

"Got it right in the gullet," was the prompt assurance. "They'll probably bring the oof with them to-morrow."

CHAPTER X

PROBABLY no promoter of such a scheme as Mr. Hiram B. Pluck's was ever blessed with easier and less inquisitive financial backers. It was not until long after they had advanced the full sum required that the brothers Underwood even visited Rawlingsey Castle, and even then it was more for the pleasure of the motor ride than out of curiosity. They returned to town a little depressed.

"I really should not wonder," Stephen declared, on their homeward journey, "if this scheme of Mr. Pluck's does not turn out to be a huge success."

"The environment," George Henry pointed out, "is at least equal to his description."

"It is the most beautiful spot I ever saw in my life," Stephen acquiesced. "The painting of the seats, too, is most artistic, and the little hotel seems as though it would be delightful."

"I have been looking through the figures again," George Henry continued lugubriously. "Our capital outlay has been rather less than twelve thousand pounds. Five per cent. interest on that is only six hundred a year. The interest is to be reckoned as a working expense, and the salaries and author's fees are ridiculously small. Here are the figures, Stephen. It seems to me, if only a quarter of the people whom Mr. Pluck expects patronize the show, and if it is only run for two months in the year, there will be a very large profit."

"There is always the weather," Stephen reminded his

brother hopefully. " Imagine a wet, cold wind and a blinding rain — what about that for a day or two? Why, no one would go near the place. With all those trees, too, the neighbourhood seems to me to be likely to attract whatever moisture there may be about."

" We must hope for the best," George Henry agreed, with a pious effort at optimism.

Rain, however, for the next few weeks seemed the most unlikely thing in the world. From early morn till evening, the sun shone down from a cloudless sky upon a parched but happy land. Mr. Hiram B. Pluck seemed to grow larger and his smile more beatific every day. His beautiful niece frequently found her way to the luncheon table behind the door at the " Milan ", and was never slow in expressing her appreciation of the wonderful generosity displayed by her uncle's backers. It was not until a fortnight before the time fixed for the opening performance that the originator of this great scheme allowed a single expression of doubt to escape him. It was a hot and breathless afternoon, and the café at the " Milan " was far more empty than usual. The sky was overcast, and there were rumours of a rapid fall of the barometer.

" What, between ourselves, gentlemen, bothers me some," he confessed, bringing his second liqueur over to the Underwoods' table, " is the fact that, as yet, scarcely any seats whatever have been booked through, what you call over on this side, the libraries. We have offered to put them in on the ground floor, but — nothing doing. Only this morning I have been to see two of the bosses. I went so far as to make a foolishly generous offer of a limited number of seats, just to get a little money on the books, but it was no good. What in thunder are they afraid of? "

" The weather," George Henry replied.

" The weather? " Mr. Pluck repeated. " Why, it's the most maligned thing in this island of yours! There hasn't been a drop of rain for three weeks. The ground's cracking down there with the heat. I've got an ice-cream shanty in the woods that'll pretty well pay its whole expenses the first day."

" If this weather should continue," George Henry observed portentously.

" Why the hell shouldn't it! " Mr. Pluck demanded, with a touch of the irritation which that morning seemed prevalent.

" The glass is falling," Stephen interposed. " What's that? " he added, suddenly lifting his head and listening.

" Rain," his brother replied, with a smile — " very violent rain."

" A thunderstorm, maybe," Mr. Pluck muttered. " It'll clear the air — do a lot of good."

" Or," George Henry remarked sagely, " it may be a break-up of the weather."

Mr. Pluck gazed at his genial little *vis-à-vis* with the eyes of a murderer.

" Well, gentlemen," he said, " I'm not one of those to meet trouble before it comes. A thunderstorm's neither here nor there. To-morrow morning the sky will be clear and the sun shining again. I've kept my face towards the bright places all my life, and I am not going back on myself now. I'll take one more of those liqueur brandies, Louis," he added, turning round in his chair, " and the storm can darned well do what it pleases. We've no rehearsal, and everything down yonder's been arranged so that a little preliminary rain won't do us a scrap of harm. Here's one more drink to the Rawlingsey Open Theatre and 'The Forest King'!"

The brothers drained the last drop of their after-luncheon glass of port, and rose to their feet. It wanted two minutes to half-past two, at which hour they invariably turned citywards.

"We shall hear from you if there is anything further you want, Mr. Pluck?" Stephen observed.

"There won't be another darned thing, sir," was the confident reply. "You gentlemen have kept your part of our bargain magnificently, and if I've stuck you for a few thousands more than I expected, it's all been open and aboveboard, and you'll get it back many times over."

A clap of thunder shook the room. George Henry gazed into the streaming courtyard with the pleased interest of a child.

"There is that possibility," he murmured.

Mr. Hiram B. Pluck stood two days of continuous rain without flinching, but on the third day he wobbled, on the fourth he was lachrymose, and on the fifth he turned up unexpectedly at the office of Messrs. Underwood and Sons, in the City. When he had divested himself of his mackintosh and sent his umbrella out into the warehouse, it became obvious that he was no longer the same man. He seemed to have shrunken into his clothes, there were little bags under his eyes, he sat resolutely with his back to the window, against which the rain was streaming incessantly.

"Gentlemen," he said, "this is the kind of luck which, at fifty years of age, finds me still a poor man."

"The continued spell of bad weather is certainly most unfortunate," Stephen acknowledged.

"There seems very little chance of any change for the better," George Henry put in, with well-assumed gloominess.

"We motored down to Rawlingsey yesterday," Stephen confided. "The prospect is most depressing."

"Hideous," his brother agreed. "There were only a few men at work, and they seemed to think it scarcely worth while going on."

"I don't know as they ain't right," their visitor groaned. "See here, gentlemen, we've got a grand scheme, but we're up against the British climate, and the British climate's going to lick us. What about cutting our losses? I think, for the matter of a few hundred pounds, our theatrical company would dissolve and allow us to break the contract."

Stephen shook his head.

"I should consider such a course premature," he declared. "We must not despair."

"Never say die," George Henry muttered lugubriously.

"Guess your principle's right," Mr. Pluck admitted, "but I am a poor man, and a sixth part of that salary is fifty pounds a week. I'd like to save that, if I could. I am counting the two thousand pounds, which is my little contribution to the show, as gone already."

"Dear me!" Stephen exclaimed, leaning back in his chair and gazing protestingly towards their visitor. "You're in a very depressed frame of mind, Mr. Pluck."

"I was at Rawlingsey myself this morning," that gentleman explained, "and there are pools of water half a foot deep in the auditorium, and the stage is a shining lake. Blast your climate, Mr. Underwood!"

Stephen leaned a little forward, with the tips of his fingers pressed together.

" I am sorry to see you so distressed, Mr. Pluck," he said, " and I must remind you that both my brother and myself have the strongest objection to blasphemy in any shape or form. However, subject to my brother's approval, I should like to relieve your mind of some of your anxieties. You have two thousand pounds sunk in the scheme, and a liability as regards the current expenses after the opening. We will, if you like, buy you out."

" Certainly," George Henry agreed. " Buy you out, Mr. Pluck."

Mr. Pluck was for a moment suspicious. The impossibility, however, of any living person possessing inside information as to the vagaries of the English climate impressed itself speedily upon him. A new eagerness shone in his face.

" How much did you think of offering me, gentlemen? " he inquired.

Stephen did not hesitate.

" We will give you," he suggested, " your two thousand pounds, and relieve you of your liabilities, on consideration that you become our manager at, say, twenty pounds a week, until we choose to abandon the enterprise."

" Put it on paper," Mr. Pluck begged hastily. " Let me see that in black and white. Let me see it over a signature."

" I will do so," Stephen agreed, drawing a sheet of paper towards him, " whilst my brother writes you the cheque."

Mr. Pluck returned to his modest rooms at the " Milan Hotel " with a cheque for two thousand pounds in his pocket, and an exceedingly light heart. It rained the whole of that night and the whole of the next day, but with trustworthy fidelity he obeyed the instructions of his employers, stocked the cold and flooded kiosks and hotel with all manner of cooling viands and drinks, and, furthermore, urged on and even encouraged the theatrical company, as though seven days' rain were nothing but a shower. It wanted only six days to the first performance, and there were few signs of a break. George Henry, however, found cause for some disquietude in the behaviour of the barometer which they had recently purchased.

" Pull up the window, Stephen," he begged that evening, " and see what it looks like."

Stephen obeyed and gazed out over the Embankment. The sound of the rain was clearly audible, the sky was black and overcast.

" Hopeless," he declared cheerily. " Have you seen the evening paper? There are floods all over the country."

George Henry stood gazing at the rising mercury.

" All the same," he muttered, " I don't quite understand this."

The next morning broke, dull and grey, but rainless, with a curious unanalysable heat. Before eleven o'clock the explanation was forthcoming. The grey mists had passed like cobwebs. Overhead was one great arc of deep blue sky, and the hottest sun which had ever shone down upon a damp and beflooded country. In two days the change was magical. The floods vanished like breath from a looking-glass. The grass became as dry as though rain had never been heard of. There was a rush throughout London for outdoor restaurants, cool drinks and Panama hats. Another two days, and men were wearing tropical helmets and carrying sun umbrellas, and the muslins of their womenkind became

more and more diaphanous. People rushed to the river
at the week-end, and Mr. Hiram B. Pluck produced
from the bottom of his steamer trunk a white linen suit
and a marvellous straw hat.   Stephen and George
Henry motored down to Rawlingsey on the day before
the opening, and were aghast at what they found there.
The place was like a paradise, an oasis in a sun-baked
island. The deep green of the lawns and trees was ex-
quisitely refreshing.   The fifty or so visitors and newspaper men, and the bulk of the theatrical company,
were lolling about in garden chairs in front of the
wooden hotel, which seemed, by some magical stroke of
genius, to have become a bower of roses. A very well-
known journalist, hearing who they were, came up and
talked to them.

" I am going to boom this show in my paper, Mr.
Underwood," he announced.   " I think you've a most
amazing success before you."

" Dear me! " Stephen replied.

" You think the weather will hold up? " George Henry
ventured.

" Not a doubt about it, I should say," was the cheerful reply.

They sought out their manager. Stephen drew him
on one side.

" Mr. Pluck," he said, " a few days ago we took
advantage of a momentary fit of depression on your
part. My brother and I have decided that to-morrow
morning it will be at your option to return to your
original position as a partner in the syndicate."

Mr. Pluck was for once in his life taken aback.

" You are princes, gentlemen," he declared, " princes,
but I will not take advantage of you until I have told
you the truth. The news has been sticking in my throat,

and that's a fact. It's magnificent for you, but cruel for me and the little lady. I've been offered, an hour ago, a fifteen thousand pound deal in seats from one of your best libraries. We spoke of a hundred per cent. profit. You are going to make nearer two."

Stephen took his brother's arm and led him away towards their waiting car. There was something funereal about their promenade.

"Our proposition stands, Mr. Pluck," he insisted. "The scheme is yours, not ours. We shall not be content unless you share in the profits."

"You are princes of the blood, gentlemen," Mr. Pluck exclaimed, as he wrung their hands in farewell. "By God, sir," he went on, turning to one of the journalists who was loitering near, "those men are going to make a fortune, and they deserve it! They've got more pluck than any Wall Street speculator I ever met. They're big men."

The echo of his words reached the brothers as they drove off, lingered in their memory after that first wonderful week, when the takings beggared all description, came back to them again a fortnight later, when they found their entire capital repaid and a fortune staring them in the face, and continually haunted them when they found themselves pointed out at the " Milan " as the men who had financed the theatrical Eldorado of modern times.

"It is most satisfactory, of course," Stephen confessed one morning at luncheon, " but ——"

"Most satisfactory," George Henry echoed, "but —"

"I dreamed of our dear father's letter last night," Stephen continued abruptly. "What would he say if he knew that we were still spending less than a sixth of our income!"

George Henry provided a little common sense for their mutual comfort.

" Stephen," he said, " we've done everything possible except throw the money away. We can't do that. The luck's been against us, or with us — whichever way you like to put it. It can't go on. Meanwhile, we've done our best."

Mr. Pluck passed through the restaurant, escorting his niece, who was very elegantly dressed in half-mourning, carried a small Pekinese under her arm, and was followed by a French maid bearing her jewel case. She paused to greet the brothers with indescribable cordiality.

" You dear, sweet men!" she exclaimed. " I shall never be able to see you without coming up and wanting to throw my arms around your neck."

" You forget," Stephen reminded her, " that it is your uncle who is responsible for the whole scheme."

She smiled up at Mr. Hiram B. Pluck, but she nevertheless shook her head.

" It was your courage in persevering, your generosity, and your wonderful foresight," she declared.

She passed on, and the brothers exchanged glances.

" I suppose we are fortunate, George Henry," Stephen observed, with a sigh.

" I should say that we were encumbered with fortune," George Henry assented gloomily.

CHAPTER XI

IT was Stephen to whom, by immemorial custom, the letter was brought soon after their arrival at the office on the following morning, but George Henry was looking over his shoulder as he broke the important-looking seal and spread out the document upon the desk. It was George Henry, too, who first grasped the doleful significance of those few typewritten words.

"The Post Office contract!" he gasped.

"And we quoted at least seven per cent. above the recommended price," Stephen groaned.

"They like our rubber," George Henry observed lugubriously.

"The stability of our firm appeals to them," Stephen muttered.

They stared for the second time, in thoughtful silence, at the unoffending sheet of note paper. George Henry made a rapid calculation on the edge of the blotting pad.

"It will mean at least another eighteen thousand pounds profit," he announced gloomily. "We have only made matters worse by putting the price up."

Stephen rose dejectedly to his feet, unlocked the safe, and brought to the desk a ponderous-looking private ledger. George Henry glanced over his shoulder.

"Our private drawings are certainly increasing," the latter remarked, with a gleam of cheerfulness. "The car has been a great help. And our weekly bills at the 'Milan' are slowly mounting to a more reasonable figure."

"A mere drop in the bucket," his brother pointed out sternly. "Our extra expenditure is very nearly covered by the profits of the Rawlingsey Open Theatre. The discrepancy between our income and our expenditure remains ridiculous. There is that letter of our father's in the safe, and we are becoming nothing more or less than misers."

For a few minutes the brothers considered this unique problem in silence — the indecent accumulation of wealth against their desire. Their dispositions resisted with difficulty the strain of such a dilemma. There was, for the moment, an expression of almost beatific satisfaction in Stephen's clear grey eyes as he studied one peculiarity of the figures.

"I fear that you are something like a hundred and fifty pounds behind me this month, George Henry," he announced. "That is after dividing our joint expenditure."

"I can explain that," was the prompt rejoinder. "It is simply because you have replaced the pearl pin which you gave to Louis with a somewhat larger one. As a matter of fact, I have decided to wear a pearl pin myself — perhaps a black one," he added defiantly. "I am told that Martier's is a most expensive shop. I shall go there this afternoon."

Stephen coughed.

"That may place me temporarily at a disadvantage," he admitted, "but I shall find means to restore the balance. These matters are trifles, however," he continued, closing the book; "the fact remains — the most disquieting fact, George Henry — that we are showing ourselves less and less able to deal with the continual increase in our profits. We have both accepted the principle that it is our duty to spend a certain portion of our income. We fail to live up to that principle."

" I have more clothes and boots and garments of every sort than I shall ever be able to wear," George Henry groaned.

" I am in the same position," Stephen declared. " We have, besides a motor car of our own, a suite at the ' Milan ' and a ridiculously unnecessary manservant. The terms of our partnership forbid our speculating upon the Stock Exchange or gambling upon horses, and the proportion of our profits to be devoted to charities is also determined by that deed. Our only outlet, therefore, is in personal extravagance or a plausible but unsuccessful private speculation. In the latter direction our efforts have only added to our embarrassments. It only needs Professor Hirschfelt to succeed in his experiments, and I really think we shall be entitled to despair."

" There is no chance of Professor Hirschfelt succeeding," George Henry declared. " I know more about rubber than you, Stephen, and I can speak with confidence upon this matter. Mind you, the man's right from the scientific point of view, or we shouldn't have been justified in going in for the speculation at all. He can get a square inch or two of rubber out of a ton of seaweed, but it will cost him fifty times the market price."

There was a knock at the door. Their managing clerk put in his head.

" Will you see Professor Hirschfelt for a moment, gentlemen? " he asked.

" Professor Hirschfelt! " Stephen exclaimed. " What an extraordinary coincidence! "

The brothers looked at each other silently.

"He has probably come for a further advance," George Henry murmured hopefully.

"Certainly we will see the Professor," Stephen assented. "Please show him in."

The Professor, in due course, made his appearance. He was a small man, with a lank, thoughtful face, heavy glasses, and he was dressed, as ever, simply in black. He shook hands with the brothers in melancholy fashion. Stephen pointed to a chair.

"The rubber coming out all right, Professor?" he inquired.

The Professor, in his reply, disclosed a strong German accent.

"It is not of the rubber I come to speak," he announced. "It is a matter of finance."

"Finance," Stephen repeated.

"You need more money?" George Henry ventured, rubbing his hands.

Professor Hirschfelt shook his head.

"No," he said, "it is not that. I come to you because I haf' a respect for you gentlemen, a very great respect for you both. You found me all the money I asked for, without question. You paid the rent of my house near the laboratory. You haf' behaved to me generously."

"I feel that you are the bearer of bad news, Professor," Stephen remarked. "Do not fear to speak out. My brother and I went into this little affair entirely as a speculation. If the money is lost — well, we can afford it."

The Professor shook his head.

"Money will be lost," he declared, "in seeking to make india-rubber out of seaweed. But it shall not be you who lose it. I haf' had an offer, and I take it.

Listen. There was a maker of elastic thread in one of your provincial towns. I take him my proposition before I come to you. He hesitates. I come to you. You find me the money. I start. Then this manufacturer, he make up his mind; my scheme — very good scheme. He comes to the laboratory. I tell him too late. He is angry. Then I consider. I say to myself, there is no more chance of making rubber from seaweed than there is of making gold out of sawdust. Here is a man whom I dislike who wishes to lose his money. There are those two kind gentlemen in London, whom I do like. They shall not lose theirs. I make another agreement with this gentleman. He has bought you out. There is a profit of one thousand pounds each for you. It is not much, but, if you had gone on, you would haf' lost all."

Neither Stephen nor George Henry were capable of saying a word. They sat absolutely silent, gazing at one another across the desk with an untranslatable expression. The Professor had drawn from his mouldy pocketbook two bank drafts. He placed one in front of each of them.

"Your shares," he exclaimed. "I haf' made a little money myself, and I shall make more. I haf' behaved honestly to you? So!"

Stephen was the first to recover himself.

"Professor," he said, "we both, my brother and I, deeply appreciate your behaviour. But this manufacturer — we do not think that we are justified in passing on our interest to him. If you have come to the certain conclusion that rubber cannot be made out of seaweed, we are prepared to share the loss."

The Professor banged the table with the flat of his hand.

"Not one penny shall you lose, either of you," he declared. "You are nice gentlemen. I like you both. My friend down in the provinces I do not like. Some day he will not like me. But that is of the future. I wish you good morning, gentlemen."

"Look here," George Henry protested, "we must write you about this. You are treating us too liberally. And this man you speak of — this manufacturer ——"

"It is finished," the Professor insisted. "We haf' signed the contract. Good morning to you both."

The situation was unique and lent itself to no known form of argument. Before either brother could frame another protest of any sort, the Professor had gone. On the table before them were the two bank drafts.

"This is the last straw," Stephen muttered.

"All the same," George Henry declared, a little peevishly, "I told you that he could not make rubber from seaweed. He admitted that. To all intents and purposes my speculation should have cost us the whole outlay, whereas your 'Singing Bird' — heaven knows where that is going to lead us to. They told me at Keith Prowse's that it seemed as though it would run forever."

"It was an entire fluke," Stephen pointed out. "You must admit that, in justice to me, George Henry. I never read the play. It would not have made any difference if I had. It is a little unfair ——"

"I beg your pardon," George Henry said contritely. "I was bad-tempered. I apologize."

They shook hands across the table. Stephen leaned back in his chair, a sudden expression of hopefulness lightening the gloom of his face. He had rather the appearance of a rosy-cheeked boy who has mischievously conceived a scheme for outwitting his refractory parents.

"George Henry," he confided, gleefully. "I have an idea."

"Capital!" his brother exclaimed.

"A part of it I will not speak of at present. I must think it out. It presents some complications. The other part is simple enough. To-night is the two hundredth night of the run of 'The Singing Bird.' We are invited to a supper on the stage. We may not wish to go, but we shall be perfectly in order in sending a small offering to Miss Blanche Whitney, the principal actress."

"Flowers?"

Stephen smiled triumphantly.

"An article of jewellery!" he declared. "And we could go to that exceedingly expensive shop in Bond Street."

George Henry approved.

"The idea is an excellent one," he admitted. "You would make it a joint gift, of course?"

"I suppose so," his brother agreed reluctantly.

"I am told," George Henry proceeded in cheerful tones, "that some of this very high-class French jewellery, although quite unostentatious to look at, is extraordinarily expensive."

"We must hope to find something of the sort," Stephen acquiesced. "We might call at Martier's before lunch, if you like. I see the car is outside."

They reached down their hats — silk hats now, instead of bowlers — and started on their expedition. Their grey business suits and square-toed shoes were altogether things of the past. They both wore exceedingly well-cut morning coats, linen and collars of the latest pattern, Bond Street ties and patent shoes. They sat side by side in their luxuriously cushioned limousine, curiously enough quite as much at their ease as in the days when they had considered a taxicab a luxury.

"We certainly," Stephen observed, with a sigh, "have the appearance of being addicted to extravagant habits."

"Every little helps," George Henry muttered, as he accepted a newspaper through a window, during a momentary block, and waved away the change from a shilling. "I got rid of elevenpence halfpenny that time."

"I have hopes of Martier's," Stephen confided. "What we want is something that will cost, say, five hundred pounds, and won't look worth more than one hundred. We must avoid all appearance of ostentation."

"Exactly," his brother agreed.

They descended outside the famous jeweller's shop and loitered for a few minutes upon the pavement, gazing in through the plate-glass windows.

"Everything seems very expensive," Stephen remarked, with renewed cheerfulness.

"That platinum watch with the diamonds, marked three hundred pounds," George Henry pointed out, "is chaste but insignificant in appearance."

"Then you can give it me for my birthday present," a girl's pleasant voice exclaimed from behind them. "Insignificant, indeed!"

They both turned around. It was Miss Peggy Robinson who stood peering over their shoulders. The two silk hats were both raised — the same height to an inch. Both brothers shook hands. Miss Peggy was looking exceedingly well, although she was plainly dressed for such a fashionable locality.

"Miss Robinson might possibly be of service to us," Stephen suggested, with an inquiring look towards his brother.

"By all means," the latter acquiesced.

"We are seeking a small gift for Miss Whitney," Stephen explained. "Will you assist us in the task of selection?"

"Fancy you two old dears thinking about such a thing!" the young lady exclaimed. "Of course I will! I've been dying to go inside Martier's all my life, but I never had the cheek."

The trio entered, and the purchase of a platinum and diamond pendant of extreme elegance was successfully concluded. George Henry showed some signs of nervousness as the shopman prepared to bow them out.

"With reference," he said tentatively, "to the small birthday offering we spoke of outside ——"

"Rubbish!" the young lady interrupted. "I was only joking. It isn't my birthday at all."

"Nevertheless," George Henry persisted, "you have been of great assistance to us, Miss Robinson, and I have for some time felt the desire to acknowledge it. I beg you to examine these wrist-watches."

"A joint offering would, perhaps, be less embarrassing to Miss Robinson," Stephen suggested anxiously.

"Better send me some flowers," Miss Peggy sighed, settling down with extreme and beatific satisfaction to examine the wrist-watches already displayed upon a strip of purple cloth. "I couldn't possibly wear anything that came from Martier's," she added, trying one on.

"A joint gift," Stephen persisted, "could arouse no comment."

"My brother's intention is amiable," George Henry said boldly, "but, in this case, I would prefer to be the sole donor."

Miss Peggy thrust her gloved hand through his arm and squeezed it.

"I can see there is no putting you off," she sighed happily. "What a duck this small one is! But just look at the price! I couldn't possibly — possibly. Oh, Mr. George Henry, how wicked of you!"

They left the shop a few minutes later, Miss Peggy wearing the watch upon her wrist. She sat in a corner of the car — she had graciously accepted an invitation to luncheon — her eyes glued upon her new possession.

"Oh, how wonderful it must be to be rich!" she exclaimed, in a tone vibrating with emotion, "to own a car like this, not to have to scheme about one's clothes, or worry about the rent — to be able to help one's poor friends."

George Henry crossed and recrossed his legs a little nervously. He was subject to the full fire of her very expressive eyes. They seemed just at the moment unduly soft.

"Your position in 'The Singing Bird' ——" he began.

"Five pounds a week," she interrupted. "It isn't exactly wealth, is it? Then there are fines, and I send a pound a week to my mother in Cumberland."

"The amount is inadequate," Stephen said sternly.

"Absolutely," George Henry agreed.

"In a sense," Stephen continued, "we, as financial backers of 'The Singing Bird', are responsible for this — starvation wage."

" We are indeed," his brother assented.

" What I want," the young lady confessed, suddenly squeezing George Henry's hand, " is for some one to take an interest in me. I want kindness even more than I do money."

" The young ladies in the company are, perhaps, not congenial," Stephen remarked.

" They all have boys — and they don't look at things as I do," Miss Peggy admitted, looking modestly down.

George Henry was a little tongue-tied. It was Stephen who still upheld the discussion.

" But you yourself," he said soothingly, " are — forgive me — attractive. How is it that you have no — no admirer? "

" Perhaps I want more than the other girls," Miss Peggy sighed. " They are all such cradle-snatchers. I like a man. I want sympathy day by day, and affection — not just suppers and lunches and motor rides. Young men," she went on artlessly, " are so selfish. They think they have given a girl all they need if they offer what they call ' a good time ', in which, naturally, they share. What I should really like — is a home."

" A very admirable sentiment," Stephen declared approvingly.

" Very," George Henry agreed, a little more limply, feeling with mingled sensations a renewed pressure upon his fingers.

" However," she continued, " why should I worry you two dear, kind things with my troubles? You have both been so sweet to me. It makes me feel better just to talk to you."

" It is possible," Stephen said, glancing at his brother, " that the financial matter you spoke of — the ridiculously inadequate compensation for your services in

'The Singing Bird' — might, through our joint inter-
vention — my brother's and mine — be altered for the
better."

" It would make the girls so jealous if it were known,"
she faltered. " They do talk so, and I wouldn't for
the world. If ——"

" If what? " George Henry asked, bravely responding
to that spasmodic pressure of his fingers.

" Let me talk to you presently," she whispered in
his ear, as the car drew up at the entrance of the
" Milan."

Stephen and George Henry, with their guest, were
ushered with ceremony to their accustomed table. They
found Harold hanging around, and he promptly accepted their rather dubiously offered invitation to
luncheon.

" Well, how goes it, kid? " was his somewhat laconic
greeting of Miss Peggy.

The young lady tossed her head and slipped her new
possession a little lower down upon her wrist.

" Very well, thank you, Mr. Margetson," she replied
haughtily, " and not so much ' kid ', if you please."

" Can't get popular this morning," the young man
complained, with a sigh. " Just put my foot in it with
Bert Stanmore over there. Some spender — Bert —
what? His father left him a hundred thou. last year,
and he's blued the lot."

Stephen leaned forward in his place. He was greatly
interested.

" Do I understand that the young man you spoke of
has dissipated the whole of his patrimony in twelve
months? " he inquired.

" Every bean," Harold assented. " Not a spondulik
left."

"Have you any idea as to the means he employed in this extraordinary dispersal?" Stephen persisted eagerly.

"Fluff and gee-gees," Harold replied, his mouth full of lobster salad. "Some old wheeze — what?"

"He had to pay Flo Manfield ten thousand pounds for breach," Miss Peggy put in. "Flo, too, of all girls in the world!"

"Breach?" Stephen repeated wonderingly.

"Ten thousand pounds?" George Henry gasped.

"Breach of promise of marriage," Peggy explained. "You two dears wouldn't know anything about that. If you made a promise, you'd keep it."

The brothers exchanged stealthy glances. The same idea was dawning upon both of them.

"A very large sum!" Stephen remarked thoughtfully. "Do you mean that the young lady was awarded that amount by the courts?"

"Bert Stanmore compromised," Peggy told them. "He would have had to pay all right, though. Flo stage-managed the whole affair beautifully."

Stephen turned abruptly towards his brother.

"George Henry," he enjoined, "do look after Miss Robinson. Remember that you particularly invited her to luncheon. She would like some more wine, I am sure. And, Miss Robinson, won't you show my nephew the little present my brother has just been privileged to offer you?"

The young lady exhibited the watch, and Harold whistled softly. During the remainder of luncheon he was, for him, unusually silent. At its termination he buttonholed his junior uncle in the lobby.

"See here, nunks," he began, "a nod's as good as a wink to a blind horse — what?"

"It is a universally accepted dictum," George Henry acknowledged.

"Put the brake on with the yellow-headed filly," Harold advised earnestly. "Peggy's a good kid enough, but this chorus gang are pinchers all the way. You see, they can't help it, nunks. The boys are out for what they can take, and it's got to be number one all the time for the girlies, or they're left planted in the middle of it, as the Frenchies say. Do you cotton?"

"I am deeply interested," George Henry assured his nephew. "Pray proceed."

"There are just two ways the girlies can get their own back," Harold continued impressively — "marriage or breach. And I can tell you this, nunks, there's more money goes into the little dears' pockets to heal their bruised hearts than any one would believe. Peggy's better than most of them, but she'd sell you like a bird for the oof."

"Would she indeed!" George Henry murmured, with a gleam in his eyes. "I am much obliged to you for your warning, Harold. I will be discreet."

The brothers, according to their newly established custom, spent a few minutes in their suite before returning to the City. An envelope upon the table attracted Stephen's attention. He tore it hastily open and drew out their weekly bill. George Henry glanced over his shoulder. Both gave vent to a little exclamation of disappointment.

"Ten pounds less than last week!" Stephen exclaimed. "I did at least hope that we could not lose ground here."

"Most disappointing," George Henry murmured absently.

Stephen threw the account upon the table. He glanced keenly at his brother.

"George Henry," he said, "you have something on your mind."

"You are right, Stephen."

"Some plan, perhaps?"

"A glimmering — just a glimmering."

"Connected with Miss Peggy Robinson?"

"Precisely!"

"You are not thinking of proposing to her?"

"That is my intention," George Henry declared heroically. "I shall, of course, change my mind the moment I have committed myself. Harold has just assured me that she will not hesitate to demand heavy damages."

Stephen frowned thoughtfully.

"Your scheme, if successful, will leave me at a great disadvantage as regards relative drawings," he complained.

"I fear so," George Henry acknowledged gleefully.

"I think," Stephen pronounced, after a brief pause, "that this should be a joint affair."

"Impossible!" George Henry objected, with unabated cheerfulness. "We can't both deceive the young lady."

"You could break the engagement at my instigation," Stephen persisted. "I am your elder brother, and in consideration of your yielding to my wishes, I offer to share in any trouble that may ensue."

The gleam in George Henry's eyes was almost cunning. He shook his head firmly.

"You must find a little trouble of your own, Stephen," he declared. "I don't want to seem ungenerous, but there's no room for two in my affair. There are, I believe, several thousand other young ladies who would be delighted to make a victim of you."

" I am older than you," Stephen pleaded.

" Three years," was the prompt reply, " a mere nothing."

" It makes all the difference which side of fifty you are," Stephen argued.

His brother shook his head.

" I do not admit the contention."

Stephen rose to his feet. His manner was distinctly stiff. He called to their servant, who was in the adjoining room.

" Adam! "

" Yes, sir? "

" You will put out our dress coats, white waistcoats and white ties to-night," Stephen directed. " We shall be attending a theatrical supper party."

" And dancing pumps, sir? " the man asked, without flinching.

" And dancing pumps," Stephen replied promptly and defiantly.

The valet bowed and withdrew from the doorway. George Henry glanced at his brother with something almost like awe in his face.

" What is the meaning of this, Stephen? " he demanded.

" I have decided that we will accept the invitation to supper of 'The Singing Bird' company, on the stage after the performance to-night," Stephen announced, with quiet heroism. " It is as you have pointed out. There are other Peggy Robinsons. It is possible," he added, " that if trouble should come of my attentions to any young lady to-night, there may be grave consequences — exemplary damages. If you are quite ready, George Henry, it is time for us to start for the City."

George Henry followed his brother from the room in gloomy silence.

CHAPTER XII

THE arrival of the brothers Underwood upon the stage of the Hilarity Theatre that evening was the signal for a really remarkable outburst of welcoming cheers. The company had just taken their places at the supper table when their unexpected guests somewhat timidly made their appearance in the wings. They were faultlessly dressed, they each carried a pair of white kid gloves, and their silk hats were the glossiest in London. In the distance they looked almost like twins, and the comedian of the party confessed later that he had taken them for an impromptu turn, thoughtfully provided for the entertainment of the party. It was Blanche Whitney who first recognized them, and her introduction made them instantly the most popular persons present. She literally rushed towards them, drew an arm of each through hers, and advanced towards the table.

"Ladies and gentlemen," she announced, "these are my two dear friends, Mr. Stephen and Mr. George Henry Underwood, my most generous backers, who made the production of 'The Singing Bird' possible. God bless 'em both, I say!"

"The syndicate!" some one shouted, and a forest of hands was outstretched. Stephen was promptly installed in the place of honour next to Blanche, and George Henry was directed to the seat on her other side. It was then, however, that the latter, casting aside all timidity, took the first step forward in his newly conceived enterprise.

"There is a young lady down here," he indicated, bowing to Peggy, "whom I have the honour to know. Would it be convenient for me to sit by her side?"

Peggy rose at once to her feet. She was at the lower end of the table, and, by what she described after-wards as an act of Providence, unescorted. She held out her very white arms towards George Henry.

"Come along, you dear man," she begged. "I'll take care of you."

George Henry was promptly installed, introduced to a young lady with jet-black hair and friendly manners, who sat on the other side, and, with an arm of each girl thrust through his, found his plate heaped with food and his glass filled with champagne.

"We'll look after you," the dark young lady promised kindly. "My name is Rose. You must drink my health at once."

"Not so much of this familiarity, if you please," Peggy broke in, a little sharply, tightening her clasp upon his arm. "You belong to me, don't you, Mr. George Henry? And don't you listen to Rose. She's a flirt."

George Henry set his teeth, leaned towards Peggy, and whispered words in her ear which had never before passed his lips. She burst into a peal of laughter and promptly kissed him on the cheek. For a single moment he flinched. He longed, yet dreaded, to look to-wards Stephen. He was profoundly uncomfortable, yet ridiculously light-hearted.

"You meant it, dear, didn't you?" she asked eagerly.

"Of course," he replied.

She clinked her glass against his.

"Please look at me while you drink," she begged.

He obeyed. She had the bluest eyes in the world —

and this was the most wonderful champagne. From across the table, Harold wagged his head mournfully.

"Oh, you giddy old nunks!" he groaned. "You'll put your foot in it before you've finished."

George Henry was rather inclined to think that he had. He settled down to place the matter beyond doubt.

On Stephen's other side was a daring-looking young lady with red hair, a green evening gown of which the shoulder straps were indistinguishable, and browny-green eyes.

"That is Tessy on your right," was Blanche's introduction, "but you must talk to me all the time and take no notice of her. She's dangerous."

"For a bride of less than a year," the young lady in question retorted, "your behaviour, Blanche, is simply disgraceful. Look at Allan glaring at you! Mr. Underwood, you seem like a man of kindly instincts. Do you wish to come between husband and wife?"

"Certainly not," Stephen assured her.

"Then don't let Blanche hold your arm, and please show me a little attention. I am free, unattached — and very lonely."

"I," Stephen declared boldly, "am in the same predicament."

"Cat!" Blanche exclaimed. "You want to take my syndicate away."

"You have an anchorage of your own, dear," Tessy pointed out, "and Allan's so jealous."

"You sound all right, but you're not exactly the friendless orphan yourself, are you?" Blanche laughed. "However, to convince you that Mr. Underwood's affections are already engaged, look at this," she invited, touching the pendant which hung from her neck.

The young lady called Tessy examined it carefully. She was a good judge of such trifles.

"Did he give it to you?" she gasped.

"The dear man did," Blanche replied, "and I am going to thank him for it — as soon as we are alone."

"You mean as soon as Allan isn't there," Tessy observed, a little spitefully.

"Hush!" Blanche whispered, in mock alarm. "Don't give me away."

"I ought, perhaps, to explain," Stephen intervened, "that the little offering you have been admiring comes to Miss Whitney from my brother and myself not only as an expression of our friendly feelings, but as a souvenir of a speculation on our part, the success of which has been due chiefly to her charm and gifts."

"So now you know, you cat!" Blanche exclaimed good-naturedly. "I told you, when they came in, that Mr. Underwood and his brother financed 'The Singing Bird' from the start, and most generously, too."

"You've all the luck, dear," Tessy sighed. "Mr. Underwood," she went on, smiling languishingly into his face, "I am an unrecognized star myself. I should make the fortune of any one who had the courage to back me."

"Don't you believe her," Blanche laughed, tightening her grasp on Stephen's arm. "She can't sing a note, and you can see for yourself how plain she is."

Tessy wiped some non-existent tears from her very bright eyes.

"The jealousy in our profession," she complained, "is too appalling. The way in which the jewel-bedecked prima donnas of musical comedy look down upon the struggling but talented aspirant, is enough to drive one to despair — and drink."

Whereupon the young lady drank off the greater part of a glass of champagne, and leaned over to recite her woes to the stage manager.

"Were you not," Stephen asked his other neighbour diffidently, "a little severe upon the young lady?"

"Oh, Tessy can stand chaff," Blanche assured him. "All the same," she added, dropping her voice, "I don't want to have you too thick with her. Tessy's a good sort, of course, but — she's clever."

"On the stage?" he inquired.

"No, off it," was the prompt reply.

"Kindly explain the innuendo," he begged.

Blanche shrugged her shoulders.

"Well," she said, "when two very unsophisticated and exceedingly wealthy men like your brother and yourself make a late entry into the world of Bohemia, you do so at your own risk. We are all tarred with the same brush. We are tolerably charming, but we've got to live. Tessy's very extravagant, very brainy, and, just at the present moment, very poor."

"I see," Stephen murmured, with a gleam in his eyes. "This is very interesting."

"Well, you be careful, dear old thing," Blanche advised him. "Remember, you declined a very promising flirtation with me, so I can't have you falling a victim to an inferior article."

"Your affections," Stephen reminded her gallantly, "were already engaged."

"Well, Tessy's aren't — or wouldn't be if you gave her any encouragement," was the dry rejoinder.

"Heard my name," that young lady remarked, breaking once more into the conversation. "What's she saying about me, Mr. Underwood?"

"The sweetest things, dear," Blanche assured her.

"Then I'll listen," Tessy declared, laying her un-ringed hand for a moment upon Stephen's. "There's a sight, Mr. Underwood," she continued, stretching out her long, slim fingers with their rather over-manicured nails, "to bring shame upon the over-opulent bachelor with credit at his jeweller's."

"Cadger!" Blanche murmured.

"You haven't often forgotten to ask for anything you wanted yourself, have you, dear?" Tessy retorted.

It was at this stage of the supper that Stephen rose unexpectedly to his feet. He was quite used to ad-dressing City companies, and he spoke simply and with-out hesitation. There was a good deal of rapping on the table and demands for silence as soon as his inten-tion became obvious.

"Ladies and gentlemen," he said, "my brother and I have a brief announcement to make. We entered to-gether into the arrangement to produce ' The Singing Bird ', with the idea of employing a trifle of surplus capital, but with no intention of making a fortune out of your brains and your talent. ' The Singing Bird ' is a well-deserved and, I am told, a phenomenal suc-cess. After the whole of the capital is repaid, it will make, I am assured, a large sum of money. It is our intention — our solicitors have already the matter in hand — to take back our original advance, plus six per cent. interest, a sum which I understand is already earned. The whole of the profits for all future time, here in London, from touring companies and in the United States, will be divided amongst you, ladies and gentlemen, the original members of the cast, in a certain ratio, according to the importance of your parts, and distributed half-yearly. My brother and I thank you very much for your kind hospitality this evening."

It took an appreciable space of time for the idea to sink in, for them all to realize that, in these few seconds, they had attained the Mecca of all actors and actresses — the something certain every week for years to come. But when they did realize it there was pandemonium. No formal speech of thanks could do more than reach its first sentence. The magnitude, the magnificence of the gift, made them almost hysterical. It broke upon them in waves, and with each wave Stephen and George Henry seemed to disappear like drowning men in a sea of white arms and nodding coiffures. Men gripped their hands, and women kissed them, frankly and unashamed. They cried for help to each other across the table. Their hair was ruffled, the shoulders of their dress coats bepowdered, their cheeks pinker than ever. That curious and unassuming dignity, of which both were certainly possessed, availed them nothing. It was not until Harold whispered in the stage manager's ear that " the nunkies might get the pip ", that their escape was connived at. Escorted by their nephew, they were led by a devious way to their car, and finally reached the " Milan " at a little after half-past two in the morning. They were both more dishevelled than they had ever been since their boyhood. They both rather avoided looking at one another. Stephen's tie had slipped round to the back of his neck, and an unsuspected tuft of hair had risen almost perpendicularly at the top of his head. George Henry's tie had escaped from vision altogether, there was a great patch of powder upon his coat sleeve, and a wine stain upon his shirt front. Harold, stretched at full length in their most comfortable easy-chair, gazed at them both through half-closed eyes with a sleepy grin.

" ' The Prodigal Uncles! ' " he murmured, " or,

' Saved by a Nephew! ' Give a quid if the mater could see you both now! ' "

Stephen frowned. The vision of his sister Amelia, a feminine edition of all that was primmest and most narrow in their past lives, rose up and reproved him.

" Your mother," he observed, " would, I trust, understand the position in which we were placed. The gratitude of those young ladies and gentlemen, the former especially, certainly took a most embarrassing form of expression."

Harold pursued his sleepy ruminations.

" Little Rose Matthews," he went on, with a quiet grin of enjoyment, " seated on Uncle George Henry's knee and tickling the back of his neck! Ye gods for a snapshot! "

" I should be obliged if you would desist, Harold," George Henry begged. " I made no response whatever to the young lady's overtures of friendship."

" Peggy saw to that! The green-eyed monster — what? " their young tormentor continued. " If it had gone on much longer, there'd have been trouble in that quarter. And Uncle Stephen, with Tessy's arm around his neck and Tessy whispering in his ear! By the by, what did she say, Uncle Stephen? Stretched herself a bit — what? Brought the colour into your innocent cheeks, what ho! "

" I was unable to gather the exact import of her conversation," Stephen replied with dignity. " Much allowance, however, must be made for these young ladies of emotional temperament, under such circumstances."

" You came the millionaire all right," Harold admitted. " Jolly sporting, I call it. Tom Dixon was working it out that it would mean at least thirty bob a week for life, even to the lowest salaried chorus girl there."

" Your uncle and I," Stephen observed, " will never regret having added something permanent to the emoluments of an exceedingly precarious profession."

" Can't think how you string the words together like that, after fizz," Harold confessed, with drowsy admiration.   " The sixth or seventh glass generally muddles me up."

Stephen, who had forgotten his tie and was fast recovering his poise, frowned severely at his nephew.

" At your age," he said, " such comments and such a style of conversation are most unbecoming.   I do not recognize any personal responsibility with regard to your actions or mode of life, but I am convinced that your mother would consider that your own presence at such a Bohemian gathering as to-night's required some explanation."

The young man's grin was broader than ever.

" That's the tophole part of it all," he pointed out joyfully.   " I got asked because you two were my uncles, and you two are the syndicate behind ' The Singing Bird.' What ho the mater's joy! Shakespeare once a year at a matinée, with tea at an A. B. C. afterwards, and thinks a revue sinful! Let's all have a drink."

Stephen accepted the suggestion without enthusiasm. He pointed to a table, on which was set out a bottle of Perrier water and some sliced lemon upon a plate. Their bottle of whisky he had carefully removed on his first entrance

" Our customary evening refreshment is there," he said. " Pray help yourself."

The young man staggered to his feet and helped himself unsteadily. He took only the briefest sip from his tumbler, which he set down with a grimace. He glanced reproachfully at his uncle.

"Nasty flat-tasting stuff, that," he complained. "Why not a bottle of the boy? Wind up the evening. Clear up all unpleasantness, what?"

"If you are referring to champagne, certainly not, Harold," Stephen refused sternly. "You have had quite as much to drink as is good for you. At your age the stimulus of alcohol should be entirely unnecessary."

"Unnecessary," Harold repeated, with a slight hiccough and a fixed stare. "Quite so!"

"You will oblige us, Harold, by taking your departure now," Stephen directed. "Your Uncle George Henry and I wish to retire."

"And quite time, too — quite time," their refractory nephew declared, frowning upon them both. "Kept me up to a shocking hour, as it is — what? Before I go — duty I owe you both — just a word of warning. I know the world. You two innocents don't. Keep off the fluff, nunkies, or you'll get stung."

Stephen opened his lips, but found himself speechless. He glanced towards his brother for support and George Henry made a brief protest.

"We find your attitude, Harold," he pronounced, "most unbecoming."

"Boil yourself, nunky!" was the prompt but inelegant reply. "You've got your own little kettle of fish stewing. It's — it's Uncle Stephen here I'm worried about. Terribly worried about you, Uncle Stephen."

"You may spare yourself any concern as to my affairs," Stephen assured him stiffly.

Harold adopted a more "man of the world" and

friendly attitude. Needing the support of the table, he clutched it with his left hand and laid his right kindly upon his uncle's shoulder.

"That girl Tessy," he continued confidentially, "she's out for the beans. She's a red-hot 'un after the oof. Draw in your horns, Uncle Stephen, or she'll have you bottled. What ho the four-fingered cheque, the sobbing child upon your shoulder, or the head line in the evening papers!"

Stephen shivered a little, but he showed a curious and not altogether displeased interest in his nephew's warning.

"I fancy," he said with dignity, "that both your Uncle George Henry and I can be trusted to meet in a becoming manner any untoward incident which might arise out of our friendship with these young ladies. You will excuse my hurrying you, Harold," he added, holding out his nephew's hat and opening the door. "It is long past our usual hour for retiring."

"That's all ri'," the young man declared amiably. "What a night we've had, eh? Look you up in your private office to-morrow morning, Uncle Stephen. Mater told me — 'Always go to your Uncle Stephen when in trouble.' Beast of a tailor — and not enough of the ready. So long!"

The young man departed. They listened to his unsteady footsteps and vehement summons for the lift.

"Blackmail," Stephen murmured.

"I fear so," George Henry assented.

There was a moment's somewhat embarrassed silence. Each had chanced to glance into the mirror, and each had made abortive attempts to improve his dishevelled appearance.

"I fancy," Stephen remarked, in a gratified tone, "that Harold was right about the young woman, Tessy."

"Indeed!" George Henry exclaimed, much interested.

"She was exceedingly anxious that I should escort her home," Stephen continued, drawing a small latch-key from his pocket. "She absolutely refused to permit me to restore this to her. She lives with another young lady, though, so she will probably not be inconvenienced. I have invited her to join us at luncheon to-morrow, George Henry."

"Most fortunate," his brother declared. "I have invited Miss Peggy."

"You found the young lady amenable?"

"Amenable but somewhat affectionate," George Henry replied, closing his eyes and painfully conscious of that patch of powder.

"Miss — er — Tessy possesses the same weakness," Stephen confessed. "I think, however, that there is no doubt as to their intentions."

"I trust not," George Henry groaned. "It would be a great pity if we had gone through all this for nothing."

"I have no fears whatever on that score myself," Stephen pronounced. "As a matter of fact, the attitude of Miss Tessy towards financial matters is already defining itself."

"Peggy, too," George Henry confided cheerfully, "is in some slight trouble owing to having assisted a friend. There are also some articles of jewellery which it appears are in the hands of a pawnbroker."

"Poor child," his brother remarked sympathetically. "Good night, George Henry. This time, I fancy, to use one of Harold's most objectionable phrases, we are on a winner."

"Good night, Stephen! Things certainly appear promising," was the hopeful reply.

CHAPTER XIII

HAROLD made a somewhat unwelcome appearance at the " Milan " grillroom on the following morning, when the luncheon party was in full swing. His uncles viewed his approach coldly, and the two young ladies, who were fully occupied, scarcely glanced in his direction.

" More festivities! " he exclaimed reproachfully, as he paused in front of the table and essayed light-hearted greetings with his uncles' guests. " Food, too! How horrible! What price an absinthe cocktail? "

" At some other table this morning," Stephen insisted. " There is no accommodation here for five."

" You can go and lunch with Julia Winch," Tessy suggested. " She's round the other side somewhere."

Harold surveyed the little party sorrowfully.

" Makes one feel like old Lear," he sighed. " The ungrateful uncles — what! Who brought you four together, I should like to know? To whom do you owe your happiness, children? Who ——"

" You are interfering with the service of luncheon, Harold," Stephen pointed out sternly. " You are also interrupting our conversation. I trust that this hint will be sufficient for you."

Harold sighed deeply and wandered away with the air of one whose feelings are past speech.

" One gets so weary of these boys," Tessy murmured, looking into Stephen's eyes.

" They are all exactly alike," Peggy echoed, touching George Henry's hand by accident. " If men only realized how we girls long for a little common sense! "

"Some one to look up to," Tessy put in.

"Some one strong enough to guide us through life," Peggy whispered, looking sadly into vacancy.

"It's like going back to the nursery and playing with dolls, wasting time with these boys," Tessy went on. "They think themselves so irresistible, too. If they only knew how they bored us!"

"It isn't as though it led anywhere," Peggy added, a little indiscreetly.

"Even if it did, who wants to marry one of these brainless young idiots?" Tessy demanded. "Selfish, empty-headed creatures, with only one idea in their heads. Give me the man of fifty every time."

"Or even fifty-five," Peggy assented, studying George Henry through half-closed eyes. "A man's at his very best from fifty to sixty."

"This is very flattering," Stephen declared, with a twinkle in his shrewd eyes.

"Most reassuring," George Henry echoed, mechanically straightening his tie.

"What are you two old dears going to do this afternoon?" Tessy inquired.

"We return to the office at three o'clock," Stephen announced.

"How early!" Tessy pouted. "Peggy and I are going shopping in Bond Street. Couldn't you find time to drive us there?"

"There must be presents," George Henry whispered furtively to his brother.

"We shall be at your disposal for half an hour," Stephen assented graciously. "You must let us know where to take you."

After that luncheon was speedily concluded, and the shopping expedition was a complete success. On the way back to the City, however, the brothers were a little thoughtful. There was a gently reminiscent smile playing about Stephen's lips. George Henry, too, seemed to find some humour in his thoughts.

" One cannot help wondering," the former observed presently, " what would have happened to Miss Tessy's purchase of hats in our absence."

" The fact that she had left her purse at home seemed to amuse the French lady who served us," George Henry remarked. " I saw her go behind the partition to laugh."

" Miss Peggy was most candid," Stephen said approvingly. " I saw her pointing out to you with great care the things she would like to have and couldn't afford."

George Henry nodded.

" Yes," he agreed, smiling, " and I noticed that the salesman immediately made out a bill for those articles and presented it to me. It saved me the embarrassment of pressing her to accept them, of course, but in other respects it seemed a little premature."

Stephen glanced towards his brother with a pleasant glitter in his keen grey eyes, and a rare smile upon his lips.

" They took us, George Henry," he observed, " for a couple of simpletons."

" I had not the least objection to that," George Henry assented, with a kindred relaxation of expression, " but I must certainly have an understanding with Peggy with reference to embraces in public."

" I quite agree with you," Stephen declared heartily. " The gratitude of both young ladies was pleasing but decidedly embarrassing."

" Not to say unseemly," George Henry pronounced.

"Miss Tessy," Stephen ruminated, a few moments later, "appears to have met with many misfortunes in life."

"Indeed!" his brother murmured sympathetically.

"Her father was a professional man," Stephen continued. "He was led into an unfortunate speculation and obliged to resign his position. He is occupied now in the uncongenial avocation of scene-shifting. For the sake of her two younger sisters, Tessy is obliged to eke out his slender salary from her own savings."

"The study of these poor girls' lives," George Henry declared, "reveals a great deal of silent heroism. No one would guess, to see them at the 'Milan' and these places, day by day, what a burden of sorrow some of them must carry about with them. Peggy's father, for instance, as I think I told you, was a country doctor, with a very unremunerative practice. He is now, unfortunately, dead, and the care of her mother and a delicate sister seems largely to devolve upon Peggy. She has her periods of great financial anxiety."

The car drew up outside the offices in Basinghall Street.

"There is no doubt," Stephen observed, as he descended and led the way to the scene of their labours, "that we have been exceedingly fortunate in coming across two young ladies who are so thoroughly deserving of the small financial assistance which we are able to tender them."

The climax arrived one morning, about a fortnight later, when the brothers were seated before their respective desks, having just concluded the task of dealing with their business correspondence. There remained only two private letters, one addressed to

George Henry in a distinctly feminine and familiar handwriting, the other to Stephen in a typewritten envelope, with the name of a firm of solicitors at the back.

"Miss Tessy," Stephen observed gladly, "has lost no time. My letter is from an unknown firm of solicitors. I understand that she declines to communicate with me personally in any shape or form — most correct."

"Peggy appears to have written me herself," George Henry declared, a little nervously. "There can be no doubt, however, as to her course of action. She has my letter, deliberately offering marriage, and my subsequent note of withdrawal without explanation or apology. My behaviour has been disgraceful. I imagine that it will cost me at least ten thousand pounds to hush this thing up."

"Tessy is, I am convinced, intensely mercenary," Stephen remarked, in a cheerful tone. "You see, she has placed the matter in the hands of a solicitor within twenty-four hours. Most promising! George Henry, I suggest that you open your letter."

George Henry did so, and his brother read it over his shoulder :—

Dear old Man,—

Your note this morning gave me a nasty start. I don't mind confessing that I have been crying most of the time since. What a beast you are to make me so happy, and then — just change your mind!

However, you're right. I should make you a rotten wife. I'm sending you back your letter in which you asked me to marry you, and let me give you a word of advice. Don't write to a girl in that way again unless you mean it. You might get into trouble. That letter would cost you a fortune if the wrong sort of girl got hold of it.

I am going to keep your presents, for luck — and the ring. You won't mind that, will you?

You are a funny old thing, and I'm rather sorry, dear.

PEGGY.

George Henry looked blankly into his brother's face. There were little beads of perspiration upon his forehead.

" This is horrible! " he muttered. " Stephen, do you realize — I'm a cad! "

" The young lady's attitude is astonishing," Stephen acknowledged. " The luck appears to be with me."

He tore open the solicitor's letter. They both read it breathlessly:

SIR,—

Our client, Miss Tessy Hamilton, has consulted us with reference to bringing an action against you for breach of promise of marriage.

" The real thing," Stephen murmured.

It has come to our knowledge, however, that the lady in question has already a husband living — a Mr. James Tanner, commercial traveller in the ironmongery business, residing in Tottenham. We have accordingly returned all documents in the case, and beg to advise you of the above-stated fact, in case any proceedings might be taken against you in other directions.

Trusting that you will appreciate our action in the matter,

We are, Sir,
Faithfully yours,

DAVIS & DAVIS.

George Henry's chuckle was significant and vociferous.

" You're no better off than I am, Stephen! "

" Our scheme," his brother admitted grimly, " seems to have ended in failure."

" After all we have been through! " George Henry groaned.

They gazed at one another blankly for several moments. Then George Henry rose to his feet and took down his hat from the peg.

" Where are you going? " Stephen inquired.

" I am going to beg Miss Peggy's pardon," George Henry announced, " and buy her an annuity, if she'll accept it."

Stephen frowned.

" That," he protested, " is rather taking advantage of me."

George Henry looked back from the door.

" You can buy an ironmongery business for Mr. James Tanner," he suggested — " if you feel like it."

CHAPTER XIV

CHRISTMAS came and went, signs of an early spring began to appear. Things were going far too well with the brothers Underwood. They had settled down into the rut of their enlarged life, with very little effort and with no desire to abandon it. It had not brought them, however, the relief they sought. Looming in the near future was the coming balance sheet, the record of another half-year of success and prosperity, and in the background the vision of that private ledger, with its utterly inadequate figures. "The Singing Bird" was still the greatest success in London and New York, and there was already a Press campaign for the early opening of the Rawlingsey Open Theatre, a course of action strongly advised by Mr. Hiram B. Pluck, who was always coming over to their table at the "Milan" to exchange greetings with the brothers, and indulging in sanguine estimates of the year's profits. Further, George Henry's appeal to Miss Robinson, who had refused the visit of a lawyer with reference to the proposed annuity, had evoked no response whatsoever. A letter from George Henry himself to the same young lady remained unanswered. She was never to be seen in the "Milan", and Miss Whitney and her husband had settled down to domesticity in the suburbs. Altogether the world was a dull place.

It was so dull that, one morning early in March, the brothers broke through their rule and, seeing Harold wandering about looking for a table, they invited him to lunch. Harold accepted the invitation readily and showed himself possessed of much *sang froid*.

" Now that we're away from the office," he said, putting down the menu, after having ordered what might be considered a very satisfactory luncheon, including oysters, a thin slice of smoked salmon, *Sole Colbert,* and a grilled cutlet, " is there any objection if I speak to you both as man to man? "

" Within certain bounds," Stephen replied, " we are willing to listen to you. We have always recognized the fact that away from Basinghall Street we meet on a slightly different footing."

" Just so," Harold agreed, making cryptic signs with his fingers which intimated to the *sommelier* his urgent need of a cocktail. " I came into Basinghall Street just a little young and you two came into the life of Bohemia just a little old. We can learn from one another."

" The preliminaries of this conversation," Stephen observed, " appear to us to be unduly extended. Kindly proceed."

Harold leaned across the table confidentially.

" You've got the pip, both of you," he declared. " Got it badly. Any one can see that. What's wrong with you both? Everything goes your way. You only have to touch a spec. and it turns up trumps. Even when you dabble with the fluff you don't burn your fingers. I suppose you heard that Tessy's gone off to South America with a wholesale fruit broker, and Miss Peggy Robinson's left the show for a time and gone up to nurse her mother in Cumberland? You two were asking for trouble in those directions. Did you get it? No! What about the Rawlingsey Theatre scheme? Old man Pluck assures me that, if he floats the company next year, you will come out of that with something like a hundred thousand of the best.   Why not sing ' Begone Dull Care? '   The spring is upon us, the dibs are in your pocket and life is short.   Yet you sit there day after day like a couple of old owls."

Stephen glanced questioningly at his brother and received a little nod of assent.

" Without going into the fullest particulars, Harold," he said, " we have decided to consult you.   It is our desire, the desire of your Uncle George Henry and myself, for reasons which do not concern you, to increase our yearly expenditure.   We have done what we can in that direction.   We have the most expensive suite in the Milan Court.   There is the car, and, as you are aware, we have abandoned the services of our former trades-people and frequent establishments where the top prices are charged for everything.   Yet that is not nearly enough.   Put yourself in our position, Harold. We desire to spend more money.   How should you set about it ? "

Harold coughed and finished his cocktail.   The speculation was full of delightful possibilities.

" There's a little lady ——" he declared enthusiastically.

" Without resort to any feminine entanglement," Stephen interrupted sternly.

Harold came down to earth.

" Right ho! " he exclaimed.   " Well then, to begin with, it's a bit late, but I should trip it to Monte. That's the place to shift the shekels."

" The suggestion has merit," Stephen acknowledged, " and I may say that your uncle and I considered the matter at Christmas time.   We do not, however, speak a word of French and we have, consequently, the strongest dislike to travelling in foreign countries. We have only been abroad once — a Polytechnic tour to Switzerland, before you were born."

"Would you like to take Trixy Holton on, with a new play she has?" Harold suggested. "I haven't read it myself, but one or two of the lads have told me that it's the goods all right. Four bedroom scenes and a ball in the South Sea Islands."

"The idea does not appeal to us at all," George Henry interposed quickly.

"The play would, without a doubt, succeed if we financed it," Stephen declared gloomily, "and we should be worse off than ever."

A ray of sunshine fell upon the tablecloth. Harold looked out towards the courtyard. There was a streak of blue sky between the tall roofs. He was suddenly inspired.

"Take a country house, a large one, with all the servants left. Somewhere close enough to town to motor up every day. You can keep your rooms on here just the same. Cost you a pretty penny, that would, I can tell you. You can let me bring a little party down for week-ends."

"A country house!" Stephen reflected. "George Henry, how does the suggestion appeal to you?"

"Favourably," was the prompt reply. "I was always fond of a garden."

"Saw an advertisement of just the thing for you," Harold continued, with growing enthusiasm, "in *Country Life* this morning. Perfectly wonderful estate. Belongs to a Lady Drummond. I'll bring you particulars this afternoon."

"We shall consider them with interest," Stephen promised.

The particulars were duly forthcoming and the brothers acted with businesslike promptitude. They paid a large deposit that evening at five o'clock, motored at once down into Surrey, signed the agreement the following morning, and spent the next week-end at Keston Court.

Their first Sunday was an unqualified success. After breakfast they walked together upon the terrace of their newly rented domain, and indulged in a morning cigarette. It was a very delightful country house of considerable size, in perfect order, with a full establishment of servants — most picturesque and satisfactory from every point of view. Both Stephen and George Henry were in excellent spirits.

" I imagine," the former remarked, looking about him, " that it will be quite impossible for us to live here without a large, a very large expenditure."

" The same thought has occurred to me," George Henry assented cheerfully.

" I understand," Stephen continued, " that we have seven gardeners to pay weekly."

" A third manservant brought me my shaving water," George Henry announced, " and from what I have seen of the butler, I should think that he would be cheap at five hundred a year. Then there is the housekeeper, the lady in black silk and old lace, whom you took for Lady Drummond herself. She has a suite of rooms of her own, and a maid to wait upon her. Her remuneration must naturally be on a liberal scale."

" And the shooting, too," Stephen pointed out. " We know nothing whatever of sport. We are sure to be robbed. I understand that gamekeepers are remarkably proficient in the art of mulcting their employers."

They stood for a moment looking across the exceedingly pleasant prospect of tree-embowered park, with cornfields and rich meadow lands beyond. Stephen laid his hand affectionately upon his brother's shoulder.

" This," he declared, " is better than any speculation. Here we have certain expenditure from which we cannot escape. The upkeep of an estate like this must be enormous, and the rent, although not so much as I had hoped, is still considerable, especially with the extra four hundred for the shooting."

" The prospect is most satisfactory," George Henry acknowledged. " I hope that, at last, we may be able to satisfy Mr. Duncan. I consider his remarks, when he sent us back our balance sheet, a little uncalled for, considering the great increase in our personal expenditure."

" I saw him yesterday at the ' Milan '," Stephen observed. " I told him that we had taken Keston Court furnished, at a rent of three thousand a year."

" Good! What did he say? "

" His remark was doubtless meant to be jocular," Stephen admitted, " but I found in it a certain satire, to the use of which I presume he felt himself entitled. He simply observed that, without doubt, we should discover gold under the tennis lawns, coal in the park, and a clause in the lease by virtue of which these became the property of the tenant! "

A personage of exceedingly august demeanour came slowly along the terrace towards them. He was clean-shaven, austere and pompous. In his morning clothes and black bow, he had the appearance of being much better dressed than either of his masters.

" I beg your pardon, sir," he said, bowing to Stephen.

"Mrs. Buxton desires to know if you will accord her an audience."

"Mrs. Buxton?"

"Your housekeeper, sir."

"We will see Mrs. Buxton in the library at once," Stephen consented.

"Very good, sir."

The new tenants of Keston Court took up a position of vantage in their magnificent library, and awaited the proposed visit. Stephen stood upon the hearthrug, his hands, however, vainly seeking the protection of his customary coat tails, dark flannel suits having been allotted to them by their valet as more suitable wear for the country on Sunday morning. George Henry supported his brother from the depths of an easy-chair. The entrance of Mrs. Buxton seemed to indicate that such support might be necessary. The perfection of her simple attire, her poise, and the manner in which she gave her orders to the maid who followed her, carrying various books, were all evidences of a status and qualities entirely unfamiliar to her new employers. She greeted them kindly, however, and accepted the chair which Stephen placed for her.

"That will do, Amy," she told her follower, as she watched the disposal of the books upon the table. "I will ring when you are required."

The maid departed and Mrs. Buxton drew the books towards her. The onus of opening the interview appeared to rest with the brothers.

"You had something to say to us?" Stephen ventured.

Mrs. Buxton smiled faintly. She seemed to wish them to understand that her request was wholly inspired by a desire for their benefit.

" I thought it best to explain to you," she said, " my system of keeping the housekeeping books, to go through the salary account with you in case you should desire to effect any reductions, and to explain my views generally as to the economical management of the household."

The brothers looked at one another a little blankly. Stephen waved away the ledger which Mrs. Buxton was opening in a businesslike manner.

" My dear Mrs. Buxton," he begged, " pray, do not trouble us with any details. Our lives, as you doubtless know, have been and are still spent in commercial pursuits, and in private life we do not wish to be worried with accounts. The recommendations which we have received are sufficient. We leave the management of this establishment entirely in your hands."

" And pray do not think," George Henry put in, " of any reductions."

Mrs. Buxton seemed a little unnerved, also more than a little surprised.

" I understood," she said, " that, being City gentlemen, you would take some interest in the economical management of an establishment such as this."

" My brother and I," Stephen explained, " have no particular desire for economy. We are, in fact, inclined — inclined to be extravagant, are we not, George Henry? "

" Most decidedly," was the prompt assent. " Anything in the nature of undue economy, Mrs. Buxton, is repugnant to us."

Mrs. Buxton was distinctly nonplussed.

" You will forgive my remarking that this is unexpected," she observed.

" You will get used to us, Mrs. Buxton," Stephen

declared encouragingly. " We ask you — our wishes are that you conduct this place in as lavish a style as possible. Spare no expense in the meals which you order for us or for the servants' hall. Let our domestics be well paid. You spoke just now of reductions. We should, on the other hand, prefer you to look through the list of servants and see whether some slight advances might not be desirable. Your own salary, for instance, Mrs. Buxton, if you will excuse me? "

" I am paid two hundred pounds a year, with the services of my maid, and a private sitting room," Mrs. Buxton announced.

" Ridiculously inadequate! " Stephen exclaimed.

" Absurd! " George Henry echoed.

" Let me suggest three hundred pounds," the former begged. " I trust that the emoluments of the house generally are not fixed upon such a paltry basis? "

Mrs. Buxton pressed her fingers for a moment against her forehead.

" Gentlemen," she confessed, " you have a little confused me."

Stephen coughed.

" Mrs. Buxton," he said, " let us take you into our confidence. We are rich men."

" Increasingly rich," George Henry added dismally.

" We have only lately realized our duty," Stephen continued, " as regards the dispersal of a certain proportion of our income. It is our wish to spend more. It is for that reason we have taken this very charming country estate. Do not cramp our efforts at the start, Mrs. Buxton. Do not wage here a campaign of economy. Get value for your money, but spend."

" You confuse me, gentlemen," Mrs. Buxton repeated.

"It has been the study of my life to effect every possible economy in the management of various households with which I have been associated. I was hoping that in your service, and with your assistance, you being City gentlemen, I might have learnt something more of the art to which I have devoted a good many years."

"On the contrary," Stephen pointed out, "we should wish you, whilst you honour us with your services, to unlearn as much as possible."

"I have succeeded," Mrs. Buxton announced, with some flickering pride, "in reducing the indoor expenses of this establishment, with four people day by day, and occasional lunches and dinner parties, to fifty pounds a week."

"My dear Mrs. Buxton!"

"My dear lady!"

"Fifty pounds a week must mean starvation for every one!" Stephen protested.

"A life of misery for all concerned," George Henry echoed.

"We are not socialists," Stephen continued, "but we wish the servants' hall to fare as well as the rest of the house. We should like you, Mrs. Buxton, to arrange a little entertainment once a week in the servants' hall — a small band for dancing, or any popular entertainers you may fancy, could be secured from Keith Prowse's. We shall not consider the expense. If more convenient, we could arrange this matter ourselves."

"We have also," George Henry informed her, "a motor car coming down, intended entirely for the use of the domestics under your control. My brother and I being in the City a portion of every day, and the staff numbering, I believe, over twenty, they will naturally have a certain amount of spare time."

Mrs. Buxton rose slowly to her feet. She was so upset that she picked up the ledgers herself and placed them under her arm.

"Gentlemen," she said, "you will forgive my saying so, but I find your views so extraordinarily opposed to my preconceived ideas, that, for the moment, I am nonplussed. I thank you very much for your offer of an increased salary, but I am not sure whether I shall be able to give you satisfaction. I have never been accustomed to conduct a household in the manner you suggest."

"Give it a trial, Mrs. Buxton," Stephen begged.

"I will, with your permission," Mrs. Buxton decided, "consider the position in my apartment."

She moved towards the door. Stephen opened it, and closed it after her. He looked anxiously towards his brother.

"Well?"

"I am afraid," the latter regretted, "that Mrs. Buxton did not altogether appreciate our point of view."

"She is evidently," Stephen remarked, "a lady of very strict demeanour. I imagine that her sense of discipline and economy will induce her before long to seek a position elsewhere. Let us try what we can do out of doors. We will see if we can discover Mr. Andrews, the gardener."

They strolled across the lawn, and at the entrance to a walled garden, one end of which was glittering with greenhouses, they came upon that potentate. It being Sunday, Mr. Andrews was dressed in sober black, and wore a black bowler hat. He carried gloves and an umbrella.

"The clergyman coming to call," George Henry whispered.

"Nothing of the sort," Stephen replied. "This is the man we are looking for. Good morning, Andrews," he went on. "Fine lot of glass you have here."

"But it's not so expensive to keep up, sir," the man assured him, raising his hat. "It's wonderful what can be done with five men and a couple of boys, properly looked after, and prices of fruit in the West End what they are. You'll be surprised, sir, when you see my books."

"Another Mrs. Buxton!" George Henry groaned.

"Do we understand," Stephen demanded, "that you are accustomed to dispose of the fruit you grow here, by selling it?"

Mr. Andrews stared at his questioner.

"You'll no understand what we do raise, sir," he remarked compassionately. "I'll just be taking you round."

"We are not interfering with your Sunday habits, I trust?"

"It's of small consequence, sir," the man replied. "You gentlemen who work so hard in the City, and have only the Sabbath for enjoying your homes, must be considered. And the church here's no to my liking, and that's a fact. You'll just follow me, gentlemen, and will the last one kindly shut all doors behind him."

The new tenants of Keston Court spent an exceedingly exhausting hour, at the end of which Mr. Andrews invited them into a small shanty rigged up as an office. Here he produced several memorandum books and some sheets of ruled paper.

"I prepared this for your coming, gentlemen," he announced, "knowing you're from the City, and keen, as it were, on the matter of figures. On this side you'll see the salary account, which, with my own wages, five men and two boys, comes to a matter of eighteen pounds a week. Then there's the cost of seeds, manure, coal, and other items — you see them there — and on the other side there's the sales — no such bad sales, either — and an allowance for such fruit and vegetables as is sent to the house and servants' quarters. You'll see, gentlemen, that the gardens and hothouses are verra nearly self-supporting. I'm proud of those figures, gentlemen. Take them away and study them, if you're willing."

Stephen adjusted his pince-nez, glanced through the memorandum book, and shook his head gravely as he returned it.

"Andrews," he said, " this is most disappointing."

"Disappointing, you call it?" the gardener exclaimed, a little taken aback. "If there's a man this side of the Tweed can show you better results ——"

"Don't misunderstand me," Stephen interrupted. "Your figures are wonderful, but in every detail your accounts show a lamentable tendency towards the vice which is our pet aversion, the vice of parsimony."

The Scotchman removed his hat and scratched his head.

"The Good Lord!" he murmured. "Parsimony!"

"Yes, Andrews," his new employer continued firmly. "Here I find that you put down your own salary — you, whom I understand to be one of the most accomplished raisers of fruit and vegetables in this country — at four pounds a week. Disgraceful!"

"It's no too much for a man like me," Andrews protested.

"Too much?" Stephen repeated. "It's too little, man! Do you want us to feel, every minute of the day, that we are slave-drivers, my brother and I?"

" Eh? What's that? "

" Your salary list all through is a disgrace," Stephen pronounced sternly. " I am not blaming you, Andrews. You are an honest man and have done your best for your employers. You forget, however, that there are others to be studied. Do you not owe something to yourself and to your family, and to those who work for you so faithfully? "

Andrews smiled in a sickly fashion. He was not at all sure that he was not being made fun of.

" You will forgive me, gentlemen," he begged. " This is strange hearing."

" We shall not quarrel," Stephen said firmly. " You are a man of the world, Andrews. You are a shrewd man. You will recognize the fact that it is necessary for you to adapt yourself to the whims and ideas of your employers. You have been drawing four pounds a week. The thought makes me shiver."

George Henry looked at his brother in silent admiration. Considering, as he well knew, that they neither of them had the faintest idea as to what a gardener's wages might be, he was perhaps justified.

" You will kindly," Stephen instructed, " draw, in future, six pounds a week. You will increase the salaries of your staff by twenty-five per cent., and you will at once discontinue this mercenary principle of sending your fruit to market."

" Discontinue? No send my fruit to market? " the man exclaimed. " Am I to make a dunghill of it, then? "

" Are there no hospitals? " Stephen demanded severely. " Think of the thousands of suffering men and women in the great London hospitals, to whom the taste of one of your peaches would be like nectar! "

" Eh, there's them," Andrews admitted wonderingly.

"My brother and I are directors of several hospitals," Stephen continued. "We shall hand you a list to-morrow. In future, the whole of the surplus fruit will be dispatched at convenient days of the week to such institutions as we shall indicate. See that the servants' hall, as well as the dining room, are thoroughly well supplied."

Andrews closed his books a little reluctantly.

"I'm no denying, sir," he confessed, "that you've given me a bit of a shock. When I heard that the place was let to two City gentlemen, I was thinking they'd appreciate my ways. I'm your servant, though, and I'll obey your orders. Eh, but it's a powerful lot of fruit and vegetables to be giving away for just nothing at all — even to the hospitals!" he added, a little sorrowfully.

"My brother and I are not in need of money," Stephen explained. "On the contrary, it is our wish to spend it."

"You're no Scotch, gentlemen, that's verra certain," Andrews observed, with a faint attempt at waggishness. "As regards the trifle of increase in my own salary, I'm not above taking it and thanking ye kindly, and I'll bear in mind your wishes with regard to the others. — There's a footpath this way to the house, gentlemen, or I'll attend you there if you desire it."

They parted company, and Stephen drew a little sigh of relief.

"Thank heaven, the man was Scotch so far as regards his own salary, at any rate," he murmured, as they retraced their steps towards the house.

CHAPTER XV

AFTER luncheon, the brothers, by previous arrangement, strolled across to the neighbouring golf links. George Henry spoke hopefully of the extravagance of sport.

"I was reading an article in one of the reviews last week," he said, "in which the writer asserted that the money spent in sports and game in the United Kingdom during a single year was sufficient to liquidate the National Debt."

"One could no doubt spend a great deal in yachting and horse-racing," Stephen acquiesced.

"Neither of those sports is open to us," George Henry pointed out. "You and I are both, unfortunately, subject to seasickness; and as regards horses ——"

"Our deed of partnership prohibits any speculation with regard to them," Stephen interrupted. "Quite right! We must see what golf will do for us."

They found the professional in his workshop. He was a large loosely built Scotchman, with stubbly, fair moustache and keen eyes. He looked them over with interest and bade them a cheerful "Good afternoon."

"We have come to consult you," Stephen explained, "with reference to our starting the game of golf."

"And why not, indeed?" was the decisive answer. "It's a healthy sport, gentlemen, and the least expensive there is."

The faces of the golfing aspirants perceptibly lengthened.

"We had an idea," George Henry said diffidently, "that if we purchased every known variety of club, indulged in a new ball for every hole, and engaged a golf professional to devote himself solely to our tuition ——"

"Eh, mon, but it's no necessary," the professional intervened. "Half a dozen clubs each in one of my hide leather bags — they're no more than twenty-five and sixpence each — will start you properly. As to a new ball at every hole, the thing's ridiculous, as you'll realize when you've played the game. And a couple of hours' tuition a day, which I can very well spare you myself, will be all that you're needing from a golf professional. A matter of twenty pounds will make golfers of you, gentlemen."

Stephen sighed.

"I have no doubt, George Henry," he said to his brother, "that we shall find the pursuit exhilarating."

"Even if it fails to help us in our present state of embarrassment," was the somewhat dismal response.

The professional glanced at his watch.

"I've an hour to spare, gentlemen," he suggested, "if you feel like taking your first lesson. There's a club or two in the shop would suit you nicely."

The acquisition of clubs, at any rate, appealed to his two visitors, and was conducted upon a scale which made their vendor, notwithstanding his nationality, indulge in a little mild remonstrance. Thereupon followed an hour, during which Stephen and George Henry, throwing dignity to the winds, endeavoured to train and develop a new sense and a new set of muscles. The result was not altogether unsatisfactory, and the professional bade them an encouraging farewell.

"You'll no make scratch golfers, gentlemen," was his

comment, " but you'll be a pair of useful half-swingers when I've done with you."

" This is all very well, so far as it goes," Stephen observed, as soon as they were out of earshot, " but I am afraid that, except from the health point of view, golf is likely to be of little use to us. The man hesitated even to accept the sovereign which I pressed into his hand as a little recognition of his efforts."

" That may have been," George Henry confessed, with a somewhat conscious smile, " because I had just given him one myself."

" You were unreasonably secretive about it, George Henry," his brother said severely. " I did not see you even put your hand into your pocket."

" Neither did I see you, for the matter of that," was the cheerful retort.

Stephen sighed.

" You are right," he admitted. " We must not allow our troubles to come between us, George Henry. We must endeavour to treat one another with confidence. — Who is this person? "

George Henry, who had once been a great reader of a certain class of old-fashioned fiction, recognized immediately the brown velveteen coat, the corduroy leggings and knobbly stick of the man who stood prepared to accost them.

" It is a gamekeeper," he declared.

" Our gamekeeper," Stephen observed hopefully. " This may be another chance for us, George Henry. I have heard that the preserving of game is very expensive."

The man touched his hat respectfully and introduced himself.

" I beg your pardon, sir," he said. " Name of

Higgs. Happening to see you come along, and hearing that you was away most of the week-days, I made so bold as to come out for a word."

" Quite right," Stephen replied. " You, I believe, are the gamekeeper to the estate? "

" Gamekeeper and vermin-killer, sir," the man assented. " There's two thousand acres of it, and a good bit of wood. There ain't many hours of the day that I'm idle."

" Two thousand acres! " Stephen repeated, in a shocked tone. " My good man, we are not sweaters, my brother and I! You must engage an assistant immediately."

" Yes! " George Henry chimed in. " Get another vermin-killer."

" We are most anxious," Stephen explained, " that our employés should be comfortable and not overwork themselves."

The man appeared a little dazed.

" I know of a likely lad, sir," he admitted, touching his hat. " I'll speak to him to-morrow. What I wanted to ask was — was you thinking of rearing? "

" Rearing," Stephen repeated, in a tone of great deliberation.

" Ah! " George Henry murmured, looking sagely at his brother.

" To tell you the truth," Stephen confided, with simple candour, " we have never before resided upon a country estate. Exactly what do you mean? "

" There's a nice few wild birds there, sir," the man explained, " but we've generally reared a few hundred, up to this year. It's full late now, but the last lot of eggs is only a week overdue, and there's hens in plenty. The coops are all ready, and if you'd a fancy for turning out a few more hundreds, it could be managed."

"The idea appeals to us," Stephen assented at once. "This pheasant rearing, I understand, is a most expensive process."

"Not the way I does it," the man replied, with a pitying smile. "With meal at its present price, and rakings, I'll turn you out a nice lot of birds as you'd hardly notice the cost of, so to speak. Mr. Helmsby, over to Wanford, has the eggs."

"Arrange for them to-morrow," Stephen directed, producing his pocketbook, "and whatever you do, don't underfeed the birds. If anything is required to add to their comfort, pray see to it. My brother and I are exceedingly fond of birds."

"We had an aviary once," George Henry remarked reminiscently.

The man dropped his stick and was several seconds picking it up. When he did so, it appeared that there was something in his eye.

"You have a book for your expenses?" Stephen inquired.

The man produced from his pocket a somewhat soiled and crumpled memorandum book. Stephen adjusted his pince-nez and glanced through a few pages.

"Do I understand," he asked, with his finger upon one item, "that your weekly wage is no more than two pounds a week?"

"There was some talk of a rise last Christmas, sir," the man explained hopefully, "but it didn't come to nowt."

"We raise your wage ten shillings a week," Stephen declared. "For the rest, here is fifty pounds for expenses. Pay for the eggs, and provide yourself with such supplies as are necessary for bringing up the young birds. Feed them well, Higgs. Be liberal in their diet."

The man placed the notes, in an awed manner, within the pages of the book, which he buttoned up carefully in his pocket.

" If you'd like to cast your eye over the partridge ground, gentlemen ——" he began.

" Partridges," George Henry interrupted. " Are you doing anything to stimulate the production of partridges? "

The gamekeeper stared at his questioner suspiciously. George Henry's expression, however, was convincingly ingenuous.

" There's a good few coveys," he said thoughtfully, " but that storm we had last month washed a good many of the young ones out of their nests."

" They must be replaced," Stephen insisted.

" What can you do about it, Higgs? " George Henry asked anxiously.

" Well, I don't rightly know what you can do, gentlemen," the man confessed. " I've heard tell of putting a few Hungarians down in the middle of the ground."

" Hungarians," Stephen repeated thoughtfully. " Exactly in what way do they contribute towards the fecundity of the birds? "

The man closed his eyes for a moment.

" Hungarian partridges," he exclaimed. " They change the breed."

" Purchase as many as you will," Stephen directed. " An excellent thing, that, to change the breed. They are doubtless expensive? "

" They cost a bit of money," the man admitted, " and they're none too easy to get hold of."

" Splendid! — I mean," Stephen went on hastily, " we must not spare expense in this matter. We have bound ourselves to keep up the estate, and the shooting is the most important part of it. My brother and I are at home every night to dinner, Higgs. Bring up to the house any further accounts you may have and we will discharge them at once."

The man watched them disappear — neat little figures, talking earnestly to each other, and having, from behind, the appearance of twins.

" Babes in the wood!" he chuckled. " Once kept an aviary! To think that simple folks like that could make money! Why, they ain't fit to be trusted with it."

His uncles were warmly greeted by Harold on their return to the house. The young man, who had come down to lunch with them, was lolling in an easy-chair in the very beautiful hall, with a whisky and soda by his side. He appeared to have been having some conversation with the butler, who was lingering in the back-ground.

" Snug little box, this, what? " the young man remarked amiably. " Ought to help you to move the dibs a bit. I've just been talking to the archbishop there. Quite a staff you've got, inside and out."

" We are pleased with the house, Harold," Stephen declared.

" We are much obliged to you for recommending it," George Henry agreed.

" You would perhaps like to walk round outside before lunch? " Stephen suggested.

Harold shook his head.

" I am very comfortable, thank you," he replied. " I know the outside pretty well by heart. Used to come down here with Jack Drummond. He was at Eton with me. Have you been making friends with your dependents?"

"We have interviewed the gamekeeper, the gardener, and the professional at the neighbouring golf links," Stephen assented. "Three most respectable men."

"Old Andrews and I used to have words sometimes," Harold ruminated. "There was a peach tree — still, I dare say he will be willing to let bygones be bygones. You've got one or two useful coverts, Uncle Stephen. Are you going to let him rear a few birds?"

"We have given the gamekeeper a free hand," Stephen declared.

"Good for you!" Harold murmured. "Used to be quite a pretty bit of shooting. Jolly glad I've got you settled down here. I think you'll like it."

The dignified butler made his reappearance carrying a silver salver on which were three glasses filled with a pale amber liquid of a cloudy character.

"What is this, Ross?" Stephen inquired.

"The young gentleman desired to know whether cocktails could be served, sir," the man replied. "I trust you will find these to your liking. I have had no experience myself with this class of refreshment, but the second footman assures me that he used often to make them for the late Lord Fallington. These are prepared according to his directions."

"And jolly good directions, too," Harold declared, drinking his off and setting down the glass empty. "My compliments to your second footman, Ross. Tell him to put it down in writing."

Stephen and George Henry toyed with their glasses and the man withdrew. Harold looked after him with admiration.

"I don't know what you have to pay him," he remarked, "but he's cheap. There was nothing like that about when I used to come down for the holidays with Jack."

The luncheon gong sounded presently. A very excellent meal was served with some state, by two menservants, Ross directing from the sideboard. Harold was pleased to express his approval of everything, especially the port. Before the butler left the room Stephen called to him.

"Ross," he said, "there was a little matter my brother and I would like to consult you about."

"Yes, sir?"

"It is with respect to the recreations provided for the domestic staff. We seem to be some distance from a town and I fear that they must sometimes find the evenings long."

"I do occasionally hear complaints, sir," the man admitted. "There is a piano in the housekeeper's room, but Mrs. Buxton is not partial to music. Some of us thought of subscribing for a gramophone."

"A gramophone shall be provided," Stephen promised. "We should like to go a little beyond that, Ross. Supposing, once a week, say, we were inclined to send down some entertainers from a London agency. Do you think that this would be appreciated?"

"I think that there is no doubt about it, sir," was the dignified reply.

"Good!" George Henry declared. "We will study Keith Prowse & Company's lists."

The butler coughed.

"If you will pardon my alluding to the matter, sir," he said, "I should like to remark, whilst I, personally, would have no objection whatever to the course you suggest, I am not at all sure about Mrs. Buxton. Mrs. Buxton is exceedingly particular — I might almost add, puritanical. It would be as well, sir, to see that the entertainments provided were of a nature to which she could take no possible objection."

"We will bear that in mind," Stephen promised, with dignity.

Harold watched the man's bow and slow departure from the room.

"I have never seen anything like it off the stage," he confessed. "Never part with him, Uncle. He is the most refreshing thing I ever saw."

"He appears to be thoroughly well acquainted with his duties," Stephen said. "And now, with respect to these entertainments, Harold."

"Leave the matter in my hands," the young man begged. "I know just the sort of thing. I will go and see the agents to-morrow morning."

"You need do no bargaining," Stephen enjoined. "Pay whatever they ask and tell them there will be a motor-bus to bring them from Guildford and to take them back at night. A hot meal will be provided and any other refreshments which they fancy."

"Rely on me," Harold declared. "I'll promise you the Solly and Tolly Quartette within the next three weeks. How often do you want them? Every Saturday night?"

"Until further notice," George Henry assented. "You will, of course, bear in mind Ross's hint as to the character of the entertainment."

"Nothing in the least vulgar," Stephen insisted.

"There shall be nothing to bring a blush to any of our cheeks," Harold promised, following his uncles' example and rising to his feet. "What about my giving

you two a lesson at pool, eh?   Just nominal stakes —
sixpence a ball.   I'll give you both a start."

"I will order the coffee to be served in the billiard
room," Stephen acquiesced.

CHAPTER XVI

STEPHEN and George Henry were lingering over their single glass of port on the eighth evening after their arrival at Keston Court. Between them lay a little pile of memorandum books, and a box of cigarettes from which it was their custom to take one each with their coffee.

"On the whole," Stephen pronounced, "I think we may consider this first week satisfactory."

"The results disclosed by the books are encouraging," George Henry admitted.

"Hungarian partridges appear to be luxuries," Stephen continued. "Mr. Andrews was fortunate, too, in finding that consignment of highly expensive chemical manure."

"The all-round increases in salary," George Henry pointed out, "have been received without complaint. Our entertainments for the servants, too, are likely to cost money. We are paying to-night, I think, twenty guineas for the Solly and Tolly Quartette."

Stephen appeared interested but dubious.

"What are they?"

"They are ragtime performers," George Henry explained, proud of his superior knowledge. "They play music, I understand, of a catchy character. That very respectable young maid of Mrs. Buxton's, who spoke to me on the stairs about them the other day, told me that they possess the gift of forcing the unwilling to dance."

"You did not forget, I trust, to give Ross orders as to the champagne for the servants' hall?"

"I told him to serve them with as much as they could drink, subject to his discretion," George Henry acknowledged.

There was a timid knock at the door. Mrs. Buxton's maid presented herself. She stood timidly upon the threshold.

"If you please, sir ——" she began.

Stephen put his hand to his ear and turned around.

"Come a little farther into the room, Amy," he invited. "What is it that you desire?"

The girl approached with some apparent unwillingness. She was as neat as usual, but there were traces of tears in her eyes.

"If you please, sir," she announced, "Mrs. Buxton wishes to know whether it would be convenient for you to see her?"

"Quite," Stephen consented. "Ask her to come this way at once. And, Amy."

"Yes, sir?"

"I trust that you are enjoying the dance?"

"Thank you very much, sir," the girl replied gloomily. "I am not allowed to go into the servants' hall this evening."

"Not allowed?"

"Mrs. Buxton," Amy explained, "does not approve of ragtime music."

"Come, come!" Stephen expostulated. "That's too bad."

"You are fond of dancing?" George Henry inquired.

"Very, sir!"

"We will intercede with Mrs. Buxton," Stephen promised.

The girl retreated, with a murmured word of grati-

tude. Mrs. Buxton followed close upon her ambassa-
dress. She wore her usual high-necked costume of
sombre black silk. A pince-nez, suspended around her
neck, rattled against a small jet purse and a bunch
of keys. Stephen rose and offered her a chair. She
closed her eyes.

"Thank you very much, sir," she said. "I prefer
to stand."

"Just as you wish, Mrs. Buxton," Stephen replied.
"My brother and I are a little tired, however, with
our day's labours in the City. You will excuse our
remaining seated."

Mrs. Buxton sank into the chair with an air of
martyrdom.

"We find the books," her employer continued, "most
satisfactory."

"I am glad you consider them so, sir," was the icy
response. "Personally, I am ashamed of them. I am
ashamed, also, of my staff."

"Dear me!" Stephen protested. "I see nothing for
you to reproach yourself with in either direction. That
the books exceed former amounts is entirely owing to
our instructions, and so far as regards your staff, my
brother and I find the service offered to us most satisfactory."

Mrs. Buxton paused to listen. The strains of the
ragtime band were clearly audible; also the rhythmical
movement of feet. There were occasionally other
sounds — a shrill whistle, something which sounded like
a cross between a post-horn and a catcall — and a good
deal of laughter.

"I have ventured to ask for this interview," Mrs.
Buxton proceeded, "to tender my resignation."

"You disappoint us very much, Mrs. Buxton,"

Stephen assured her. " Have you any complaint to make? "

" None, sir."

" Then why do you wish to leave? " George Henry interposed pertinently.

" Because," Mrs. Buxton explained, " I find here no scope for such poor qualities as I may possess. It has been my ambition to keep my books at a certain fixed figure, according to the number of domestics and the number of guests. Your instructions leave me all at sea. You, gentlemen, appear to approve of extravagance. My efforts at economy find no favour with you. A person of no experience whatever could administer your household, when neither discretion nor economy are required. Furthermore, I am losing my hold upon the staff. Richards, the second footman, met me in the corridor on my way here, and invited me to indulge in, what I believe he called, a bunny-hug. I caught a glimpse just now of my domestics dancing, and I can only say, sir, that I was shocked to think that these were the young men and women whom it has been my pleasure and duty to train. They are losing alike all sense of deportment and discipline. Next week I understand that a troupe of nigger artists are coming down. I can only guess at the character of their performance. I prefer not to countenance it in any shape or form."

" My brother and I," Stephen said, " are exceedingly sorry to hear this, Mrs. Buxton."

" Grieved," George Henry murmured.

" We placed the matter of the entertainments in the hands of the best agents in London," Stephen continued. " I cannot think that they would send us anything of an objectionable character."

Mrs. Buxton rose to her feet.

" I am perhaps old-fashioned," she confessed.   " I shall be glad if you will appoint my successor as speedily as possible.   I have no interest in a household where discipline is fast becoming impossible and where economy is not a consideration.   You will pardon my discussing the matter further, sir."

Mrs. Buxton turned towards the door.   George Henry coughed.

" The maid," he reminded his brother, in an agitated undertone.

" Quite so," Stephen assented.   " Mrs. Buxton? " The lady turned round.

" Sir? "

" Your maid, Amy, who was here a moment ago, seemed somewhat distressed at not being allowed to share in the entertainment we have provided."

" The young person, sir, is in your employ, not mine," was the cold reply.   " I will convey to her your wishes."

The housekeeper closed the door behind her firmly. Her employers exchanged somewhat doubtful glances.

" Mrs. Buxton," Stephen said, " is obviously of an austere school."

" An unsympathetic person," George Henry declared. " We shall certainly be able to find a housekeeper who will enter more into the spirit of our wishes."

" At the same time," Stephen observed, a little nervously, as a louder catcall rang through the room, " I am not quite sure that we should not have been well advised to have exercised a little more discretion in our choice of amusements.   Something in the nature of a magic lantern, now, or some part singers."

" We left the matter entirely in Harold's hands,"

George Henry pointed out. " He understood the necessity for a judicious selection."

They finished their port in silence. The catcalls continued.

" I think," Stephen suggested, rising to his feet, " that we had perhaps better witness this performance, George Henry. If we find anything in it in the least objectionable, we can call at the agency to-morrow."

" Precisely," George Henry assented. " Don't you think, however, that our presence would rather disturb their enjoyment? "

" We will glance at them from the gallery," Stephen replied. " I have noticed a small place of that description over the clock."

They made their way furtively towards this post of vantage, and gazed below. At first sight it appeared that a certain number of fashionable young ladies in evening dress were indulging in a kind of Swedish exercise with a similar number of languid young gentlemen of fashion. Mr. Ross, with extraordinary dignity, was crossing the floor with a pompous strut, slowly pushing before him Mrs. Buxton's young maid. Mr. Andrews, very stiff, and with a gardenia in his buttonhole which he made frantic efforts to hide as soon as he perceived his employers, was engaged in a similar occupation, except that, as his partner was the cook and a lady of ample proportions, his task appeared the more formidable. The whole of the noise appeared to proceed from the four coloured musicians, who were doing all they could to induce the dancers to adopt a less serious view of their responsibilities. Stephen and George Henry looked down with growing approval.

" I see nothing whatever in this," the former observed, " to justify Mrs. Buxton's criticisms."

"The dancing," George Henry declared, "is most decorous. The polka in which we sometimes used to indulge is certainly a dance of more movement."

Mr. Ross at that moment caught sight of his employers. He leaned in a dignified fashion towards the leader of the musicians. A moment or two of misunderstanding followed. Mr. Ross, however, was not to be denied. With the tips of his right fingers still retaining his partner's, he whistled a little air. The four black faces suddenly lit up. They bent over their instruments. In a moment the tune was changed, without, apparently, disconcerting the dancers, who solemnly pursued their perambulations to the tune of "For he's a jolly good fellow." Mr. Ross looked towards the gallery and bowed. A whisper ran round. One and all joined in the chorus. Stephen and George Henry acknowledged the compliment. As soon as the strains had died away, the former looked down with a smile.

"I trust that you will all enjoy yourselves," he said simply. "My brother and I have been very interested in watching your dancing to such very inspiring music."

There was a burst of applause. Stephen and George Henry retreated.

"Most gratifying!" the former murmured

"Entirely so," George Henry assented. "I think that we can retire to our beds with a clear conscience. Fortunately, our rooms are on the other side, so the noise will not disturb us."

Stephen opened the library door. A bottle of Perrier water, two tumblers and two slices of lemon were displayed upon the table.

"Most thoughtful of them not to have forgotten our customary refreshment," Stephen declared. "Between

ourselves, George Henry, I don't fancy that we shall
miss Mrs. Buxton.   Notwithstanding all my instructions, I discovered in her weekly books indications of a
desire to avoid perfectly justifiable expenditure."

"It was scarcely kind of her," George Henry said,
"to keep that exceedingly well-mannered maid doing
needlework in her rooms whilst the others were enjoying
themselves."

"We will find a housekeeper," his brother concluded,
as he prepared to retire, "of more liberal views. And,
by the by, we must ask Harold down for next week-end.
He would, I am sure, enter into the spirit of this sort of
thing."

The engagement of Mrs. Buxton's successor was by
no means a difficult task.   A Mrs. Harmon-Browne,
whose references were unexceptionable, duly presented
herself for the post and was engaged without hesitation.
She was a distinctly good-looking woman of youthful
middle age, with a politely reserved manner and a most
demure expression.   Her hair was copper-coloured, with
variations.   It appeared that she had some acquaintance with Harold, who was the first to recommend
her.

"A treasure, I believe," Stephen decided, the evening
of her installation.   "She received my few remarks on
the subject of lavish expenditure with enthusiasm.   I
think we shall find her of considerable assistance."

"She seems to have brightened up already since she
came," George Henry observed.

"The loss of her husband at such an early age,"
Stephen remarked, "was doubtless a heavy blow to her.
Harold did not tell us that she was a widow.   We must
see that she has a comfortable home."

Mrs. Harmon-Browne showed every inclination to arrange that for herself.   At the end of the first week she had lifted her drooping eyes.   A smile, half plaintive, half seductive, played frequently about her lips. She showed a disposition to linger when she brought her books in for approbation.   There was a certain brief space of time when George Henry had met her unexpectedly in the corridor, which remained with him a disturbing but unrevealed memory.   At the end of another week she had certainly found herself.   She was the life and soul of the entertainments below, and the number of visitors whom she received from outside grew daily.   Nevertheless, a slight uneasiness concerning her entered into the minds of both the brothers at practically the same moment.   Unused to keeping secrets, they became confidential on the subject one night about six weeks after her arrival.   Harold had been expected for dinner, but had not yet arrived.

" George Henry," Stephen asked, as he took his first sip of port and looked around to see that the door was securely fastened, " what is your candid opinion of Mrs. Harmon-Browne? "

" I am afraid," George Henry admitted, " that she is not what you might consider an entire success."

" She is amiable," Stephen continued judicially, " and hospitable.   The servants like her, and she undoubtedly helps them with their entertainments.   At the same time, there are certain things about her which to my mind are not wholly satisfactory."

" I agree with you," George Henry assented.   " I agree with you, Stephen, absolutely."

" For example," the latter proceeded, " I scarcely think that she was acting in entire accordance with her position when she sent down her compliments to us from the housekeeper's room on Tuesday night, and asked us to make up a rubber of bridge with a friend of hers who had motored over from the barracks."

" I must admit," George Henry agreed, " that I thought it indiscreet."

" Then on Thursday night, a motor car arrived with guests for her, quite late in the evening. The piano was going, as you remember, until after two o'clock, and it was not our fault that, rising very early the next morning, we found the door of her sitting room wide open and the table decorated with numerous empty champagne bottles."

" I am not entirely clear," George Henry said, " as to the privileges of a housekeeper, but I should be inclined to say that Mrs. Harmon-Browne exceeded them. One of the young men, I am informed, slept in the house."

" Ross felt it his duty to mention the fact," Stephen assented. " He added that the young man was too ill to be moved. I noticed that he lingered for a moment on the word ' ill.' "

" To any one else," George Henry observed, " he would probably have said ' drunk.' "

" She appears, also," Stephen continued, looking steadfastly at the colour of his port, " to be a sleep-walker. I have heard footsteps in our corridor on several occasions. Last night I was able to open my door noiselessly and look out. I do not consider it becoming that our housekeeper should perambulate the place in a rose-coloured dressing-gown covered with lace."

" And bare feet," George Henry put in. " I saw her the night before."

" And some sort of headgear which is, I presume, the

modern equivalent of a nightcap. If I am not mistaken, George Henry," his brother went on, after a moment's hesitation — " it may have been my fancy or did I hear the sound of voices? "

" She saw me looking through the door," George Henry confessed, " and invited me to explain the pictures to her."

" Dear me! " Stephen exclaimed. " How embarrassing! "

" I spoke to her as severely as possible, under the circumstances. I was unfortunately in my pyjamas and not able to continue the conversation. I considered her deportment, however, unbecoming. She stood and laughed at me, and ——"

" Most unbecoming! " Stephen interrupted. " We cannot have her wandering about our corridor. I am afraid, George Henry, that, although she is extremely satisfactory in some respects, we must get rid of Mrs. Harmon-Browne. — What on earth! "

There was a thump at the door. In reply to their invitation to enter, there was a moment's pause, the sound of half-stifled voices, and then the sudden entrance of the lady in question. She was wearing an extremely décolleté evening gown, and she was leaning heavily upon the arm of a young man who was vainly trying to escape. The young man was Harold.

" Brought friend in to introduce to you," she explained — " Mr. Harold Margetson."

" Not my fault, Uncle," the young man pleaded. " I couldn't get down before and Mrs. Harmon-Browne told me that you had finished dinner and insisted on my having something served in her room. I thought the message came from you."

" I think, madam," Stephen said sternly, " that you

are somewhat abusing your position as housekeeper here."

"Housekeeper!" Mrs. Harmon-Browne repeated in derision. "Get on with you, old thing! I'm a guest in the house, that's what I am. Looking after things for your uncles, Harold. Great friends of mine. Lady companion to them both. Going to teach them to dance. Come on, Mr. George Henry. I saw you twinkling at me out of your bedroom door the other night! Come and let me teach you the one-step."

"Madam," was the indignant response, " I have no desire to learn that or any other dance."

"Mr. Stephen, then," the lady suggested, turning towards him. "Teach you in two turns. Give you the time of your life. You're giving in too early, that's what you boys are doing. Nothing like living while we're young. What about a whisky and Perrier? Or there's champagne in the servants' hall? "

"Harold," Stephen said severely, "whatever excuse there may be for your presence here under these circumstances, and your recommendation of this lady, we will consider afterwards. If you desire us to make allowances for you, you will at once conduct her to her apartment and lock her in."

Mrs. Harmon-Browne wrenched herself free from her escort's arm.

"Think I've had too much to drink," she asked, swaying a little on her feet, " just because I want to be friendly? I hate all this stuck-up business. Why don't you come out of your shells, you two, and leave off talking as though you were frost-bitten. I'll teach you a thing or two."

"We rely upon you, Harold," George Henry appealed, almost pathetically.

Harold whispered in the lady's ear. His speech appeared to have some reference to liquid refreshment, for she immediately clutched his arm.

"Come along, billikins!" she invited George Henry. "No? Well, we'll come back and fetch you, later on."

Stephen and George Henry stood at the door and watched the couple out of sight. Then stealthily, but with some haste, they ascended the staircase and locked themselves in their respective rooms. They wished one another good night through communicating doors on the inside.

"George Henry," his elder brother said firmly, "Mrs. Harmon-Browne will have to go."

"Without a doubt," was the fervent rejoinder.

"I don't know whether it struck you," Stephen continued, "but it appeared to me ———"

"She was undoubtedly drunk," George Henry interrupted. "I fear that her example in the servants' hall will be most pernicious."

"I have noticed a lax tone there myself, since the departure of Mrs. Buxton," Stephen sighed.

"To-morrow morning," his brother declared, "we must dismiss her."

"I fear that it will be our duty," Stephen admitted. "We must sleep upon it. I must confess that I shall feel more comfortable when she is out of the house."

The next morning, however, brought its own problem. Stephen passed across to his brother, with a little gasp of dismay, the solitary letter which he drew from the post-bag. They read it together. It was from their solicitor and it contained an enclosure.

Dear Mr. Underwood,—

I think I can do no more than send you on the enclosed, which speaks for itself.

Faithfully yours,

Robert Jardine.

The enclosure was from another firm of solicitors, and was addressed to Mr. Jardine.

Dear Sir,—

Re the letting of Keston Court to Messrs. Stephen and George Henry Underwood.

My client, Lady Drummond, desires me to write you on the above subject. She has learnt, with the utmost pain and dismay, of the proceedings at Keston Court since her departure, and she is astonished that two clients recommended by your firm, and in possession of seemingly unexceptionable references, should countenance behaviour there entirely unseemly and inadmissible. She understands that the housekeeper in charge is a lady lately connected with the stage under the name of Miss Florence Watkins; that weekly entertainments and dances of a highly objectionable character are given in the servants' hall, under the countenance of this lady; that unlimited quantities of champagne are provided and drunk; and that, in short, the entire discipline and moral tone of the establishment are destroyed.

Under these circumstances my client herewith gives you notice that she desires to avail herself of the clause in our agreement which gives her power to refuse to sign the lease if, at any time within the three months covered by the agreement, she should come to the conclusion that the proposed tenants are undesirable.

She desires me to add that, under no circumstances, will she reconsider her decision, and she begs me to point out that the place must be vacated on the thirty-first of next month.

She is making it her business to inquire into the bona fide character of the references given by City houses of stability as to the personal character of Messrs. Stephen and George Henry Underwood.

Faithfully yours,
MILES & MILES.

Stephen laid down the letter with a groan.

" I fear," he regretted, " that our entertainments in the servants' hall were a little too lavish.   As to Mrs. Harmon-Browne, I cannot see how we can be blamed for engaging her from the references which she presented.   They were undoubtedly false, but how were we to know it? "

" It appears to be the most dangerous thing in the world," George Henry declared, " to raise the salaries of domestics.   They immediately become dissatisfied and suspicious."

" Wherever we turn," Stephen added, in a tone of despair, " with the object of dispersing a little more money, disaster seems to wait upon us."

" And there is still," George Henry muttered, under his breath, " Mrs. Harmon-Browne to be dealt with."

They finished their breakfast in silence.   The same idea seemed to occur to both of them.   George Henry rang the bell, but it was Stephen who commanded the presence of their valet.

" Robert," he directed, " we shall dine in town tonight, and sleep.   Have our bags packed and placed in the car.   Kindly let Mr. Harold know that we are starting in half an hour."

They drove away half an hour later.   A very depressed Harold had made a late appearance and taken the seat by the chauffeur.   Mrs. Harmon-Browne was still asleep.   Keston Court, with its glittering array of greenhouses, its walled gardens, its gamekeeper's cottage with the long line of coops, was a peaceful and a pleasant sight.   They turned and bade a sad farewell to it.

" I fear," Stephen sighed, " that we have involved some of these excellent people in difficulties."

" Mr. Higgs' late pheasants," George Henry reminded his brother.

" And the Hungarian partridges! " Stephen murmured.

" Mr. Andrews' connection for the disposal of his fruit will have been severed, too," George Henry pointed out.

" It will be our duty," Stephen declared, " to deal munificently with these people."

" Even then," was his brother's bitter comment, " we shall have wasted these last two months."

" Absolutely," Stephen groaned.

They leaned back in the car, their brows furrowed with care.   City men, hastening to the various stations on foot, glanced at them significantly.

" Even these millionaires," one remarked to a friend, " have to worry a bit to keep what they've got."

CHAPTER XVII

IT was the close of a long and painful discussion between the brothers — a discussion which had taken place, this time, in the sitting room of their suite in the Milan Court. On the table before them lay the rustling sheets of parchment, the document which they had opened that morning in fear and trembling, and which had confirmed their gravest apprehensions. By its side was a letter — another letter from Mr. Duncan.

" It all comes back to the same thing," Stephen said firmly. " We have raised our expenditure to the limits of our capacity, and the discrepancy between it and our income remains, as I can see, from Mr. Duncan's point of view, ridiculous. Let me read you once more what he says."

Stephen unfolded the letter, adjusted his pince-nez, and read:—

MY DEAR FRIENDS UNDERWOOD,—

I address you in this familiar way because I knew you as lads and because your father and I were at school together and inseparables through life. I am not writing you these few lines in any spirit of reprobation. It is my duty, however, to point out that, though I honestly believe you have made efforts in that direction, you have not yet increased your personal expenditure to anything like the figures enjoined by your father. I recognize the difficulties you have been labouring under in the great prosperity of your business and the successful issue of several of those speculations in which you might reasonably have been expected to lose money. But, at the same time, I must write you frankly. I have made, as you will see, enormous reserves in the present balance sheet. I have written everything down that could be written down. Your profits are still stupendous and seem likely to increase. You must spend more money. You must not let me feel that, with the memory of your father's letter before me, I am continually putting figures before you which show that you are not yet spending a tenth part of your income. I do not ask for impossibilities, but I do expect and hope to see, within the next six months, an added sum against your names in the private ledger, of at least twenty thousand pounds. Don't disappoint me.

Sincerely yours,
THEODORE DUNCAN.

"A kindly and yet a peremptory letter," Stephen announced, folding it up and slipping it inside the folds of the balance sheet.

"I agree with you," George Henry said, "but we have done our best."

"Unaided, we could do no more," Stephen acknowledged. "A wife and an establishment are all we have to hope for."

"Wives," George Henry muttered, "would make the matter fairer."

Stephen shook his head judicially.

"I myself," he said, "have reached the time of life ——"

"Stop, stop!" George Henry insisted. "You are only three years older than I am."

"That three years, at our time of life," Stephen declared, "is equivalent to a decade. If we could have foreseen this earlier," he added, with a gentle but somewhat hypocritical sigh, "I should have felt it my duty to have sought out some congenial companion."

"Why not do it now?"

"We will put the impossible on one side," Stephen suggested, with a little wave of the hand. "The fact remains that you are the younger, George Henry. The younger has privileges. He has, also, obligations. When marriage becomes a necessity for one of two men, it is the younger on whom that duty must fall."

"And whom do you propose that I should marry?" George Henry asked.

"Miss Penelope Jones," was the firm but unexpected reply.

George Henry stared at his brother with wide-open, grey eyes.

"You mean the niece of Lady Jenkins?" he demanded. "Why, I scarcely know her. I took her in to dinner the night we dined there. I think I had only seen her once before."

"That is quite enough," Stephen replied. "You must see, George Henry, that marriage, when approached by men of our age, is dealt with in a more deliberate fashion than with these haphazard young people. I will confess that I have dropped a hint to Sir Peter. They would welcome the connection. I have Sir Peter's assurance for that."

"But the young lady herself is probably wealthy," George Henry objected.

"I have satisfied myself on that point," Stephen assured him. "She has not a shilling and Sir Peter does not propose to give her any money or leave her any! She is an undowered bride, George Henry, with, I be-

lieve I am right in saying, extravagant tastes.   That is
what makes the situation so interesting to us."

George Henry sighed.

" I am afraid," he confessed, " that I am far too set
in my ways for such changes."

Stephen merely tapped the balance sheet and the
letter lurking in its folds.

" It may be a sacrifice, George Henry," he said, " but
there is nothing else left for us.   I shall invite the
Jenkins to dine on Wednesday evening."

For the next few days, life was more or less of a
nightmare to George Henry.   He woke in the middle of
the night — a thing he was entirely unaccustomed to —
and gazed with horrified eyes at a presentment of himself, carefully dressed for the occasion by his tailor,
walking down the aisle at a fashionable West End
church, with an unknown young woman in white satin
clinging to his arm.   He tried to fancy his new surroundings, a host of old habits interfered with, some
one else to choose his meals, a different walk to the
City.   He conceived a new and passionate affection for
his cosy suite of rooms, the genial atmosphere of the
place, the pleasant sense of freedom with which he made
his way here and there.   Day by day he became more
depressed.   On Wednesday morning he swore at a
porter.   On the way home from the City that afternoon he flatly ignored some pleasant little remark of
Stephen's.   He lacked the courage to rebel altogether.
The situation without his sacrifice seemed insoluble.
But he was depressed and irritated.

The fatal hour drew near.   At a few minutes after
half-past seven, the brothers stepped out of the lift
and made their way into the thinly peopled lounge
of the hotel.   George Henry, who was still in the

same irritable condition, glanced at the clock and
frowned.

" We have a quarter of an hour to wait," he grumbled.

" That is a fault upon the right side," his brother
replied cheerfully. " We could not risk having our
guests arrive before we were here to receive them. If
you will wait here and keep an eye upon the door, I
will go and have a word with Victor."

He vanished into the restaurant and George Henry
gave himself up to a few moments of gloomy reflection.
He affected not to notice the almost extraordinary
urbanity of Stephen's manner on his return.

" The table is looking most attractive," the latter
announced. " Victor assures me that the dinner has
received his personal attention. Nothing better will be
served in the restaurant to-night."

George Henry declined to show any interest. Somewhat defiantly he summoned a passing waiter.

" A cocktail," he ordered. " I don't care which sort
— anything."

Stephen appeared a little shocked.

" I was not aware that it was your custom, George
Henry," he observed severely, " to take anything before
your wine at dinner time. As a matter of fact I have,
in accordance with the fashion of the day, ordered cocktails to be placed upon the table."

" I don't care," George Henry snapped, " I want one
now."

Stephen settled himself in his chair, hitched up his
well-creased trousers and turned towards his brother.

" George Henry," he said, " I fear that the direct
object of our festivity this evening does not commend
itself to you."

" It does not," was the prompt acknowledgment. " I

have thought the matter over seriously. I do not wish to get married. I am very comfortable and happy as I am."

Stephen sighed. He had the air of one seeking to conciliate an unreasonable child.

" Let me remind you," he begged, " that we did not come to our present decision without very grave reasons."

" *We* didn't come to it at all," George Henry retorted, grasping the cocktail which the waiter had just brought to him. " It was *you* who came to it. I contend that, if an enterprise of this sort was necessary, we should have gone into it in partnership."

" My seniority ——" Stephen began.

" Rubbish! " George Henry interrupted, emboldened by his cocktail. " We are practically the same age."

" Hush! " Stephen begged beneath his breath. " Our friends have arrived," he added, rising briskly to his feet. " Lady Jenkins — Sir Peter — Miss Penelope, we are delighted to welcome you."

Lady Jenkins, very fat, very dark, very Semitic, with a moustache upon her lip and many diamonds around her neck, shook hands and smiled. Sir Peter, who amply fulfilled *Punch's* idea of a London alderman, puffed out a few good-natured remarks. Miss Penelope, Lady Jenkins' niece, a somewhat personable young lady in the later twenties, who was greeted by Stephen with marked attention, and by George Henry with a sort of pathetic resignation, justified a reputation for vivacity by breaking out at once into a little stream of pre-dinner conversation. A gloomy and morose young man, whom the alderman introduced as his nephew Joe, stood at the edge of the group and seemed to be on the point of bursting into tears. The appearance of the head waiter, however, with a whispered message for Stephen, affected his spirits for the better.

"We have no other guests and dinner is ready," the host announced simply.   " Will you permit me to show you the way, Lady Jenkins."

The little party trooped into the restaurant and took their places at the flower-smothered table. George Henry sat between Lady Jenkins and her niece. Conversation, after the decorations had been duly admired, was rendered somewhat difficult by Sir Peter's frequent and vociferous allusions to the fluctuating state of that day's markets. Miss Penelope Jones looked up at George Henry with a little frown.

" I do wish my dear uncle could leave Mark Lane and Mincing Lane and all those places behind him sometimes," she whispered.   " I am sure you don't talk about your business when you have left the City, do you, Mr. Underwood? "

" Not as a rule," George Henry admitted, " unless Stephen and I are alone."

Miss Penelope sighed. She had very fine eyes, and she was rather fond of using them.   George Henry, who had drunk his second cocktail at a gulp, was prepared to admit that they were, in their way, attractive. It was a curious fact, however, that he found himself comparing them disparagingly with Miss Peggy Robinson's.

" Of course," she said, " one realizes that business is a necessity, but when it is finished for the day, there are so many things better worth thinking and talking about. Don't you agree with me, Mr. Underwood? "

" As, for instance? " he asked cautiously.

" Art — music — the theatre," she replied enthusiastically.

" Just so," he acquiesced.

"I think," she continued confidentially, proceeding on lines already suggested by her aunt, " that two people who feel alike about these things can so easily find happiness."

"I go to the theatre sometimes," he ventured. "I like musical comedy."

Miss Penelope concealed the lower part of her face with a fan of white ostrich feathers, and shook her head at her neighbour.

"Bad man!" she exclaimed. "But there, you're all the same. — Isn't this a great place for actresses?"

"One or two whom I know slightly," George Henry confessed, " sup here sometimes."

"Great place for supper," Joe declared, suddenly breaking into the conversation. "Did I ever tell you, Pen, about meeting Ginger Morris and Stella here one dance night?"

He leaned forward and continued his conversation in a lowered tone. George Henry turned towards Lady Jenkins with some idea of justifying his position as joint host, and found her regarding him with a fat and placid smile, which seemed to remain there even during her arduous consumption of a much appreciated *vol-au-vent*.

"Your niece tells me that this is one of her favourite restaurants," he remarked.

Lady Jenkins' voice was hushed almost reverently. She seemed indisposed for conversation.

"Such cooking!" she murmured.

George Henry listened idly for a few moments to Sir Peter's account of a recent commercial deal, glanced furtively at Lady Jenkins' unchanged and disconcerting smile, and finally, finding Miss Penelope still whispering with her cousin-in-law, permitted himself a closer scrutiny of her personal appearance than he had as yet attempted. She was wearing a steel-grey gown, with little touches of blue appearing in unexpected places; there was a broad band of blue ribbon in her hair, turquoise earrings hung from her ears. Without any particular distinction of type, she was nevertheless by no means unattractive. Conscious of his preoccupation, she broke off her conversation and turned smilingly towards him.

"Joe and I are such enthusiastic play-goers," she confided, as though in explanation of her temporary absorption.

"It will give my brother and me great pleasure," he suggested, "if you and Mr. Ransom will visit the theatre with us one evening, Miss Jones."

She laughed at him in a disturbing manner.

"Won't you take me alone, Mr. Underwood?" she replied demurely. "Joe goes far too often as it is, and I don't believe your brother would care about it."

It was at this moment borne in upon George Henry that Miss Penelope Jones had certainly made up her mind to marry him. She had, by what he considered a most artful stroke, deliberately established confidential relations. The silent smile upon Lady Jenkins' face had now taken a knowing, almost a roguish, turn. Sir Peter winked across the table.

"Getting on, Underwood, my boy," he observed. "A glass of wine with you! What did you think of the price of jute to-day?"

Thereupon the conversation became freer and less formal, until the thing happened which, so far as George Henry was concerned, put an entirely different complexion upon the whole matter. For a person of somewhat ingenuous appearance, he was possessed of singularly shrewd powers of observation, and he became suddenly and indubitably aware that secret correspondence was being carried on underneath the table between his prospective inamorata and the bulky young man whom she addressed as " Cousin Joe." George Henry's emotions were, in a sense, curious. His first impulse was one of relief, his second of indignation, his third of curiosity. It seemed impossible that, brought to this feast with a definite object in view, by relations on whom she was wholly dependent, Penelope should choose those few minutes for a somewhat risky flirtation with a man whom she was probably in the habit of seeing every day. On the other hand, the moment during which he had stooped down to pick up his cigarette case had been illuminating.

" Why are you so silent all of a sudden? " she whispered in his ear.

He detected the note of covert apprehension. A second before, he had noticed a reproving frown on her face as she had glanced towards Joe.

" I am not a great talker," he said simply. " I think I have been listening to the music."

" What play shall you take me to when we go to the theatre? " she asked under her breath.

" The choice will be yours," he answered.

She shrugged her shoulders ever so slightly. For some reason or other, every one at the table seemed conscious of a cloud. Stephen, with a silent gesture, anxiously directed the filling of his brother's glass. Sir Peter tried to enliven matters by the story of a recent bargain of his in jute. Penelope complained of the cold and a waiter was sent for her fur. She was some time adjusting it to her satisfaction around her neck, and again George Henry's keen eyes brought him disquiet. He saw her hand, a few minutes later, steal under the tablecloth. Then he slowly drank the remainder of his glass of wine, and bade a final adieu to certain visions, half terrifying, half fascinating. A most amazing and mysterious revelation had been vouchsafed to him.

CHAPTER XVIII

AT their host's suggestion, the little party adjourned upstairs for coffee and liqueurs. At the entrance to the lift Joe drew out his watch.

"Got to see a man in a few minutes," he announced. "Think I'll be toddling. Many thanks, Mr. Underwood, for a wonderful dinner."

"Do me the favour of trying one of my cigars and some old brandy first," Stephen begged, "or I shall regret not having proffered these in the restaurant."

"I might come back," the young man began, hesitatingly.

"My brother and I," George Henry interposed, with unusual earnestness, "would be greatly hurt if you did not spare us another five minutes of your time."

Joe floundered for a moment. He was obviously exceedingly anxious to get away. His uncle, however, cut matters short.

"Don't be a fool, Joe," he enjoined. "Come upstairs with us at once. You can go and meet your friend later on."

The young man stepped into the lift after another moment's curious indecision. Penelope seemed still to be suffering from cold. She shivered repeatedly, she was distinctly paler, and a great deal of her vivacity seemed to have left her. Stephen did the honours of the very luxurious sitting room, accepting with quiet dignity the loud encomiums of his guests.

"We have a spare room, Lady Jenkins," he pointed out, "if you would care to leave your cloak. I think that Miss Jones will find it quite warm enough here."

With that — disclosure! Penelope removed the fur wrap from her shoulders and shrieked. Lady Jenkins became a little mottled in the face.

"My pearls!" she gasped. "I knew something would happen if I lent them to you. Where are they, Penelope?"

The young woman's hands were clasped around her naked throat.

"They were there when I sat down to dinner," she faltered.

"I saw them," Sir Peter assented.

"And I," Stephen agreed. "Pray do not discompose yourself, Lady Jenkins. If you will excuse me, I will step down myself and see the head waiter. I expect they have been discovered by now. If not, there is a detective in the hotel."

"I'll run down as well," Joe declared briskly, picking up his hat and coat.

The two men hurried off, but parted at the bottom of the stairs. Stephen made his way towards the restaurant. Joe lingered behind under the pretence of lighting a cigarette, and glanced furtively towards the swing doors. He had taken only a single step in that direction, however, when he felt a touch upon his arm. It was George Henry, very much out of breath after running down three flights of stairs.

"Mr. Ransom," the latter said, "I must speak to you at once."

"I'll come back directly," Joe promised. "There's an old pal of mine across there I want to have a word with."

George Henry's manner became very grave, not to say peremptory.

"I must speak to you," he insisted, "before you

approach your friend. Sit down on this divan, if you please."

They were in a small recess opposite the lift, sheltered to some extent from observation. An ugly spot of colour flamed in Joe's cheeks, and the veins were standing out on his clenched white hand. But for a certain lack of decision in his pallid face, his appearance was distinctly threatening.

" I'll talk to you as much as you like later on," he replied gruffly. " At present I have no time."

He would have swung away, but George Henry's grasp upon his arm was unexpectedly powerful.

" Mr. Ransom," the latter persisted, " if you do not sit down upon that divan this moment, I shall ask the commissionaire there to assist me in detaining you until a policeman can be brought. I am well known in this hotel, and they will take my word for anything."

" What the devil ——" Joe began, and then all his bluster died away. There was something very steely about the eyes of this simple-faced, quiet-mannered man. He sank back upon the divan.

" I had the misfortune," George Henry said quietly, " to see Miss Jones unfasten her necklace whilst she arranged her fur, and, a moment later, pass it to you under the tablecloth. I think it will be better, under the circumstances, for you to confess that you picked it up from the floor and were keeping it as a joke."

" Who the hell would believe that! " Joe replied, with gloomy resignation. " They know I'm bust. The old woman won't leave me alone for a moment with Pen, as it is."

" You are, I presume, attached to your cousin? "

" Oh, we've always been pals," the young man assented. " No chance of ever marrying, though, or anything of that sort. Penelope's never had a bob, and I have had the devil's own luck. Now I am in a worse hole than ever I was before. Pen knows that unless I can raise a thou. by to-morrow, I'm finished. That's why she agreed to risk this."

"The pearls must be restored to Lady Jenkins, and at once," George Henry insisted.

"You mean that I am to own up?" Joe demanded fiercely. "I tell you it's no use trying on that stunt about a joke. Old Sir Peter knows I'm in Queer Street."

"Give me the necklace, and I will arrange the matter without reflection upon you or Miss Penelope," George Henry promised rashly.

The young man drew a string of pearls from his pocket, handed them over and stalked sulkily away. George Henry rang the bell for the lift, ascended to his apartments, and entered a room fervid with hysterics. Stephen had returned from his unsuccessful quest, Penelope was looking like a ghost, and Lady Jenkins like a fishwife. The newcomer closed the door behind him.

"Lady Jenkins and Miss Penelope," he began, "I have a confession to make."

They all stared at him. He held out the pearls.

"I have been guilty," he went on, "of the worst attempt at a joke a man ever made. The pearls were never lost at all. They were always perfectly safe. Permit me to restore them."

He handed them to Lady Jenkins, whose mouth now was as wide-open as though she had been in the dentist's clutches. Penelope, still deadly pale, was gripping the sides of her chair. Her eyes were fixed upon George Henry. She seemed wholly incapable of speech. Stephen was watching his brother with lowered eyebrows.

"I have no excuse to offer," the latter concluded, "except that I yielded to a momentary impulse. Allow me, Sir Peter, to give you your belated brandy, and I may say that, although neither my brother nor I know anything of cigars, we are assured on good authority that there is nothing finer in London than these Partagas. Lady Jenkins, will you take some *Curaçoa?*"

"Well, I'm damned!" Sir Peter exploded.

The ejaculation appeared to relieve everybody. Lady Jenkins alone said nothing. She gazed alternately at her recovered jewels and at George Henry, who had crossed the room and was standing by Penelope's side.

"You must please drink this liqueur," he begged. "I am sorry that my clumsy joke has so distressed you. Pray endeavour," he added, dropping his voice a little, "to recover your spirits. Your aunt ——"

Lady Jenkins had found her voice, only it sounded as though it had come from behind the counter of a pawn-shop in Whitechapel. She had sprung to her feet, her doubled-up fists were clenched. She was a most unpleasant-looking object.

"What sort of a game is this?" she shouted. "These aren't my pearls! I don't wear imitation trash!"

There was an awestruck silence. George Henry stood perfectly still. They were all bending over the necklace, which Lady Jenkins had thrown contemptuously upon the table. He looked into Penelope's face and he began to understand. Lady Jenkins brushed Stephen unceremoniously on one side. She pointed to George Henry.

"Look here," she went on fiercely, "you've got to answer me a plain question. You may be the wealthiest man in the City of London, Mr. George Henry Underwood, but if this is a joke, it's gone far enough, and if it isn't a joke, you give me back my pearls or I'll go straight from here to the police-station."

"My dear! — My dear!" Sir Peter spluttered.

"My brother, I am sure, can explain everything," Stephen intervened with dignity. "I must say that I agree with Lady Jenkins," he added, "that if this is a joke, George Henry, it has gone far enough."

"It is a joke," his brother confessed bravely, "which has ended in disaster. If through my clumsiness your pearls are temporarily lost, Lady Jenkins, I can only express my humble contrition and assure you that any sum at which you value them shall be at your disposal at Martier's, or any jeweller you may fancy, as soon as the banks open to-morrow morning. Your husband, I think, will guarantee my financial integrity."

"My dear," Sir Peter insisted fussily, "Mr. Underwood's word is good enough to buy the Crown Jewels with. If he has made a mistake, which no doubt he will explain later, take it, I beg you, like a sensible woman."

"Those pearls cost three thousand nine hundred pounds," Lady Jenkins announced, her eyes fixed upon the culprit.

"Pearls have increased in value," George Henry reminded her. "I shall deposit five thousand pounds at Martier's to-morrow morning before eleven o'clock. If your pearls have been lost through my folly, I shall ask you to replace them. If I am able to return the pearls, I shall still ask you to accept a solatium for the inconvenience and trouble I have caused you."

Lady Jenkins' expression suddenly changed. She said not a word, but she began to smile. Every one felt the relief. No one noticed that after that first

wondering gaze at George Henry, such a gaze as had
never before shone from Penelope's wonderful eyes, that
young lady had retired into a distant corner of the
room, and was sobbing quietly to herself.

"Come, come!" Stephen intervened, breaking up a
silence which was still somewhat electric. "I do not
quite understand what it all means, myself, but I can
assure you that there will be no trouble about that five
thousand pounds. Fashions change, Lady Jenkins, even
in jewellery. You may see something at Martier's that
you like better. — Now, I insist upon it that every one
takes a liqueur. Every one, mind! There is *Benedictine* and *Crême-de-Menthe*, as well as the brandy.
George Henry, look after Miss Penelope. Sir Peter, I
am glad to see, has helped himself. Lady Jenkins, I
think you said *Benedictine*."

George Henry poured out some *Benedictine*, and took
it over to Miss Penelope. He spoke a few words of
ordinary courtesy to her. Then he dropped his voice.

"I think it would be as well," he advised, "if you
resumed your place with us. Your aunt is beginning
to wonder at your agitation. You can take my word
for it that nothing unpleasant will happen."

Penelope showed that her eyes could be beautiful with
real meaning. She rose to her feet.

"I do not know why you are so kind," she murmured, suddenly squeezing his hand as she passed.

They all sat round the hearthrug like a family party.
George Henry cleared his throat and offered his explanation.

"I have been guilty," he confessed, "of an unpardonable attempt at an unpardonable jest. When I picked
up Miss Penelope's pearls from under the table, I intended to return them to her immediately she discovered

her loss. I slipped them into my pocket, however, and for a few minutes I quite forgot that they were in my possession. I, in fact, forgot all about them."

"Good, so far," Sir Peter intervened. "But, first of all " — waving his pudgy forefinger at George Henry — " why did you hesitate to produce them when my wife announced her loss, and, secondly, how can you explain the fact that the string of pearls which you now produce is not the string which you picked up from under the table? "

"That's right," Lady Jenkins declared, with a belligerent wag of her head. "Let's see how you explain that, Mr. George Henry."

"Madam," George Henry replied, " your discomfiture was so immense and your manner so menacing that, for a moment, I lost my head. I remembered that Stephen had gone downstairs to advertise the loss of your necklace. I admit, with contrition, that it was my intention to bring it back as having been discovered under the table. Lady Jenkins' manner, I must confess, alarmed me."

"We'll pass that so far," Sir Peter observed, " but how do you explain the fact that this isn't the necklace at all? "

"I cannot explain it," George Henry acknowledged. " All I can say is that I stuffed the pearls carelessly into my waistcoat pocket, that I was jostled by a good many people in leaving the restaurant, and that I stopped in the bar for a moment on our way to the lift, to make sure that a particular bottle of brandy had been sent up. The only possible explanation is that the necklaces were changed by some up-to-date thief. In any case the responsibility is mine and I have assumed it."

"There is no more to be said," Sir Peter decided. "We will forget the incident. Dry your eyes, Penelope. How can you expect a young man to take any notice of you when you sit there looking like a scared rabbit? Go over and read a little lecture to Mr. George Henry on practical jokes."

From thenceforward the evening proceeded according to plan. When their guests had departed, however, there was a moment almost of awkwardness between the brothers — a rare, almost an unprecedented thing. A couple of sentences were all that passed between them on the subject.

"You are not a good liar, George Henry," Stephen remarked.

"Very bad," George Henry admitted, with a gloomy shake of the head. "I am surprised at any one even pretending to believe me. You will find me readier, Stephen, when I tell you the truth, in a few days' time."

Stephen nodded in kindly fashion and mixed two very weak whisky and sodas.

"I think on this occasion," he said, "we will leave the Perrier water. It must have been a very trying evening for you. Shall we sit down for a few minutes? I notice that the small steamer, *Land of Burmah,* which we chartered in Japan to bring over that cargo of indigo, has arrived in the Thames. We must consider carefully as to our course of action, George Henry. It would not be wise, I think, to disturb the market too much."

CHAPTER XIX

A FEW afternoons later George Henry descended from his automobile before a certain number in a long terrace of untidy but pretentious-looking residences, in a suburb which had ceased to even call itself residential. He passed up a narrow strip of path, overhung with weeds, carefully avoided glancing into an unwholesome-looking area, and was admitted to the house after a brief delay by a slatternly looking maid-of-all-work. After a few minutes' waiting in an apartment which showed signs, olfactory and otherwise, of the recent service of a meal, the visitor was relieved by the abrupt entrance of the young lady of whom he was in search, and the consequent cessation of angry voices from the room beyond. Shocked as he was by many of the circumstances of his visit, George Henry was even more shocked by Penelope's appearance. There was a spot of angry colour in her cheeks, and her eyes were still aglow. Her hair was not altogether tidy, she was smoking a cigarette with a defiant air, and there was something unanalysable about her carriage, the daringness of her deshabille, which further disturbed him. She flung the cigarette into the tiled hearth as she held out her hands, and for a moment her face softened.

" So sorry to have kept you waiting! " she exclaimed. " You see what's happened to me. I am sent here in disgrace, and I hate it. Sit down, please, if you don't mind Tottenham Court Road plush."

George Henry seated himself upon an uninviting-looking chair. She threw herself into a similar one opposite to him.

" It's good of you to come," she continued, " but then you are the most extraordinary, the most wonderful person I ever heard of. I wanted to explain. I couldn't be happy until I did."

" I fancy ——" George Henry began, hesitatingly.

" I dare say you have guessed the whole story," she interrupted, " but you'll have to hear it from me. Joe and I have been sort of sweethearts all our lives. I think I am the only person who has ever kept him reasonably straight. If I had had a little money and they'd let me marry him, I should have made a man of him. But that's all over now. He's been unlucky in the City, and he had to have a thousand pounds to save him from disgrace. We planned that little affair, although of course we never meant to bring you into it. I was to let the real necklace slip to the floor when I put on my furs — I suppose you saw me do it — and afterwards, some time or other, he was going to give me the imitation string, and I should have put it on in the cloak room or somewhere, before we went home. Aunt is so short-sighted that she would never have noticed, and, as soon as the pearls were back in her strong box, no one would have been able to say when the exchange had taken place. You spoilt it with your hot room and your insisting that I should take my furs off, before Joe had had an opportunity to give me the imitation."

" I am sorry," George Henry murmured mechanically.

" Sorry! It was nothing to do with you," she replied. " You were just nice and courteous and all that, but of course it upset the whole scheme. Joe would have passed me the imitations at the dinner table, but we both fancied that you were watching us, and we got nervous and clumsy. I was perfectly satisfied to rob aunt. She is a pig who never parts with a penny unless she gets something for it, and my uncle's as bad. If I'd known how the thing was going to turn out, though, I'd have cut off my right hand before I'd have done it."

"I beg that you will not distress yourself," George Henry said. "My brother and I happen to be in the curious position of being encumbered with too much wealth. Your aunt, I believe, is perfectly satisfied with the necklace she has chosen."

"That doesn't do away with my feeling horribly ashamed of myself," Penelope went on bitterly. "As regards Joe, he has had luck. He raised the money on the pearls, paid the thousand pounds he'd — well, I may as well use plain words — stolen, and he tells me that he has found an excellent situation in the City. Here's the ticket for the pearls. They are pawned for a thousand pounds. I suppose they really are worth three or four thousand."

George Henry accepted the ticket and placed it in his pocketbook.

"We have found Mr. Ransom," he told her gravely, "a place in our countinghouse. We think that we shall be able to make a man of him."

The girl's eyes suddenly filled with tears. She leaned over and clutched her visitor's hands. For the first time George Henry knew what it was to feel a woman's kiss and the splash of a salt tear upon his finger.

"I beg of you," he said, a little stiffly, though very kindly, "not to distress yourself. I am sure we shall find Mr. Ransom very useful. May I add that I am sorry to see you in such uncongenial surroundings."

"I am not staying here," she explained, her tone

becoming harder. "I simply couldn't stand it. I am going on the stage. I can get a small part. I shall get on somehow."

George Henry shook his head.

"I hope that you will do nothing of the sort."

"What is there left for me?" she demanded. "Uncle and aunt won't have anything more to do with me, because they think that I have fooled away my chance with you. My income comes to exactly eleven shillings a week, and I like nice things."

"Your uncle and aunt are a little premature," George Henry declared. "I wrote to Sir Peter this morning, saying that I should be glad to pay my addresses to you, and accepting his invitation to dine next Thursday, on condition that you were present."

She came and knelt before him, a proceeding which very much embarrassed her suitor. He set his teeth firmly and kissed her on the forehead.

"My proposal," he added, "is for your acceptance or refusal. If you feel that your attachment to Mr. Ransom is of such a nature that you prefer to wait until he is in a position to marry you ——"

"I want to marry the most generous man I have ever known in my life," she faltered, "and no one else."

The engagement appeared to give every one an immense amount of pleasure. Penelope was duly reinstated in her aunt's household, and several cumbersome dinner parties were given, with the object of making George Henry feel perfectly at home amongst his new connections. The latter's deportment towards his inamorata elicited the entire approval of the Jenkins *ménage*. His gifts were of a princely nature, and his ideas as to a future establishment eminently satisfactory. Penelope herself was the only one whose deportment was not exactly as expected. She seemed to have lost all her taste for gaiety and extravagance, and, with them, a certain buoyancy of manner, known in her aunt's circles as "liveliness", which had been accounted her principal charm. Yet her manner to George Henry left nothing to be desired. She received his very hesitating advances willingly and even tenderly. She made no demands upon his time, and, whenever she could, sought to restrain his distinct penchant for making expensive presents. This latter course of action was the subject of one of the many conversations between the brothers.

"I find in — er — Penelope," George Henry complained, "most disturbing symptoms of economical propensities. She is continually begging me not to spend so much in flowers and trifles."

"The young lady shows excellent common sense," Stephen said approvingly. "Wait, my dear brother, until your establishment is started. I am convinced that you will find a most gratifying increase in your expenses. You must remember that Miss Penelope is absolutely penniless."

"That, of course, is a great advantage," George Henry acquiesced.

"I found Sir Peter," his brother continued, "most amenable on the question of settlements."

"Settlements?" the prospective bridegroom exclaimed, a little startled.

"The absence of them, I should say," Stephen explained. "He was also entirely of our opinion as to the husband's right to provide all domestic articles necessary for an establishment. They are giving a trousseau and a silver tea set."

George Henry shivered for a moment. Then he turned towards his brother, and, if such a thing had been possible, one might have believed that the gleam in his eyes had something in it of malice. They were finishing their luncheon in the grillroom at the " Milan ", and were lingering over the inevitable single glass of port.

" Stephen," he said, " I fear that these new arrangements into which you have entered on my behalf, will place me at a very great advantage in our expenditure account."

Stephen set down his glass and turned towards his brother hastily.

" That," he pronounced, " I have already considered. I have spoken to the accountants, and arranged that the whole of our drawings shall be pooled."

George Henry smiled, but again there was a gleam of something not altogether analysable in his kindly eyes.

" Nothing," he protested, " would induce me to accept so generous a proposition. The very idea of it is intolerable. Why, for instance, should you pay a share in my wife's dressmaking bills? "

" This matrimonial arrangement is a joint one," Stephen declared.

" I can assure you that it is nothing of the sort," his brother objected firmly.

" I mean, of course, so far as regards expenses," Stephen explained, blushing. " Why, the whole idea was mine."

" Yes, but I am the victim of it," George Henry pointed out. " I have never accepted your views as regards the difference in our positions. You are three years older, but I have a cough every winter and my eyesight is not nearly so good as yours. I consider that you are the better preserved man."

" It is a little late, now," Stephen said with dignity, " for you to adopt this attitude."

George Henry rose to his feet.

" If you desire to place our financial position upon an equal standing," he suggested, " Penelope has a sister, just three years older than she is."

At that moment Sir Peter, who had just entered the place, bore down upon them; florid, verbose, excited. He forgot to shake hands. He stood before them in a state of great excitement.

" If you fellows," he exclaimed in a tone of profound envy, " haven't the luck of old Nick! Did Penelope get on the telephone to you this morning, George Henry? "

" I have had no communications with Miss Penelope since yesterday," the latter replied. " I was unfortunately not in when she telephoned."

" Got a cable early this morning," Sir Peter went on breathlessly. " Old Morse has died, out in the West Indies — her mother's uncle — and left her two hundred thousand pounds. Think of that, my boy!" he went on, patting George Henry on the back. " Two hundred thousand pounds! "

The brothers exchanged unutterable looks. They rose slowly to their feet. They were a most dejected-looking pair.

" We do have the devil's own luck!" George Henry groaned.

On the way down to the City, however, a gleam of hope came to them. George Henry became quite excited about it.

" Listen, Stephen," he said, " what's that girl marrying me for? Money! Not a doubt about it! There was no other sort of — er — attraction. She was marrying me at her aunt and uncle's instigation, for money and a position. She's a good-looking girl — very attractive indeed. Now that she's got the money, why not select a young husband?"

"Joe!" Stephen exclaimed.

"Precisely," his brother agreed.

Stephen sighed.

"It will place us in a very awkward position financially," he declared.

"We're in that now," was the brisk reply. "Penelope is a girl of rather generous disposition. She will insist upon paying her share of the household expenses. We shall not be a penny better — I mean worse off than we are at present, and this sacrifice which you are imposing upon me will have been made in vain."

"The sacrifice does not fall on you alone, George Henry," Stephen objected gaily. "I was contemplating the breaking up of our more intimate association with the greatest distress."

George Henry held out his hand, which was promptly seized by his brother.

"I am glad to hear you say that, Stephen," he declared. "Very glad indeed. We will approach Ransom at the first opportunity. The matter must be dealt with tactfully."

"With great tact," Stephen agreed.

They sent for Joe immediately they arrived at the office. Young Mr. Ransom was very busy, and was able to announce the completion of a somewhat intricate piece of business, upon his handling of which the brothers congratulated him.

"Ransom," George Henry said earnestly, "we wish to speak to you in confidence."

"Yes, sir?"

"It has come to my knowledge that there has been an attachment of long standing between you and Miss Penelope Jones."

"That's over and done with, sir," the young man assured them, with resignation. "After your wonderful generosity, I hope you will believe that I should never permit myself to think of Pen — of Miss Jones again."

George Henry looked and felt distinctly crestfallen.

"But your feelings?" he persisted.

"Don't ask me, sir," the young man begged drearily.

His questioner cheered up.

"I have news for you, Ransom," he said. "Miss Penelope Jones has become an heiress. She has been left two hundred thousand pounds."

Ransom stood the shock well. He picked up the ledger and prepared to leave the room.

"I am sure, if I may be permitted to do so, I congratulate you, sir," he ventured.

"Stop!" George Henry cried. "I have a personal question to ask you. Supposing, under these altered circumstances, Miss Jones should be indisposed to carry out her present matrimonial arrangements ——"

The young man drew himself up.

"Miss Jones has a very high sense of honour, sir," he interrupted.

"But, damn it all, what are your feelings in the matter?" George Henry demanded, in exasperation. "Would you marry her if you were free to?"

"I shall never marry any one else, sir," was the gloomy reply.

George Henry beamed.

"See that Miss Jones is shown in directly she ar-

rives," he directed. " I gather from a telephone message that she is on her way here."

The manner of Penelope's coming was scarcely encouraging to her fiancé's new hopes. She swept into
the room in her new furs, looking very handsome and
very delighted. She took both George Henry's hands,
and, but for a tactical evasion on his part, would have
embraced him.

" Such news! " she exclaimed. " I can't tell you how
happy I am about it. You've been such a dear, generous man to me, and now, after all, I'm not a pauper.
I've had two hundred thousand pounds left me! Just
fancy! I'm not a charity girl any longer. I am going
to buy my own trousseau and — and everything. It
makes me so happy to think that I sha'n't cost you a
penny."

George Henry handed her to a chair.

" My dear Penelope," he said kindly but firmly, " I
hope you will realize that this completely alters our
arrangements."

" In what way? " she demanded.

" I engaged to marry a poor girl," he continued.

" But aren't I just as nice rich? " Penelope protested wonderingly.

" You are not so suitable a wife for me, my dear,"
George Henry pointed out. " I have already more
money than I know what to do with. My chief object
in looking for a wife was to disperse a larger portion
of my income than has been possible under bachelor
conditions."

She looked a little bewildered.

" Then you don't really like me? "

" I have the most profound admiration for you," he
hastened to assure her, " but my conscience has been

uneasy for some time. I have felt that I was taking
an unfair advantage of my position as a man of wealth."

"Do please be more explicit," she begged. "Are
you trying to get out of marrying me?"

George Henry shook his head with hypocritical sad-
ness.

"Penelope," he said, "I will tell you why my conscience troubles me. There is a young man in our employ, a young man whose work has been most creditable,
and who has given us every satisfaction, who I am sorry
to say is most profoundly unhappy."

"Joe!" Penelope faltered.

"Your cousin," George Henry assented. "Day by
day I have watched that young man, and I have felt a
sense of guilt from which I cannot escape. He loves
you, Penelope. With two hundred thousand pounds
you can both be happy."

Penelope was suddenly very pale. There was a tell-
tale sparkle in her eyes.

"But I want to keep my promise to you," she murmured wistfully.

George Henry banged the bell and rested his hand
upon Penelope's shoulder.

"My dear," he said, "I know that you do. Conditions, however, have entirely changed. I only do my
duty when I give you back your freedom."

"But I ——"

"Not another word," he interrupted, trying not to
be conscious of a lump in his throat as he saw the wonderful things in her eyes. "Joe," he added, turning
around, "come in. Come in at once. Put down that
book. Now then, sir," he went on, bustling towards
the pegs and taking down his brother's hat and his
own, "Miss Jones wants to talk to you. Get it all

over before we come back.   Stephen, a cup of coffee, I think, at the ' Mecca.' "

They made the most hurried exit they had ever attempted from their own office.   When they reached the street, George Henry took out his handkerchief and dabbed his forehead.

" Stephen," he declared, " we'll start a yacht or endow an opera house, but we'll leave matrimony alone. Let's go where we can get a liqueur with our coffee."

CHAPTER XX

THE marriage of Miss Penelope Jones to Mr. Joseph Ransom was accepted by the bride's relations with very modified approval. So much so, indeed, that, although the ceremony took place in Sir Peter Jenkins' very fine house in Berkeley Square, it was not made the occasion of any very great rejoicing. Sir Peter had flatly refused to go to the expense of a reception, and Lady Jenkins was, for once, in agreement with her spouse. The affair took place, therefore, at eleven o'clock in the morning, at the neighbouring church, and only a few intimate friends of the family were invited to take a glass of wine afterwards and inspect the presents. Stephen and George Henry Underwood were amongst the distinguished guests invited. In the interval of waiting, whilst the bride changed her gown, they amused themselves by looking at the presents. Lady Jenkins, seeing them at the long table, deserted a little group of matrons at the refreshment counter, and hastened over to them. She drew their attention to the very magnificent pearl necklace which bore their joint card.

"You're a generous man, Mr. George Henry," she declared. "Never knew any one like you — you and your brother too. What a husband that poor girl has missed."

"You are very kind," George Henry replied. "I think that the loss, if any, has been mine. My brother and I have both come to the conclusion that we are a little too settled in our ways and habits for married life."

"Old fogeys, you know, Lady Jenkins — old fogeys," Stephen observed.

"Not a bit of it!" that lady protested amiably. "I'll find you a wife before I've done with you, Mr. George Henry — and Mr. Stephen too, if he wants one. I've some more nieces coming up from the country next week. Fine girls, two of them. I'll have you both in to dine. You shall hear Marion sing. — Look here, let me show you why I came across. I was looking last night at that pearl necklace which you've given Penelope. Does anything strike you about it?"

The brothers bent over and examined it. George Henry was looking preternaturally solemn.

"It meets, I trust, with your approval?" he asked. "We are not great judges of such things, but we bought it at a high-class establishment."

"Oh, it's all right," Lady Jenkins declared, "but can't you see for yourself that it's the very spit of that one which was stolen from Penelope at the 'Milan' that night, and which you had to replace."

"Dear me!" George Henry murmured. "No, it had not occurred to me. And now I look at it closely," he added, bending down, "I notice that the clasp is set with diamonds. Now, unless my memory fails me, the clasp of the necklace in question was set with two or three small turquoises."

"That's quite right," Lady Jenkins agreed. "I hadn't noticed that, I must confess. Still, a thief would naturally have the clasp changed before he endeavoured to dispose of it."

"A thief, you silly woman," Sir Peter, who was standing near, intervened, "would have unstrung the pearls and sold them separately. No one but a half-baked idiot would keep a pearl necklace about which there was the slightest question, in its original condition."

"Quite so," George Henry agreed.

"No one but a positive idiot," Stephen murmured.

"H'm! I suppose that's right enough!" Lady Jenkins acquiesced. "All the same, those middle stones ——"

"Not nearly so handsome as those you stuck Mr. Underwood for," her husband interrupted once more. "Good job for you if the others never turn up, I should say."

Lady Jenkins abandoned the subject in the excitement caused by Penelope's reappearance. Every one crowded around the young couple, and George Henry was subjected to an embrace which left him breathless. He escaped with his brother into the street as soon as was possible.

"I am quite sure," he declared, "that the young lady could never have looked as happy as that if I had been the bridegroom."

"All is perhaps for the best," his brother assented graciously. "It would have been a great ordeal for both of us."

"I hope," George Henry remarked, "that Lady Jenkins will not pursue the subject of the pearls."

"I can answer for it that she will not," Stephen replied. "I had just a word with Sir Peter on the subject. I explained that you were very sensitive as regards that — er — contretemps. He promised that it should not be alluded to again."

"Under those circumstances," George Henry observed, "I think that our wedding gift was both well chosen and appropriate."

They made their way back to the "Milan" and at

a quarter past one precisely took their accustomed table in the grillroom. George Henry, attuned to extravagance, threw down the luncheon menu a little petulantly. Nothing was expensive except the things he most disliked.

"I will take half a dozen oysters, some roast beef and baked potatoes, and cheese," he decided.

The well-trained waiter accepted this somewhat surprising order, considering the source from which it came, without comment, and retired. George Henry turned to his brother.

"Stephen," he said, "we lay too much stress upon small things. For weeks I have searched the menu here for the most expensive dishes I could find, and have had to face indigestion for the sake of getting rid of a few pounds. The whole thing is insignificant."

"I am inclined to agree with you," Stephen declared. "Still, you must remember that in converse fashion our grandfather's fortune was started by economy in small ways."

"That may be so," was the dubious reply, "but I am perfectly certain that no one can ever succeed in dissipating one by these minor extravagances. For the first time for a month I have ordered exactly what I want to eat and drink. The difference in the bill will be barely half a sovereign. We must put our heads together, Stephen. Some justifiable expenditure, or plausible investment — surely we can think of something."

Stephen squeezed the lemon on his oysters.

"Life," he groaned, "has become one continual struggle against the adversity of success."

Harold put in an appearance a few minutes later, and, by special invitation, took a seat at the table. It was understood that, in these days of greater industry

on his part, luncheon in the West End should be limited
to twice a week. On this occasion, however, special permission had been granted so that he might bring news
of any untoward incidents in the City during the unusual absence of the senior partners.

"Plenty of business down yonder," he announced,
"but no difficulties. Nothing to make a special report
about. Seven pages full of orders I copied in myself.
Mostly export."

"Quite satisfactory," Stephen murmured. "Pray
decide what you fancy for luncheon, Harold."

"I'm inclined to be peckish," the young man confessed, giving a somewhat considerable order. "Looking a bit glum for wedding guests, what! Not regret-
ting the little filly, are you, Uncle George Henry? You
take my word for it," he went on, leaning confidentially
across the table, "you're well out of it. I know the
breed. They don't wear. Look at that aunt, and just
imagine what might come to Miss Penelope. It's a
great tip of mine I always pass on to my friends, to
just cast an eye over a girl's elder relatives before you
make up your mind. Lady Jenkins' moustache, Uncle!
What ho!"

George Henry frowned.

"The young lady made a perfectly charming bride,"
he declared. "We must all grow old, but it is scarcely
fair to anticipate."

"Let us tell Harold the truth," Stephen intervened.
"Our depression arose from an entirely different
source. We are very much in the same position,
Harold, as when we consulted you before taking Keston
Court."

"Still can't get rid of the oof, what?" Harold exclaimed. "Bad luck! Now, in my case ——"

Harold paused tentatively. His Uncle Stephen smiled faintly and shook his head.

"It will be exactly three weeks and two days, Harold," he reminded his nephew, "before the subject of any further pecuniary advance can be broached between us."

"That's all right, Uncle," the young man answered airily. "I wasn't going to do more than just drop a hint — deserving poor and that sort of thing, you know! But if you want an idea I will give you one. Pictures."

"Pictures," Stephen meditated.

"Thought of it only as I came in this morning," Harold went on, "when I saw those two hideous old daubs hanging in the entrance hall, lent by some Johnny who spends hundreds of thousands on that sort of thing. I thought to myself, 'Why don't they take an interest in art?'"

"Art," George Henry murmured pensively.

"Pictures, bronzes, statues, all the sort of truck they get together at Christie's," his nephew explained. "Pictures would be my choice. Something medieval, with plenty of the female form divine, what? You'd get something for your money, anyway. You can't be swindled at Christie's unless you're an out-and-out mug, and you can make a hole in the banking account of a Rothschild if the thing grows on you."

"Pictures," Stephen observed approvingly, "are a great adornment. They give pleasure to many people besides the possessor. I am inclined to consider favourably the acquisition of a certain number of pictures. What do you say, George Henry?"

"The idea appeals to me," the latter replied. "Our rooms upstairs are very bare. I have always understood that the collection of pictures and antiques of every sort is a strain on the most elastic income."

" How should you recommend us to get in touch with a reliable adviser? " Stephen inquired.

Harold scribbled a few lines on a card and handed it to his uncle.

" There is a pal of mine who will show you the ropes," he declared. " Mind you, I wouldn't trust any of these art coves further than you can see them, but he's as likely to give you a square deal for your money as any one. They say he's filled half the houses in Park Lane with old masters."

" We will call upon him this afternoon," Stephen decided. " The sooner the better, I think, George Henry? "

" The sooner the better," George Henry assented.

CHAPTER XXI

As soon as they had finished their luncheon, Stephen and George Henry entered their car and drove to the address in Sackville Street, designated on Harold's card. Mr. Shollitt Douglas, who was a youthful to middle-aged man, with a black moustache, an exceedingly acquiline nose, and rather narrow eyes, was very pleased to see them.

"My nephew," Stephen explained, "has mentioned your name. He tells me that you are a judge of pictures, and that you also deal in them commercially. We wish — my brother and I wish — to acquire some."

A beatific expression shone for a moment in Mr. Douglas's face. He wrestled with it, however, and resumed his customary imperturbability.

"There is no finer or more satisfactory way of spending a surplus income," he declared.

"We have, at present, no technical knowledge as to values," Stephen continued, "but our likes and dislikes are somewhat marked. We want your advice, at such fees as you think well, as to whether the pictures which we design to purchase are intrinsically worth the money which may be asked for them. It is possible that you might have, from time to time, pictures of your own which appealed to us and which we could purchase."

Mr. Douglas held on to the table hard. On the whole his deportment was restrained and excellent.

"Sit down and smoke a cigar with me, gentlemen," he invited. "We will talk the matter over. There are one or two small things in my gallery here which might interest you. As a rule, however, I buy on commission at the various sales. I have not the capital to hold a large stock."

For an hour or so Stephen and George Henry lounged in easy-chairs and walked up and down the narrow gallery in which were displayed several masterpieces — chiefly of ladies who, by a singular coincidence, were either just about to make their toilets or who had just succeeded in divesting themselves of the greater part of their clothing with a view to impending ablutions.

" Eighteenth Century French School," Mr. Shollitt Douglas remarked.

" Just so," Stephen answered, a little hastily. " There is a small landscape there in the corner."

" Charming little piece," George Henry assented.

" I congratulate you both," Mr. Shollitt Douglas declared. " You are connoisseurs. You have an eye to value. An eye to value, believe me," he went on impressively, " is one of the most difficult things to acquire in the picture world. There is money in that picture. You realized it."

" I do not think so," Stephen replied. " I liked the colouring."

" The cow in the foreground is exceedingly natural," George Henry put in.

" It is," Mr. Shollitt Douglas announced, adjusting his spectacles, and peering for several moments at the right- and left-hand corners of the painting, " by Gustave Send. You know the name, of course."

" I doubt," Stephen rejoined, " whether we should know the name of a single painter of repute. I have explained our position. We are somewhat attracted by that picture. If it is for sale, we should be glad to know the price."

"Certainly," George Henry acquiesced, " the price. We should like to know how much you want for it."

" I would sell it to you," Mr. Douglas said, speaking very slowly, " for one hundred guineas. I would rather the price were never mentioned. I bought it below value myself, and I am content to sell it below value. But it would do me no good in the trade — profession, I should say — if it were known that I had parted with a genuine Gustave Send for one hundred guineas."

" We will not mention the price," Stephen promised. " If you will give me a pen and ink I will write you a cheque."

The transaction was concluded. It was arranged that the picture should be delivered at the Milan Court that evening.

" I congratulate you upon your start, Mr. Underwood," the picture dealer said. " A little gem! A perfect gem! "

" It will look well over the sideboard," George Henry reflected.

" If, by any chance," Mr. Shollitt Douglas continued, " you had an hour to spare this afternoon, I think I could put you in the way of acquiring something really good — something a little more important than the Send Landscape, you understand."

" We have the remainder of the afternoon to spare, if necessary," Stephen acknowledged.

" There is a sale on, starting at once," their mentor explained — " not at Christie's — at Aldersley's — and there is a picture there you ought to buy."

He produced a catalogue and handed it to Stephen.

" Number forty-three," he pointed out — " *Study of an Italian Lady*. It is by an unknown artist, but it is an exquisite piece of work, and it will be worth a lot of money some day. In the meantime it is pleasing, it is an adornment to any wall. The colouring is rich, almost lurid. It recalls the sunny skies and passionate atmosphere of Italy."

George Henry moved his head towards the gallery.

" Is the lady — er ——? " he began.

" Not at all," Mr. Shollitt Douglas interrupted. " She is in costume. Voluminously draped, in fact. It is only certain schools of art that run to the nude."

" Perhaps it would be a good plan," George Henry suggested, " if Mr. Douglas accompanied us to the sale."

" I will look in as soon as I possibly can," Mr. Douglas promised. " But the fact of it is that I have a man from Leeds coming in this afternoon to buy some pictures — a good client, whom I can't afford to lose. He buys a picture a week on an average, and he won't look at one unless I am there. I am going to give you a note," he continued, drawing a half-sheet of paper towards him and scribbling on it, " to a Mr. Mosenchein whom you will find there — just to let him know that you are friends of mine, and they won't interfere with you in the bidding too much. Number forty-three, mind! And don't go above five hundred pounds. Anything else you fancy you might talk to me about when I get down there."

He put the note he had written into an envelope, sealed it, and handed it over.

" I shall telephone Mosenchein to let him know that you are on your way," he went on. " He will put you right on anything you want to know about. Don't buy too much all at once. No use rushing things. Aldersley's is just at the back of Stafford Street, barely a hundred yards or so away. I won't say good-bye. See

you again. Very glad to have made your acquaintance.
You will never regret having bought that Gustave
Send."

The brothers thanked him and departed on their fate-
ful errand. Stephen presented the card to Mr. Mosenchein, who was waiting for them at the entrance of the
salesrooms — some not very imposing premises in a back
street. Mr. Mosenchein welcomed them both, and introduced them to various friends who were dotted about
the sparsely filled auction room, and who might well have
been his first cousins. Places just underneath the auctioneer's desk were found for the newcomers, and they
watched with interest the various pictures that were offered — not one of which appealed to them in the least.
Number forty-three, however, was not altogether without charm. It was the picture of a woman of ample
proportions, dressed in a loose, medieval gown of Italian
design, and gazing over the balcony of a palace at a
cramped and impossible perspective.

"What do you think of that, George Henry?" Stephen whispered.

"I like it," his brother announced.

"You think that we should do well to acquire
it?"

"By all means," George Henry assented. "You do
the bidding. I think that it is a delightful picture."

The bidding started, after some delay, at fifty
guineas, and eventually reached four hundred and
seventy-five. At that there was a pause. Stephen was
conscious that he had one opponent only — a man who
stood somewhere in the vicinity of Mr. Mosenchein. He
rose to his feet, adjusted his pince-nez and studied the
picture carefully — then resumed his seat with his customary deliberation. He had decided, upon the whole,

that there was something about the woman's face which did not please him.

"If you are agreeable, George Henry, I will let it go," he whispered. "I am not sure about the woman's expression, and it is a large picture for our present rooms."

"Just as you say," George Henry assented, a little disappointed.

"Four hundred and seventy-five pounds against you, sir," the auctioneer remarked, looking down at him. "Going at four hundred and seventy-five."

Stephen shook his head.

"I will let it go," he said.

Stephen, immersed in his catalogue, was unaware of something that approached a sensation at the back of the room. The hammer descended, and the picture was carried away. Mr. Mosenchein, who had hurried to the front, was engaged in an animated conversation with the auctioneer's clerk — a conversation which continued long after the next picture was offered. Stephen, utterly unconscious that his withdrawal from the contest for the Italian lady had excited any particular interest amongst the remainder of the buyers, studied for the first time with real pleasure the small canvas which was now exhibited. It represented the figure of a boy driving a harrow, attached to a team of horses, down the steep slopes of a brown field — a boy who was gazing with something like wonder in his eyes at the sunset over the valley, a yellow-green Coleridge sunset, lit with all the poet's melancholy.

"What about that, George Henry?" Stephen inquired.

"Don't miss it," George Henry begged. "It is a nice size, and I am not sure that the absence of any female figure does not make it more suitable for bachelor apartments."

The picture was started at twenty-five pounds. Stephen promptly bid fifty. There was a little disturbance in the back of the room. Mr. Mosenchein himself made the next bid, a little hesitatingly. Stephen's nod, however, was full of decision, and Mr. Mosenchein went round the room holding his head in his hands. At a hundred guineas Stephen bought the picture, handed up his cheque, and engaged one of the warehouse men to take it out to the car.

"There is nothing else in the catalogue," Stephen remarked, glancing down it, "likely to be of any interest to us. I think, if you are agreeable, George Henry, we might go down to the City now. There are the daily reports which it would be as well for us to look through, and the letters to be signed."

"Certainly," George Henry acquiesced. "I am quite ready."

Mr. Mosenchein followed them, breathless, out on to the pavement, and laid his hand on Stephen's shoulder.

"Mr. Underwood," he said, "I think that an arrangement can be made with regard to number forty-three. A friend of mine bought it for four hundred and seventy-five. Very cheap — very cheap indeed! But he has bought rather more than he intended. Very tempting when you see pictures going at something like half their value, as they did to-day. If you felt inclined to spring a tenner, or even a five-pound note — business might be done."

Stephen shook his head.

"Will you present my compliments to your friend," he begged, "and thank him exceedingly for his generous offer. I really lost my taste for the picture after a more critical examination, and I am very glad indeed that I did not buy it. My brother agrees with me."

Mr. Mosenchein's face was a study.

" But I thought," he gasped — " Douglas thought that you were going to give five hundred pounds for it."

" If I had taken a fancy to the picture," Stephen exclaimed, " or even if my brother had taken a fancy to it, the price would not have been a primary consideration."

" What about the little one that you bought for Mr. Douglas? " Mr. Mosenchein asked anxiously. " I see they've put it in your car."

Stephen began to move slowly away.

" I think there is some misunderstanding," he, said gently; " I had no commission from Mr. Douglas. I bought this picture for myself. I like it very much, and I should have paid a good deal more for it had it been necessary."

" Good God, man! " Mr. Mosenchein exclaimed. " Of course you would! It is a genuine Tiernay! We were all there for it, but we let you have it because we'd agreed with Douglas ——"

" Some misunderstanding, perhaps," Stephen, who had taken a dislike to Mr. Mosenchein, interrupted. " Mr. Shollitt Douglas knows my address if he desires to communicate with me — Basinghall Street, Smithers."

The car drove off. Mr. Mosenchein remained, bare-headed and blasphemous, upon the pavement.

" I did not altogether like that place," Stephen confessed.

" I am rather surprised that Mr. Shollitt Douglas should have sent us there," George Henry acquiesced.

" There were more loafers than buyers," Stephen

pointed out, " and the bidding seemed to be conducted upon a strange principle."

" I have never come across such a thing, but one might almost have imagined that there was a ring there," George Henry ventured.

" I was impressed with the same idea," his brother assented. " Under the circumstances, I am glad that we decided against the Italian lady."

CHAPTER XXII

THERE was a very definite understanding between Harold and his two uncles that private or domestic affairs should at no time be alluded to in Basinghall Street. Some arrangement of the sort had become necessary owing to the fact that Stephen and George Henry, feeling their way into an unfamiliar world, had occasionally been glad to take their nephew's advice on various minor and unimportant matters. And Harold, without any actual desire to take advantage of the position, had, nevertheless, drifted into the habit of bringing items of news of a distinctly unbusinesslike character into the private office at untoward moments. It was an understanding to which Harold had faithfully subscribed, but on the morning after his uncles had commenced their career as patrons of art, he displayed marked signs of restlessness. Twice he lingered in the private office with a wistful expression upon his face, only to be given some orders connected with the business of the firm in a peremptory tone. He restrained himself, therefore, for the interdicted period, but Stephen and George Henry had barely seated themselves at their usual table for luncheon when he entered the room and approached them with a little less than his usual nonchalance. Stephen looked at him coldly.

"This is not one of your usual days for lunching in the West End, Harold," he remarked.

"Promised I'd have a word with you," Harold explained, ordering some liquid refreshment from the waiter but indicating that, for the purposes of luncheon, he was engaged elsewhere.

"Promised whom?" Stephen inquired.

"Shollitt Douglas. I say, Uncle Stephen, you didn't half rub it across him," Harold added, in a tone of mild reproach.

The brothers exchanged glances. They were both genuinely puzzled.

"Explain yourself, Harold," Stephen begged.

"We do not understand what you mean," George Henry observed. "We fail to see in what respect our behaviour towards Mr. Douglas was — er — unbecoming."

"Listen," Stephen expounded. "We called upon Mr. Shollitt Douglas with your note and were received very politely. I bought a small picture from him, and he told me of a sale that was going on in the vicinity. It is true that he advised us to go to five hundred pounds for a certain picture, but, as you must be aware, personal preference is a great factor in such matters, and I was conscious of taking a dislike to the subject just after it had reached four hundred and seventy-five pounds. I thereupon, with your Uncle George Henry's sanction and approval, ceased to bid. I have never been able to understand, to this moment, why Mr. Douglas's friends, who were present at the sale, seemed annoyed with me."

"It absolutely beats the band," Harold declared to an imaginary audience. "What about the genuine Tiernay which you bought for an old song?"

"We are very pleased with it."

"Very pleased indeed," George Henry echoed.

"It is a delightful picture," Stephen continued, "but

I bid for it quite in the ordinary way, and it was knocked down to me with very little competition."

Harold drained the contents of his glass and regarded his uncle for a moment almost with reverence.

" Uncle Stephen," he said, " I sent you to Shollitt Douglas because I knew that he wouldn't skin you more than any other picture dealer, and he happens to be — a — well, a kind of a pal. The picture for which you went to four hundred and fifty would have been sold for about fifty, only that Duggie had sent word round to the ring that you would be certain to bid up to five hundred. So they got landed with it. Then the Tiernay had been promised to Duggie — every one knew that — and Mosenchein, knowing that Duggie had sent you there, thought that you were buying it on his account. You fairly laid it over them."

" I am sorry," Stephen acknowledged, with a very faint smile, " if we proved in any way a disappointment to your friends. I must confess that neither your uncle nor I liked Mr. Mosenchein, nor, after what you have told me, have I a great deal of confidence in Mr. Shollitt Douglas. I shall probably take advice in other directions as to what pictures to buy, and shall be guided — your uncle and I will be guided — in large measure by our inclination. On the other hand, I will make a point of engaging the services of Mr. Shollitt Douglas, when the opportunity offers, as a buying agent, paying him, of course, an adequate commission for his services."

" Oh, he's not squealing," Harold remarked, rising to his feet. " He's too good a sport for that, but, if you mean to lose a lot of money buying pictures, you'll have to go about it a little differently. Duggie tells me that that Tiernay you bought for a hundred is worth nearer a thousand."

"Lord Grim, who has rooms on our floor and is a very famous connoisseur, has since offered me five hundred," Stephen confessed.

"Absolutely beats the band!" Harold repeated, as he took his leave.

Miss Blanche Whitney, flamboyant, perfumed, a miracle of frills and rustles, beatifically escorted, paused at their table.

"Don't get up, you dear men," she begged. "I positively must shake hands. My heart warms every time I see you."

"The play goes well, I trust?" Stephen inquired politely.

"I think that it will run for ever," was the confident reply. "We are all making our fortunes. You won't live long enough to have the chance of another theatrical speculation, Mr. Underwood."

George Henry coughed. This was an opportunity for which he had been waiting a long time.

"By the by," he inquired, with an air of elaborate carelessness, "there was a young lady, Miss Peggy Robinson, a young lady in the chorus, with blue eyes, who used sometimes to come in here for lunch. Do you know what has become of her?"

"Nearly all the girls in the chorus," Miss Whitney observed, "have blue eyes and lunch here when they get the chance. But Peggy — of course I remember Peggy. Why, I introduced you to her, and I shall never forget how disgracefully you flirted with her the night of the party, raising her hopes like that and all for nothing. It wasn't nice of you, Mr. George Henry."

"When you have finished chaffing me, please," George Henry said meekly, "could you tell me what has become of her?"

" No idea," Miss Whitney replied indifferently.   " She got wrong with the stage manager, somehow.   Then she sprained her ankle.   I did hear something about her having gone home to Cumberland.   Anyhow, she's out of the show now. — Do come and see us again soon, both of you, and give us all some supper afterwards."

Stephen murmured a courteous but vague promise, and the reigning queen of musical comedy fluttered away to rejoin her escorts.   The brothers proceeded with their luncheon.   George Henry's appetite, however, was spoilt.   Every now and then he found himself glancing at the table to his right, occupied this morning by a minor novelist and a lady whom he was proposing to adopt as his next heroine.   There had been something different about Peggy Robinson.   Notwithstanding the extravagance of her dress, the brevity of her skirts, the unabashed use of her eyes, there had been a certain instinctive self-respect which lingered still in the memory of the man who watched her empty place. Besides, there had been that letter, of which he was never able to think without experiencing a cold shiver of shame.

" Your beef is perhaps a trifle too underdone," Stephen remarked, looking critically at his brother's plate.

" It is just as I like it, thank you!"

" You are thoughtful."

" The fact is," George Henry confessed, " I was wondering whether it might not be possible, notwithstanding her cold reception of my previous efforts, to extend some help to the young lady of whom our friend was speaking."

" I should be delighted to associate myself with any such undertaking," Stephen agreed hastily.

George Henry frowned.

"Not at all necessary for both of us," he declared. "Miss Whitney was rather by way of being your protégée. Why not send her another diamond necklace to mark your appreciation of her success?"

"I find that such gifts," Stephen rejoined, a little stiffly, "lend themselves to misconstruction."

Harold was coming down the room, his watch in his hand, and with a great appearance of being in a hurry. He was due at Basinghall Street in a quarter of an hour. George Henry stretched out his hand and detained him.

"Don't keep me, Uncle, will you?" the young man begged. "I've an awfully busy afternoon. They'll be held up in the rubber department if I'm not back punctually."

"I shall not detain you for a moment," George Henry assured him. "I was just wondering whether you happened to know the present whereabouts of Miss Peggy Robinson?"

"Little Peggy Robinson!" Harold repeated thoughtfully. "Let me see, she was the girl you used to trot around, wasn't she? One of the quieter sort. Always bothering old Lovell to give her a small part."

"She is a young lady for whom I have always felt the utmost respect," George Henry said firmly. "I hear with much regret that she has fallen upon adversity. I should be glad of her address."

Harold sighed.

"You two do take some looking after," he observed. "I'll see what I can do for you, Uncle. Nice little thing, what I can remember of her, but a bit too straight for her job. You can easily get rid of a few thousands if you begin hunting for chorus girls in distress."

"Miss Robinson has already proved," George Henry declared, "that she has no mercenary instincts. I should consider it a favour, Harold, if you could procure her address."

" Do the best I can," Harold promised. " I'll toddle round the back to-night and make inquiries. It may cost me a quid or two. Old Barnes, the doorkeeper, don't give addresses away for nothing. They say that he owns a row of villas at Peckham, all acquired through trading on the susceptibility of you young fellows."

" That will do, Harold," his uncle said, waving him away. " I will reimburse you for any outlay you may be put to in the matter."

Harold took a graceful leave of his relatives and flung himself into a taxicab outside.

" Item number one in the search for Miss Peggy Robinson," he murmured. " Taxicab, four — say five shillings. The search, I fear, will be a prolonged one. What those old dears would do without me, I can't imagine! "

CHAPTER XXIII

Mr. Duncan lunched with the brothers one morning, a few weeks later. Stephen was anxious to assure him that their troubles were at an end, that they had at last discovered a means of spending an income larger, even, than their own. Mr. Duncan was a grave man, with a dyspeptic countenance and dreary expression. He drank hot water with his lunch and was inclined to take a gloomy view of life. He listened without enthusiasm to Stephen's explanation as to their new hobby.

"I must admit," Stephen said, "that we are indebted for the idea to my nephew Harold. He has several times made helpful suggestions to us — suggestions which, however, have not materialized exactly as we should wish. This time, though, I think there can be no mistake. My brother and I have been able to spend eight thousand pounds during the last six weeks, buying art treasures."

"Eight thousand pounds is a great deal of money," Mr. Duncan assented grudgingly.

"We have not proceeded in the matter rashly," Stephen assured him.

"By no means," George Henry put in — "not in any way rashly."

"We have secured the advice of experts," Stephen continued, "and we have bought what we fancy. Half an hour a day at Christie's, or some of the picture exhibitions, has been quite sufficient for our purposes."

"We have extended our lunch hour a trifle," George

Henry explained. "We find that our nephew Harold is becoming of more use to us in the business."

"I am glad to hear it," Mr. Duncan observed, with an air of some surprise.

"We have first of all fixed upon something that we like," Stephen went on — "a picture, a bronze, or, in one case, it was a set of Japanese prints — we have then secured the best expert advice as to their value and, finally, made the purchase through an agent."

"A man whom we do not trust," George Henry put in, "but to whom we feel ourselves under some slight obligation."

"Just so, just so!" Stephen assented. "We shall be happy to show you our little collection after luncheon, Mr. Duncan."

Mr. Duncan sipped his hot water thoughtfully.

"Am I to understand," he asked, "that these *objets d'art,* which you have accumulated, are, to use a commercial term, 'good value'? Are they worth the money you paid for them?"

"Every one of them," Stephen declared. "In fact, one small thing we picked up quite accidentally is, we are assured, worth a great deal more than we paid for it."

For the first time an expression of furtive cheerfulness flickered into Mr. Duncan's face. He was about to launch a thunderbolt.

"I am very interested to hear about your new hobby, Mr. Stephen," he said, "and yours, Mr. George Henry; but I cannot conceive how you imagine that the accumulation of art treasures in the manner you have been explaining, fulfils, in any way, the last request of your father."

The brothers were thunderstruck.

"I do not understand, Mr. Duncan," Stephen confessed.

"We have been spending money like water," George Henry protested.

"That is just what you have not been doing," Mr. Duncan pointed out. "You have been making investments. You have actually been saving money, hoarding. You have collected the capital from your income, and you have invested it in sound securities. You have locked it up. That is precisely the course of action which your father begs you to avoid."

"God bless my soul!" Stephen exclaimed.

"You follow that, I am sure," Mr. Duncan went on. "The very fact of the care with which you have made your purchases shows that you were desirous of securing value for your money. You haven't spent the money. You have it still, or its equivalent."

It was a shock. Stephen, to whom the picture buying had become a delightful occupation, remained silent. George Henry was the first to recover himself.

"Explain then, Mr. Duncan," he demanded, "the method of spending which you would consider in accordance with our dear father's instructions?"

The momentary gleam of cheerfulness had passed from Mr. Duncan's face.

"Well," he said, "it is a matter for common sense and clear vision. In a small way you are precisely carrying out your father's desires by occupying a flat here instead of living at Hampstead, by lunching and dining here instead of at Prosser's. It is by the spending of money for which you get no tangible return that you obey the spirit of that letter. Such forms of spending would include all sorts of personal extravagance. Your clothes, for instance, hospitality which you might offer to your friends, your car — which was quite a sound idea — the employment of a manservant — of whose services, I understand, you seldom avail yourselves — attentions to ladies, including suitable offerings ——"

Mr. Duncan paused. Stephen had suddenly looked away, and seemed interested in the ceiling. George Henry was searching in unlikely places for the salt. It was obvious that Mr. Duncan had heard rumours.

" Sport," the latter continued, after that suggestive pause, " any form of sport would serve the purpose. You must understand that it is the dissipation of money as well as the actual spending of it which was in your father's mind. He wished it to go from your pockets into the pockets of some one else."

" The trouble of it is," Stephen sighed, " that it generally returns to our own. The one or two private speculations which we have made have turned out to be ridiculously successful. Even the gentleman who was going to make rubber out of seaweed returned us our capital."

" You have certainly been fortunate — or unfortunate, whichever way you like to look at it," Mr. Duncan acquiesced. " Why not concentrate upon sport? Golf, perhaps? "

" We bought some golf clubs once," George Henry reminded his brother.

" We even went so far as to have a few lessons," Stephen recollected. " We discarded the game because we came to the conclusion that there was no money in it."

" My brother means," George Henry explained, " that there was no money to be spent on it."

Mr. Duncan stroked his chin.

" I am not sure that you were well advised," he said.

"One can always spend money on one's hobbies. At golf, for instance, you can give cups, present needed articles to the clubhouse ——"

"Stop!" George Henry exclaimed. "I follow you. Stephen, there is common sense in what Mr. Duncan is saying."

"What we need, then," Stephen remarked, "is to join a golf club. Perhaps you are acquainted with one, Mr. Duncan?"

Mr. Duncan shook his head.

"My health," he said, "precludes my enjoying any form of outdoor exercise. There is your nephew Harold, though, who has just come in. You know, of course, that he is a famous golfer. I believe that his handicap is plus one — whatever that may mean. He should, at any rate, be able to put you in the way of joining a club."

"A needy one, if possible," George Henry commented. — "Stop, Harold! One word, Harold!"

The young man, who had been leaving the room, approached the table where his uncles were seated.

"We were wondering, Harold," George Henry said, "whether you know of a golf club which your uncle and I could join?"

"A not too prosperous one," Stephen put in. "A club where a little money might be spent."

Harold took to the idea at once.

"I ought to have thought of that before," he admitted. "Are you going to play the game or just take an interest in it?"

"We shall certainly play," Stephen declared.

"Most decidedly," George Henry echoed.

"We are already provided with clubs," Stephen announced.

" We have had a lesson," George Henry reminded his brother — " several lessons, in fact."

" I know the very place for you," Harold exclaimed, with a sudden gleam of inspiration. " Absolutely top-hole it might be, but they're short of money. Suitable situation, not more than thirty miles from London, and I can get you in at once, especially if you would be willing to pay the entrance fee on the nail."

" If you will take the matter in hand for us, Harold," Stephen decided, " we shall be much obliged. We will accompany you down there as soon as it is arranged."

George Henry looked up at his nephew a little wist-fully.

" Any news yet? " he inquired. " That address, I asked you about? "

" Not yet," Harold replied. " The old doorkeeper is at home with bronchitis. If he is not back in a day or two, I will find out his diggings."

" Good! " George Henry declared. " The sooner the better, you understand, Harold? "

Harold departed with a solemn wink.

" We are obliged to you for this suggestion of golf," Stephen said, turning towards their guest. " I wish we could persuade you to join us in our glass of port? "

" You'd have to carry me out a corpse, if I did," was the gloomy reply. " I don't know that you wouldn't do better to take a big shoot."

" My brother and I have considered such a step," Stephen admitted. " We should very much like to avoid it, if possible. For one thing, the indiscriminate slaugh-ter of birds does not appeal to us, and further, we are entirely inexperienced in the use of firearms. We have sought professional advice, and have been told that it would take us much longer to learn to shoot than to play golf. Besides, we should need guests and, as very few of our acquaintances are addicted to that form of sport, we should be dependent upon the society of comparative strangers, who accepted our entertainment very much for what they could get out of it."

"We are, at all times, happy to entertain our friends," George Henry explained. "The more expensive tastes they have, the better; but — we have talked this matter over, my brother and I — we find it a little undignified to offer hospitality to strangers."

"There is yachting," Mr. Duncan observed.

"Yachting appeals to us even less," Stephen replied. "Most of our friends, we found on inquiry, suffered from seasickness, as my brother and I do. A party under those conditions would scarcely be agreeable."

"Most disagreeable," George Henry echoed. "Although," he went on, with a little sigh, "the estimates for the upkeep of even a moderate-sized yacht were most attractively large."

"Horse racing," Mr. Duncan said, "is prohibited."

"We do not regret it," Stephen declared. "We have no inclinations in that direction. My one recollection of a race course is that it was a most disagreeable place."

"Noisy," George Henry agreed.

"Most uncouth set of people," Stephen added. "No, we will see what can be done with golf. In the meantime, Mr. Duncan, we are very disappointed at the attitude you take up towards our picture buying. We feel, however, that you are right. We shall continue to buy a few pictures as a hobby, but we shall understand that we must not look upon it as a material aid to our ultimate object."

"One of you ought to get married," the accountant suggested maliciously.

Stephen shivered. So did George Henry.

"We are content to leave that ——" Stephen began, with dignity.

"For a last resource," George Henry interrupted. "We are not marrying men."

"We have been bachelors for so many years," Stephen pointed out.

Mr. Duncan took his leave.

"I have done my duty," he said, "in drawing your attention to these few matters. Personally, with every respect to the dead — and your father was my greatest friend — I think that letter was a great mistake. As it was written, however, and as we are agreed that its terms must be carried out so far as possible, I feel it my duty to supervise to some extent your efforts. Let me know how the matter of golf turns out."

CHAPTER XXIV

THE expedition to the golf links was undertaken on the next Saturday, Harold pleading for that day in preference to Sunday, with a view to avoiding the crowd. The links were pleasantly situated on the edge of a somewhat remote Surrey village, and extended over a common plentifully besprinkled with heather and small plantations of pine trees, through which, however, wide avenues had been cut. Stephen and George Henry expressed the utmost satisfaction with the prospect as they descended from the car, each carrying his bag of clubs.

" Very finely situated indeed," Stephen observed.

" Most bracing air," George Henry remarked.

" An hour or so here every week," Stephen continued, " should prove an excellent tonic."

" The place, too, seems to want a little money spending on it," George Henry considered, glancing around at the clubhouse, from the front of which little patches of plaster had fallen away, at the somewhat scanty row of geranium plants and the cheap cane chairs.

" Want any balls or anything? " Harold inquired. " Or shall we go straight in and see the secretary? "

" Balls," Stephen repeated. " I have only six in my bag. We must certainly purchase some."

Harold led the way to the professional's shop and introduced his charges.

" Flete," he said, " these are my two uncles, Mr. Stephen and Mr. George Henry Underwood. They are joining the club. Look after them well for my sake, and when you have sold them everything you have in the shop you can come out and play me a game."

Flete was a thin-faced, eager-eyed little man, who had the appearance of having fallen upon slack times. He welcomed his prospective patrons gladly.

"I'll be able to play with you with pleasure, Mr. Margetson," he assented. "There's been scarcely a soul down this week. Glad to hear you're joining the club, gentlemen," he went on. "We're needing a few new members."

"What golf balls do you recommend?" Stephen inquired.

"Silver Queens," was the prompt reply.

"And the price?"

"Three shillings each, sir."

"We will take two boxes," Stephen decided.

"Each," George Henry put in.

More amazing things had happened to Flete in his life, but he seemed to have forgotten them. He stood with his mouth open for a moment.

"You can take one ball out of each box as commission for the lad," Harold suggested.

Flete recovered himself, dusted the four boxes — his remaining stock — and laid them on the edge of the table. His two customers looked hungrily around, as though in search of something else they could buy.

"Do you know, Stephen," George Henry ventured, "I am not sure that I am altogether satisfied with my driver."

"Curious that you should mention it," his brother remarked. "I failed badly with my brassy the last time that I endeavoured to use it. Perhaps Flete had better look at our clubs."

"They may not be as well adapted for this course as for Horsley," George Henry suggested.

One by one Flete drew the clubs from the bag, examined them, essayed a half swing and laid them down again. An air of gloom and doubt appeared to pervade his whole being. He glanced at the maker's name and sighed. Harold, entering into the spirit of the thing, swung lightly one or two of the discarded ones, setting them down at once with an air of disgust.

"Well, what do you think of them?" Stephen asked anxiously.

"They might suit some," was the guarded reply.

"Not quite the clubs for us, eh?" Stephen persisted.

"You may play a peculiar game, gentlemen," the professional observed. "I'm not one of those who would ever say a word against another man's clubs. But, for a driver now — well, just swing this one yourself," he suggested, taking one down from a rack by the wall. "Just let it play round in your wrists. You'll perhaps notice a difference?"

"Amazing!" Stephen responded. "George Henry, we have been handicapped with our clubs."

"And for brassies now," Flete continued, somewhat emboldened; "let the other gentleman just try a swing with this."

George Henry's expression was almost ecstatic.

"Beautiful!" he exclaimed. "This is a club I shall never part with. You must find my brother one like this."

"I have an idea," the latter suggested, "that we had better place ourselves unreservedly in Flete's hands. Select for us, Flete, of your own make, a complete set of clubs."

"With bags," George Henry put in.

" Certainly, with bags," Stephen acquiesced, " and let us find them here when we return. We will play with our own this morning. We will settle with you when we come in, if you will have the bill made out."

" I'm sure I'm very much obliged to you, sir," Flete declared. " You'll understand, I hope, gentlemen, that it wasn't so much the clubs I was objecting to as their suitability. A piece of dead wood, that brassy, though, and the mashies were neither of them laid back far enough."

" Let our new mashies be laid back as far as they will go," George Henry enjoined.

" Precisely," Stephen agreed. " We leave ourselves in your hands, Flete."

" We'll pop in and see the secretary before you start off," Harold suggested, as they left the professional's shop. " I've ordered some caddies. They'll bring your clubs along."

He piloted his charges into the clubhouse and into the secretary's office. The latter, however, was upon the first tee, where they presently found him.

" Brought my uncles along to have a look at the course, Doll," Harold explained. " Mr. Doll, secretary of the club — Mr. Stephen Underwood, Mr. George Henry Underwood."

Mr. Doll shook hands warmly. He was a short, rather rotund man, whom nature had evidently intended to be of a cheerful disposition until circumstances had intervened.

" Very glad to welcome two new members, I can assure you, gentlemen," he said.

" Delightful situation here," Stephen remarked.

" Wonderful view," George Henry murmured.

Mr. Doll sighed.

"And believe me," he declared impressively, "a very fine golf links — structurally speaking."

"They look in very good condition," Stephen agreed.

"We do our best," was the secretary's rather dreary assurance. "Of course, we've been very much handicapped by this dry summer."

"The greens ——" Stephen began.

"Precisely," Mr. Doll interrupted. "I felt sure you would notice that we have no water laid on. Entirely a matter of expense. We did start a scheme for the issuing of debentures, either small ones which would take the place of an entrance fee, or larger ones which would carry life membership. But we met with very little encouragement! Some clubs," Mr. Doll added lugubriously, "seem to boast of any number of rich members. We, on the other hand, although our members as a class are very good fellows, seem to have no one who is able to put his hand in his pocket. We couldn't even raise twenty pounds to send our pro. to the championship."

If two such amiable countenances could admit, for a moment, of such an expression, one might have fancied that there was something almost wolfish in the faces of Mr. Doll's listeners. There was certainly a gleam in Stephen's eye and an answering light in George Henry's as they exchanged glances.

"You interest us very much, Mr. Doll," Stephen declared. "My brother and I do not call ourselves rich men, but we have been of a saving disposition, and the time has arrived when we feel that the necessity for caution has disappeared."

"A beautiful course like this without any water laid on the greens!" George Henry murmured, with an under-note of indignation in his tone.

" A little money spent upon these links," Mr. Doll ventured, " would be the soundest investment any one ever undertook."

His remark was received without enthusiasm.

" One does not necessarily expect a financial return," Stephen began, " for money — er ——"

" Advanced for the purposes of sport," George Henry interposed.

" Just so," Stephen agreed. " My brother and I, Mr. Doll, would like to take advantage of this beautiful sunshine and play round your links. If we have the good fortune to find you in the clubhouse upon our return, we should be glad to have you put before us the financial proposals to which you alluded."

" I shall be delighted," Mr. Doll promised. " If you will allow me, as you seem so much interested in the course, I shall be glad to walk round with you for a few holes. There are several things I should like to point out to you."

" We shall be glad of your company," Stephen answered courteously.

Mr. Doll pointed out the first green. Stephen took out his driver.

" We ought, perhaps, to explain to Mr. Doll," George Henry suggested, " that we are beginners at the game."

" Quite so," Stephen assented. " We have only had a few lessons, Mr. Doll."

" The game attracts us, though," George Henry declared.

" We are determined to persevere," Stephen asserted.

It was a somewhat singular circumstance, considering neither Stephen nor George Henry had devoted a thought to athletics since their youth, that the possession of a clear eye, a healthy body and steady nerves had made them exceedingly apt pupils. They never forgot that the end and aim of each shot was to hit the ball. They never lost control of their club; they seldom, if ever, foozled. They were naturally short, but they were straight. They halved the first hole in six, and both successfully carried the bunker at the second.

"Good sound eighteen handicap players," Mr. Doll commented, " and I should say that, if you took the game up seriously, you wouldn't stay at that very long. If you'll forgive my saying so, gentlemen, I never saw beginners who got the middle of the club so often to the ball as you do."

"We are much gratified," Stephen murmured.

"It is our intention to practise regularly, now that we have joined the club," George Henry declared.

Mr. Doll waxed eloquent about the course. He pointed out where the pipes might be laid for the water supply, where some small shelters might be built, certain stretches of the fairway where a larger and better type of mowing-machine should be employed. Presently he strolled across to Harold, who was playing behind with the professional.

"Very desirable members, your uncles, Harold," he said. "Have you got any more like that?"

"There aren't any more, laddie," Harold assured him. "The pattern's been destroyed. Doll, old man," he went on earnestly, "don't you let them out of your sight. Mind, I know what I'm talking about."

"They're pretty well off, I suppose," Mr. Doll observed.

Harold gripped his arm.

"They've got it to scatter with both hands," he declared solemnly. "What they told you was quite true — in miniature. They've piled it up so long that they're beginning to be afraid of it. They want to part. Mind, they're not mugs," Harold continued, watching a particularly fine brassy shot run on to the edge of a distant green. " It isn't so easy to spoof them, but, if they see a scheme which appeals to them, they're all over it. 'Nuf said, Doll. I'll join you when I come in."

Both Stephen and George Henry thoroughly enjoyed their round. They further enjoyed a very neatly served tea, on the veranda of the clubhouse, from which position of vantage there was really a very fine view. Afterwards Mr. Doll invited them into the committee room. They broke through their rules to the extent of each accepting a cigarette. Mr. Doll sat between them at the green baize-covered table, with a sheet of foolscap spread out before him.

" Briefly speaking," he explained, " this is the situation. The club has not enough members to pay. The reason people hesitate about joining is, first of all, because our quarters here are cramped, we need a new dressing room and dining room; secondly, because the greens can never be good until we have water laid on; and thirdly, because we cannot keep the fairway quite in proper condition, owing to the fact that we haven't got the machines and cannot afford the labour. Now, the scheme I have drafted out is this," Mr. Doll went on, " only I must tell you frankly that I have failed to find the financial support necessary. The laying on of water would cost fourteen hundred pounds. New machines, I put down at five hundred. To redecorate the clubhouse completely and extend it according to this plan would cost two thousand five hundred. My idea was to raise five thousand pounds by means of debentures of varying amounts, carrying privileges proportionate to the holding. The debentures would be fairly well secured by the buildings, entire property of the club, including machinery and domestic appliances, and the lease."

The two visitors whispered together.

" My brother and I," Stephen announced, " would like to see the existing accommodation of the club."

" I'll show you round with pleasure, gentlemen," Mr. Doll assented.

They made a leisurely but close inspection of the whole of the premises. Afterwards George Henry and Stephen walked together for a few minutes, arm-in-arm, along the veranda. Mr. Doll sat anxiously in the committee room. He had a strange feeling that miracles were about to happen. Presently his visitors knocked at the door and entered.

" We are not altogether satisfied with your proposals, Mr. Doll," Stephen began.

The vision of a miracle seemed to recede in Mr. Doll's mind, but he was used to disappointments.

" I am sorry to hear that, gentlemen," he replied. " In what respect ——? "

" Stop, stop! " George Henry interrupted. " Do not misunderstand us. My brother and I do not consider that your proposed additions to the clubhouse are sufficient."

" We think," Stephen explained, " that you should extend the kitchens — you have plenty of space at the back — and we think you should add at least ten feet to the dining room, and throw out a bow window in the smoking room. Further, in the dressing room, we think that three shower-baths should be provided."

" But, my dear sirs," the secretary gasped, " this would cost money."

" There is nothing in the world worth having which does not cost money," Stephen rejoined. " We have decided, my brother and I, that, if you will adopt our suggestions and employ a good architect, so that the work is creditably done, increasing the amount of the debentures to, say six thousand pounds, we will take them."

" What! The whole of them? "

" Between us," Stephen replied, " certainly. That is to say, three thousand to my brother and three thousand to myself."

" Stop, Stephen!" George Henry exclaimed.   " I have an idea."

They whispered together. Mr. Doll sat quite still, tearing up a piece of blotting paper. Stephen turned once more towards him.

" My brother has made an excellent suggestion," he said. " We were introduced here by our nephew Harold. We desire to recognize his services. One thousand pounds' worth of the debentures, for which, of course, we will pay, can be issued in his name. The remainder can be divided equally between my brother and myself."

" This is a very wonderful suggestion, gentlemen," Mr. Doll found breath to say.

" We are very pleased to make it," Stephen assured him. " To tell you the truth, there is a certain amount of selfishness in our point of view. My brother and I feel that, if the debentures were issued publicly, there might be a great increase in your number of members. We prefer to take them all to avoid this. We do not like crowded links."

" We prefer not to have to wait on the tee," George Henry explained.

"It is a very princely proposal," Mr. Doll declared. "The Committee meet late this afternoon. I wonder whether I could induce you to wait and discuss the matter with them?"

"There is no necessity," Stephen replied. "We are anxious to start back to town shortly."

"We are attending the theatre this evening," George Henry announced.

"We have, therefore, to dine early," Stephen pointed out. "However, give me pen and paper, and I will place our proposal in writing. I will also give you the name of our solicitors. Do not let the matter be unduly delayed. If an advance of money is needed before the debentures can be prepared, our solicitors will be authorized to make it."

"And when shall we see you again, gentlemen?" Mr. Doll asked, in a dazed fashion, as the brothers rose.

"Next Saturday, at the same time," Stephen replied. "My brother and I have it under consideration," he went on, "to devote one afternoon during the week to recreation. If we are able to arrange it, we shall spend that afternoon here."

"You will be exceedingly welcome at any time," Mr. Doll declared warmly. "I must say — I never expected anything like this."

Stephen wrote out an abstract of his proposal. Mr. Doll, who was recovering from his stupefaction, grew more eloquent at every moment. Harold, whose presence his uncles had not encouraged, was summoned in and told the news. He highly approved of the whole proceeding.

"This," he insisted, after he had read the document and watched Mr. Doll fold it up, "is an occasion for celebration. The bar here is most comfortable, and amply provided with means for the same. What about it, Doll?"

"If your uncles will honour me?" Mr. Doll begged, leading the way.

Stephen and George Henry brought up the rear of the little procession. They made their way into a cosy little apartment, fitted up with easy-chairs and a lounge, and hung with the usual collection of sporting prints.

"One whisky and soda?" Mr. Doll pleaded.

"May as well complete the breaking out," Harold suggested. "Just a tiddly to drink success to the club. The ride home will sober us."

The brothers conferred in whispers. Stephen announced the result judicially.

"We wish to show ourselves free from prejudices," he said. "We are glad to have met Mr. Doll. We like the club, and we are happy to be of service to it. We will take one small whisky and soda, divided into two portions."

"Dear old sports!" Harold murmured beneath his breath.

CHAPTER XXV

" I can conceive of no form of recreation superior to this," George Henry declared, as he sat upon the veranda of the Golf Club one afternoon about three weeks later, with the memory of his last cleanly hit putt still present in his mind.

" A most enjoyable pursuit," Stephen assented.

" I was lucky to win the match," George Henry confessed modestly.

" You played steadily all the time," his brother admitted. " I had a bad hole at the eleventh. What is the technical term, George Henry, for a ball which starts straight and curves to the right? "

" A slice? "

" Precisely. Well, I never recovered from my sliced ball at the eleventh. It probably cost me the match."

" I see that our handicaps are on the board," George Henry remarked. " We are both eighteen. There are some twenties and twenty-fours, I see. It is evident that the secretary was impressed with our skill."

" He has made several polite remarks to me on the subject," Stephen acquiesced. " Flete, the professional here, too, seems immensely impressed by the fact that we had not touched a club for six months. He considers our precision remarkable. But, George Henry."

" Yes, Stephen? "

" You know that I had a game last Wednesday afternoon with Harold. Have you seen him drive? "

" I have watched him from the tee," George Henry

answered. " As you know, I have never played with him."

" Harold," Stephen continued, " has no muscle whatever. I have felt his arms. They are disgraceful for a young man of his age. He is thin, as you know, and lanky. In any trial of strength he would be unable to compete with either of us. Yet he strolls on to the tee, with a cigarette in the corner of his mouth, swings lazily at the ball, there is just a little click, and away it goes two hundred and fifty yards to our one hundred and fifty."

" How does he do it? " George Henry asked.

" I know," Stephen declared triumphantly. " I cross-questioned him diligently as to his methods, and I hinted that the matter of his taking Mr. Hardman's trip to Paris was receiving our favourable attention. He took the utmost pains to impart his secret to me. What do you think it is, George Henry? "

" I have no idea," his brother acknowledged.

" Wrist," was the terse pronouncement. " Just wrist. Nothing more."

" Wrist! " George Henry repeated meditatively.

Tea was brought out to them — tea and buttered toast — which they ate with an excellent appetite. Stephen was still full of the subject of that extra length. George Henry was waggling his wrists in a mysterious fashion.

" Of course," Stephen explained, " the application of the wrists at the right moment is, without doubt, a matter of practice."

" A knack," George Henry agreed. " Just a knack."

" It may be difficult to acquire," Stephen continued, " but it would be an exceedingly interesting study. The idea seems to be to keep your left arm as straight as possible, taking the club back, and then to complete the swing with a slight fall of the wrists. So far, so good."

" Precisely ! "

" The difficulty, of course, comes in," Stephen went on, " in the latter portion of the stroke. Harold seems to turn his wrists over at the last moment with a little click. The effect upon the ball is marvellous."

" Have you tried it yourself? " George Henry inquired.

" Not yet," Stephen confessed. " I have been a little afraid of interfering with the steadiness of my tee shots. To tell you the truth, George Henry, I have engaged Flete for half an hour this evening. It may interest you, perhaps, to share such instruction as he can impart."

" I will join you with pleasure," was the prompt response. " Here comes Mr. Doll. He apparently wishes to speak to us."

Mr. Doll came out to them bareheaded. Metaphorically speaking, he was always bareheaded when he addressed either of the brothers Underwood.

" I should like you, gentlemen, to see the cup which has come down from the Goldsmiths' Company," he begged. " I am afraid that there must be some mistake."

" Mistake," Stephen repeated.

" What sort of a mistake? " George Henry asked.

" The cup is suitable for a world's championship," Mr. Doll declared. " It would be a magnificent trophy for the International Yacht Race. It would be a worthy offering to the victor of the Olympian Games. As a handicap prize at the Fursedown Hill Golf Club it is, if I may say so, a little astounding."

Stephen frowned slightly. They had wandered into the committee room, and were surveying a very magnificent cup which stood upon the side table.

" I dislike anything savouring of ostentation," he observed. " The cup, in these surroundings, of course does appear a little formidable."

" It was reduced in price because of its size," George Henry confided. " I don't believe for a moment that they would consent to take it back."

" If I might make a suggestion," Mr. Doll said, " why not make the meeting an open one? It would be a great advertisement for the club. The news of the cup will certainly spread, and we shall have entrances from far and wide."

" Open? " Stephen queried.

" Not confined to members of this club," Mr. Doll explained. " If the news of the cup gets about, we shall have competitors from all over Great Britain. We are in a position now, I am glad to say, thanks to your princely assistance, Mr. Underwood, to be independent of new members, but that only makes the situation more interesting. We can choose whom we like. Some of the best known people in the golfing world might like to join."

" Let it be open by all means," Stephen assented, after a glance at George Henry. " My brother and I would prefer it so."

From that day on, the cup to be won at the Fursedown Hill Golf Club was the universal topic of golfing gossip. There were pictures of it in the papers. People living at a distance made up parties to have a round on the links and a view of it. Entries rolled in. After a week a time limit was fixed. Even then, on the closing day, telegrams continued to arrive until the last minute.

Mr. Doll was beside himself with work and excitement. He telephoned up to London for help and advice. There were three hundred and forty entries. Commencing at half-past eight, the last couple could not start until twelve o'clock. It was prodigious.

"We must take a day off," Stephen declared. "We must certainly watch the play."

"Watch it!" George Henry replied. "We are going to play. I've entered our names."

Stephen was at first startled, then the little creases by the side of his eyes began to appear. The idea struck him as being genuinely humorous.

"Why, my dear George Henry," he pointed out, "we have only played golf for a few months. All the cracks from every part of England are going to be here, according to Mr. Doll."

"We need tell no one our score," George Henry persisted. "It will be amusing to see what we can go round in and deduct our handicap."

"Just as you like, of course," Stephen acquiesced, a little dubiously. "We must decide, then, to take a whole day's holiday on that date."

"It will be expected of us," George Henry said. "The donors of the cup must naturally be present on such an occasion."

Harold was waiting for them outside, with an air of great importance, when they left the office for lunch that morning. He handed a folded-up strip of paper to George Henry.

"Cost me — well, I shouldn't like to say what it did cost me — but there it is."

"There what is?" his uncle demanded.

"Peggy Robinson's address. Little bit of fluff, you know, that you nearly came a mucker with."

George Henry glanced at the scrap of paper, and placed it carefully in his waistcoat pocket.

"I am very much obliged to you, Harold," he acknowledged gratefully. "We will discuss the subject of your expenses this afternoon."

"If you mean to do anything for the lassie, well and good," Harold declared, looking with loathing eyes at the crowded hostelry opposite, where his luncheon was to be taken, and enviously at the great, perfectly kept car, into which his uncles were stepping. "From what I can hear, she's completely down and out. Got wrong with them at the theatre, and hasn't clicked since. Be careful, Uncle George Henry. Innocent though they may seem, every one of these young ladies is tarred with the same brush. Don't overdo the 'elderly benefactor visiting the attic' business, or you'll find the sobbing lassie in your arms and —— Here, I say!"

The car had started suddenly, at George Henry's imperative orders. Harold recovered his equilibrium, and crossed the road with reluctant footsteps.

"Ought to have been worth a lunch," he grumbled. "However, here goes for the nimble chop!"

CHAPTER XXVI

GEORGE HENRY speedily made use of the information procured for him by Harold. At half-past six the same evening, assisted by the chauffeur, he reached the fifth story of a block of flats in Chenies Street, and deposited outside the door the hamper which they had been carrying.

" You can go down and wait, Smithers," his master directed. " I shall require to get my breath before I ring the bell."

The man obeyed with a respectful salute. George Henry sat upon the basket and mopped his forehead. On the other side of the door he was conscious of the monotonous sound of a typewriter being struck very slowly and after long pauses, as though some one were practising with one finger. Suddenly the door was opened, and Peggy, leaning a little upon a stick, looked out at him in blank amazement. George Henry staggered to his feet.

" You! " she exclaimed.

" I must apologize," her visitor gasped weakly.

" But what are you doing there, sitting on that basket? " she demanded. " I thought I heard some one."

" You see," George Henry explained, " we carried it up and it was rather heavy. These stone stairs are a little tiring. I was taking a rest before I rang the bell."

" You were coming to see me, then? "

" I was venturing to take that liberty," he admitted, very humbly.

She laughed.

"Well, do come in," she begged, after a moment's hesitation. "It's a terrible little place, and I think you are the first man who has ever crossed the threshold. But what on earth have you got in that basket?"

George Henry's suddenly revealed glimpse of the poverty of the apartment brought an extraordinary huskiness to his voice for which he was quite unable to account.

"I heard a report," he said diffidently, "that you were ill. I ventured to hope, therefore, that I might exercise the privilege of an old acquaintance and bring you some few articles such as one is generally permitted to — er — offer to an invalid."

The huskiness was suddenly very much worse in George Henry's throat, for behind the light of pleasure in those very hollow-set blue eyes there was an ominous gleam of something grimmer. It was, unhappily, a fact that, for the last three weeks, Miss Peggy Robinson had not had enough to eat.

"How perfectly wonderful!" she exclaimed unsteadily. "Do bring it in and let's unpack it. I never had such a delightful surprise in my life."

The unpacking was a lengthy affair, and the various ecstatic remarks suggested by its contents brushed away that first feeling of embarrassment. Peggy laughed and cried alternately. For a girl who had lived for two months and paid her rent on the scanty savings from thirty-eight shillings a week, the sight of pots of caviare, *pâté de foie gras*, cold roast chicken, country butter, brown eggs, and a variety of gold-foiled bottles, peaches as big as apples, great green muscatel grapes, pear-shaped, and with the bloom still upon them — the sight of all these things made ordinary miracles seem insipid. Presently she sat down and cried. George Henry gazed at her like a helpless child. Then he had an inspiration.

"Miss Peggy," he said, "it was a long climb up those stairs. Might I venture to open one of these small bottles?"

She sprang up with delight.

"You dear thing!" she exclaimed. "Of course! Let me get you some glasses. And do you know, I have been practising and practising away at this wretched old typewriter — they say I sha'n't be fit for the stage again for a year, even if I get a job — and I quite forgot my lunch."

"Louis rather failed us at luncheon to-day," George Henry observed, as he followed her to the cupboard. "We had an *entrecôte* which was distinctly tough, and, my digestion not being what it was, I was obliged to leave a considerable portion. Just one glass of wine, Miss Peggy, before you do another thing."

The girl looked as though she needed it. The delightful roundness of form, which had given her a place in the front row of the chorus, had vanished. Her cheeks were almost hollow. Her plain black dress, spotlessly neat though it was, shone a little from frequent brushing. Her hair had lost its burnish. Nevertheless, after those first few moments of weakness, her spirits seemed to return in a marvellous manner. She seated herself on the edge of the table and drank with sheer and unpretending joy the wine which her guest poured out.

"How did you hear of me?" she asked.

"My nephew Harold made inquiries," he told her. "I believe that he obtained his final information from the doorkeeper at the Garrick Theatre. You were very difficult to find."

"I intended to be," she acknowledged. "I am sure

the girls meant to be kind, but I simply couldn't bear
it when they got to sending me trifles from their salary,
and that sort of thing. Perhaps you knew that I had
a kind of a disagreement with Mr. Lovell? "

" What was it about? " he inquired curiously.

" Oh, the usual sort of thing! He thought I needed
sea air towards the end of the week, and I suppose his
vanity was hurt."

George Henry's rubicund cheeks paled a little, and
the inward turn of his lips was almost vicious.
Thoughts were passing in his mind which it was as
well for Mr. Lovell that he knew nothing of.

" Well, anyhow," Peggy went on, " they stopped my
salary dead, and here I am trying to learn the typewriter."

" Before we go any farther," George Henry said,
" I am the bearer of a message from my brother. He
has seen Mr. Lovell personally on the subject of your
dismissal, and has pointed out to him that the offer
which he made when he handed over forthcoming profits
on the production of ' The Singing Bird ' to the company, referred to the company as it existed at that
moment, unless any one of them should voluntarily with-
draw or be guilty of conduct necessitating dismissal.
Those are the words which Stephen's lawyer used in the
agreement. Consequently the company owe you, at the
present moment, your share of the profits from the day
that you left and they will continue to owe it weekly
until you voluntarily resign."

" But, Mr. Underwood," she exclaimed breathlessly,
" it is too wonderful! "

" Nothing of the sort! " George Henry protested.
" You were one of the beneficiaries under the arrangement and you remain one. We get our interest on the

capital invested. We do not desire any more. The scheme was accepted by the company, they have all profited by it enormously, and I know I can say truthfully that there is not a single one of them who is not only too anxious for you to have your share."

"Money of my own!" she murmured brokenly. "This isn't charity or anything?"

"My dear young lady," her visitor enjoined sternly, "please do not be absurd. It is simply your share of our arrangement with the company. As soon as you are well enough to go back, you will help to earn it. I have here," he went on, drawing an envelope from his pocket, "a statement which my brother insisted upon Mr. Lovell preparing. It shows a balance due to you of twenty-seven pounds and eighteen shillings, for which, I believe, there is a cheque enclosed. A sum, varying from thirty shillings to three pounds, will, in future, reach you every Monday morning."

She walked away from him to the window and stood there for several minutes with her back towards him. When she turned round, although there were traces of tears in her eyes, she seemed younger.

"Finished!" she cried. "I am not trying to thank you. You found me here. You know what you have done. — Now I am going to lay the cloth."

For the best part of an hour she chattered and ate, and her visitor experienced to the full the joys of the appreciated philanthropist. When she had cleared away, she lit a cigarette from the box which he had brought and watched the coffee in the battered little pot on the hob. George Henry cleared his throat.

"So you thought of going in for typing, eh?" he asked.

"I thought of it," she confessed ruefully, "but I am very, very slow."

"You've had the best advice about your foot?" he asked.

"Absolutely," she assured him. "It cost me nearly my last guinea, but I went to the best man. I shall not be able to dance or even to walk without a slight limp for a year. What I want to do is to earn enough by typing to keep me until then. I was worrying about it dreadfully," she admitted, "but it isn't half so bad now. I feel secure from starvation, at any rate."

"You have no regular work in typewriting?" he inquired.

"Nothing regular," she admitted, with a sigh.

"Then there is an opportunity, perhaps," George Henry said, "of your being of service to us. My brother and I desire a typist at our warehouse in Basinghall Street, to make out certain lists of prices every morning. These lists need not be rapidly done, but fidelity to detail is essential. There is a private office and we would endeavour to make you as comfortable as possible. The salary, at first, would be four pounds a week."

Peggy breathed a sigh of intense relief.

"You dear, dear man!" she exclaimed. "Why are you so kind to me?"

George Henry was, for a few moments, the picture of woe.

"My behaviour to you once ——" he began.

She suddenly put her hand over his mouth. He had never felt the proximity of soft, warm fingers upon his lips before, and he found it extraordinarily pleasant.

"You are not to allude to that again," she ordered. "I have forgotten it completely. So must you. The only thing is," she added, a little wistfully, "I did rather wonder what made you so kind to me."

George Henry looked away for a minute. Very dimly he thought he knew, but he was quite sure that he would never find the words to tell her.

"I have wished to make amends," he said, "for my intolerable conduct."

"No other reason?" she persisted.

"We have, my brother and I, a great regard for you."

"Your brother and you!" she repeated, with a little grimace. — "When may I start work, Mr. George Henry?"

"To-morrow morning, if you will," he answered. "The office will be ready at any time. The work is merely copying, though intricate. Harold will be able to make everything quite easy for you."

"Shall I ever see you?" she asked.

"Frequently," he assured her.

"I think," she decided, "that I shall start to-morrow morning."

CHAPTER XXVII

THE Fursedown Hill Golf Club Open Meeting was held on a Saturday early in May. Never before had such a stream of people made their way up to the very picturesquely situated Golf Club. They came by train, by motor car, on motor bicycles, and even in vans. The little enclosure for cars was chock-full and a line of them extended all down the hill.

Stephen and George Henry, who were amongst the early arrivals, wandered round the place with an air of very tempered satisfaction.

"One would think that a fair was being held here," Stephen remarked.

"There are actually competitors having breakfast in the dining room," George Henry declared.

There was already a little crowd surrounding the first tee. Harold, swinging his driver, strolled over to them.

"All the talent here this morning," he exclaimed. "Thank heaven it's a west wind! It will suit my hook."

"Tell me," Stephen demanded, "what is the cause of this extraordinary gathering? Are all Open Competitions patronized to this extent?"

"Bet your life they ain't," Harold replied. "It's the Cup."

"The Cup," Stephen repeated.

"Is there anything unusual about it?" George Henry asked.

Harold drew his uncles a little away from the crush. He remained kind, but there was a note of gentle reproof in his tone.

"Now that we are alone, tell me, what did you give for that Cup?"

Stephen frowned slightly.

"Quite a reasonable price," he declared.

"Silver is dear just now," George Henry murmured.

"I won't press the matter," Harold conceded graciously. "The point is this — twenty pounds is, as a rule, the outside value of any cup that can be won outright at an Open Meeting. There have been hundreds of guesses as to the value of this one and they mostly put it down at about five hundred. That's what's brought them all scurrying to Fursedown Hill. It isn't often that an amateur gets such a chance of doing himself a bit of good. I'm off in a tick. So long."

Harold returned to the tee and the brothers made their way into the committee room and gazed at the Cup over the shoulders of the small crowd. It presented a magnificent but colossal appearance. They gathered from the gossip around that it was reputed to hold a dozen bottles of wine.

"It is, perhaps, a little ostentatious," Stephen sighed.

"Not at all," George Henry said stoutly. "I won't have it."

"We must not forget," Stephen whispered, "that it represents five hundred pounds of genuine expenditure."

"Two hundred and fifty each, Stephen."

"It was an excellent idea. If comments are made, we need take no notice of them."

Mr. Doll came hurrying up. He was perspiring but happy. It was distinctly the day of his life.

"Can I speak to you for a moment outside?" he begged.

They followed him out to a comparatively retired corner of the veranda.

"Look here," he began, "I am in a difficulty. It is the custom in all Open Meetings that relatives should not play together. With you two, of course, it doesn't matter, as I suppose you would scarcely consider yourselves serious competitors. But a very valuable new member, Sir Philip Woodman, the banker, is down to play with his son, who is scratch."

"We know Sir Philip Woodman," Stephen said.

"An excellent firm," George Henry murmured.

"Could I induce you," Mr. Doll suggested, "to divide up? I know you prefer, as a rule, to play together, but if you, Mr. Stephen, would play with Sir Philip Woodman, and you, Mr. George Henry, with his son, it would help us very much."

The brothers exchanged glances. They had played a good many rounds, but never with a stranger.

"I am acquainted with Sir Philip," Stephen admitted.

"I know his son by sight," George Henry declared. "He seems a well-behaved young man."

"If this arrangement would help you, Mr. Doll," Stephen decided, "we should be glad to fall in with it."

"Quite glad," George Henry echoed.

Mr. Doll was much relieved.

"In that case, you, Mr. George Henry, will start within the next quarter of an hour," he announced. "I'm afraid that you, Mr. Stephen, have only your own very late time to rely upon."

"I prefer to start late," Stephen replied. "There will be no trouble at all about that. It interests me very much to see the starting of the other competitors. That drive of Harold's, for instance," he added, pointing down the first fairway.

"Wrist," George Henry declared with significance.

" Undoubtedly wrist," Stephen acquiesced. " Thanks to Flete, we know something about that now."

It was a morning full of disaster to many well-known amateur golfers. A strong breeze was blowing right across the course from left to right at the majority of the holes, and the slightest slice brought untold difficulties. The Fursedown Hill course was never an easy one and its architect seemed to have been inspired by a fiendish desire to punish the commonest fault of the mediocre golfer. The first few couples began to come in some time before Stephen and his partner started out. Their language was vigorous, their walk weary, their mien depressed. They gathered together in little knots, recounting their disasters. Nearly all of them would have done wonderful rounds but for a single hole. A great many were off their putts, a condition which they seemed to resent as due to an unfair interposition of Providence. There were others who had found themselves in an unplayable place after quite a reasonable shot, and who had wasted an untold number of strokes in their return to the fairway. With common consent they all, however, sought the same means of consolation. The Bar was packed to such an extent that Mr. Doll ran about explaining that refreshments could also be procured in the dining room and in the tent. Almost automatically the spirits of the unsuccessful competitors revived. It appeared to take the average golfer about half an hour to leave behind him the stage of depression, abuse of the course, and his own luck, and to discover that there were still bright spots in the world. The luncheon rooms filled up, pipes were lit, a babel of cheerful conversation drowned the thin murmurs of disappointment and disgust from many of the returning couples, and at one o'clock, when quite half the competitors were in, the best return was Mr. Harold Margetson's, of eighty, plus one — eighty-one. There were no less than fourteen returns of eighty-two, each one of which would have been a stroke better but for a fallen twig upon the green, a stone in a bunker, an ill-cut hole or the presence of a bald spot due to an unreplaced divot in the very middle of the course, or some other contributory cause equally accidental. One by one the formidable competitors were accounted for. Harold took a pilgrimage into the committee room and stood looking at the Cup.

" Nice little bit of stuff," he remarked to his bosom friend, Jimmy Dean, a young man of somewhat similar outlook upon life.

" Tophole! " was the laconic but somewhat sad reply from the unhappy youth who had taken twenty putts on five greens.

" Gives one quite a queer feeling," Harold continued, " to think that in half an hour's time that bit of plate may be in my pocket, metaphorically speaking."

" You'll have to fill it," was the gloomy reminder. " It will cost you a fiver at least."

Harold smiled in a superior manner.

" Filled it shall be to the very brim," he promised, " but it won't be ' yours truly ' who will pay for the stuff. I have uncles, Jimmy — elderly uncles, fussing around with money to burn. They will be enthused with family pride. They will see to the replenishment of that comely pot."

" Old jossers who gave the thing," Jimmy observed.

" A little more respect, if you please," Harold insisted. " They are pets of mine."

" What shall you do with it, anyhow? " Jimmy inquired, studying the Cup from all angles. " Use it for a bird bath, or a baby's christening font? It's too big for any reasonable purpose."

"What I should like," Harold admitted wistfully, "would be to transmute it into oof."

"Not a chance, dear boy," Jimmy assured him. "Your avuncular blessings will keep their eye upon it. It will be 'Harold, where's the Cup?' whenever they come to see you at your humble abode. You won't even be able to pop it."

"You're in a damned unsympathetic frame of mind," Harold complained, a little testily.

"If I had taken my aluminium out," Jimmy murmured, "I might have been better. A putting-cleek is the very devil if you begin to go off it. On that fourth green, Harold ——"

"Chuck it!" the latter interrupted, turning away. "Let's watch the last few couples come in."

On the veranda sat George Henry, enjoying a bottle of ginger beer and waiting anxiously for his lunch.

"Enjoy your round, Uncle?" Harold asked pleasantly.

"Very much indeed," George Henry replied. "I completed the first nine holes in fifty-one."

"Jolly good," Harold commended. "And afterwards?"

"At the twelfth," George Henry explained, "I found my ball embedded in some vegetable matter of an unpleasant nature. I saw no reason why I should distress myself unnecessarily and my companion had already torn up his card, so I removed the ball to the fairway. We had a very pleasant match home."

"Where's Uncle Stephen?" Harold inquired.

"He is ascending the hill now to the last hole," George Henry pointed out. "I had hopes," he added, glancing at his watch, " that he might have retired from the contest before now. It is an hour later than our usual time for luncheon."

" Just been to have a look at the Cup," Harold confided.

" I suppose you know," Mr. Doll, who had just strolled up, remarked, " that it is practically a certainty now that the Cup remains in the family."

" I was about to congratulate my nephew on his very fine score," George Henry declared. " At the same time, such a win was not exactly what we had anticipated. Harold shall certainly receive some form of recognition for his effort, but it is just possible that his Uncle Stephen may consider the desirability of allowing the Cup itself to pass to the next competitor."

Mr. Doll laid his hand upon George Henry's shoulder. He had the air of a man who is on his knees.

" Mr. Underwood," he said, " I am going to make you a very earnest request. There are fourteen competitors who tied for the place below your nephew. They have practically sent me here as a deputation. They wish you to conform to the generally accepted principles at such a meeting. They wish you to consent to the Cup going to the person by whom it is won. There is not the slightest reason why our friend Harold here should be disqualified simply because he is your nephew. It would have been just the same if you had won it yourself."

" There's a huge sweep for the other Johnnies," Harold remarked.

" Just so," Mr. Doll acquiesced. " Several of the fourteen who have tied are anxious to leave, so they sent me to beg for your decision. I am sure you will not hesitate. They are unanimously of opinion that the Cup must go to the actual winner, and they think it would be a very seemly thing if the sweep were divided amongst the eighty-twos. May I ask for your assent, Mr. George Henry?"

"If they are unanimous," George Henry replied, "certainly."

"This relieves me of some responsibility," Mr. Doll declared. "I will now devote myself to the task of apportioning the sweep."

A ball landed with a plop on the green in front of them, from the unseen valley below. They watched its course with interest. It took two more little jumps, and then settled down to a gentle and businesslike run towards the hole. As it drew nearer and nearer every one got up to watch it. In the end it gently surmounted a hummock, took the proper semicircular course from it, deliberately avoided a small worm cast, hovered on the edge of the hole and, finally, relapsed into it.

"Some one has holed out an iron shot!" Harold exclaimed. "Good for them! I thought all the competitors were in."

"It is your uncle and Sir Philip Woodman," George Henry announced. "I am very glad they are here. I am in need of my lunch."

Two heads appeared over the rise. First of all Sir Philip, without a hat and mopping his forehead. A few paces behind came Stephen. He appeared unperturbed and he was not unduly flushed by the exertion, but, to a close observer, there was a new look upon his face. He had a rapt and a detached expression. He appeared to see nothing of the little crowd upon the veranda. He reached the edge of the green and looked all over it. His caddy stood by his side. Sir Philip, with his putter on his shoulder, joined him. There was a chorus of shouts from the veranda. In accordance with the directions, the trio moved towards the hole.

"By our Lady of Threadneedle Street!" Sir Philip exclaimed. "You've done the hole in two!"

Stephen looked down at the ball, a quiet and gentle gleam of affection in his eye. The caddy lifted it up and handed it to its owner. Sir Philip produced a card from his pocket and commenced to add it up.

"Good for you, Uncle!" Harold remarked, strolling across the green. "Kept your card all the way through?"

Sir Philip looked up, a massive gold pencil in his hand.

"What's the best in?" he demanded.

"Eighty, plus one — eighty-one. My little effort," Harold replied modestly.

"Then your uncle has won the Cup," Sir Philip declared. "Forty-four and forty-seven — ninety-one, less twelve — seventy-nine."

CHAPTER XXVIII

THERE was general confusion and hubbub as the news was flashed around. The last green was crowded with loiterers from the Bar and smoking room.

"The thing is ridiculous," Stephen declared. "I shall not, of course, take the Cup."

"I am afraid, my dear sir," Mr. Doll protested, "that you have no alternative. Owing to the fact that there are fourteen scores tying for third place, I extracted from your brother a promise, for the purpose of allotting the sweep, that the Cup should go to the actual winner."

"But I thought that it was Harold," George Henry remonstrated.

"'The actual winner' was the term used," Mr. Doll insisted firmly.

"Have you pledged your word to this, George Henry?" Stephen asked.

"I am afraid so," his brother admitted.

Harold suddenly appeared from the committee room, bearing the Cup. He set it down on the green baize table. A little stream of waiters, with gold-foiled bottles, made their appearance from the dining room. Harold crossed the green and shook his uncle by the hand.

"Good old sportsman!" he exclaimed, patting him on the back with his disengaged hand. "Ninety-one gross on a day like this after six months' golf! Tophole! Look here, I've given the word to the steward there. They're opening the bubbly. That's all right, what?"

Stephen, confused for a moment, suddenly realized the situation.

" By all means," he assented hastily. " But, Harold — stop! The Cup must be yours."

" Not on your life," Harold replied. " I'm pinching the sweep, or most of it. Two thirds of seventy pounds. Come on and gaze at your treasure."

They all stood round the Cup.

" Jimmy, my lad," Harold went on, addressing his friend, " I've got a quid on with you that it will hold a dozen. They've just poured in the seventh bottle and it looks like nothing but a puddle."

" You win all right," Jimmy assented gloomily. " It's not my day out."

Stephen, on the outskirts of the crowd, drew Mr. Doll on one side. There were little beads of perspiration upon his forehead and his hair had been blown about by the wind.

" Mr. Doll," he exclaimed, " this is most embarrassing! A most unlooked-for *dénouement*. It is absurd for me to take my own Cup."

" It is very frequently done," Mr. Doll assured him. " And in the present instance it was the unanimous wish of the whole of the players occupying the next position. You see, they come from all parts of the country and they none of them wanted to play another round this afternoon. I am afraid you must accept the inevitable."

Stephen groaned.

" Of course, I am very proud," he said. " But ——"

" If I might make a suggestion," Mr. Doll interrupted, " you might, if you cared to, offer some little prize for an Open Meeting next year."

Stephen became instantly more cheerful.

" My dear Mr. Doll!" he exclaimed. " Next year!

284 THE INEVITABLE MILLIONAIRES

Nonsense! Let us have an Autumn Open Meeting. I will give a Cup the exact replica of this one, and my brother George Henry shall also give a prize. We will decide upon its nature later. I shall also provide trifles for a competition amongst the ladies."

" It is most generous of you, Mr. Underwood," Mr. Doll declared. " We shall speedily become the most popular club in Surrey."

The announcement was received with great enthusiasm. Glasses were distributed right and left. Harold, with a ladle which he had borrowed from the kitchen, served out champagne with untiring hand. George Henry sidled over to his brother.

" It is long past our usual hour for lunch, Stephen," he whispered. " Our digestions ——"

" I am entirely of your opinion," Stephen agreed. " Let us slip away."

They found a quiet corner in the dining room and many people anxious to wait upon them.

" George Henry," Stephen announced solemnly, " I am beginning to believe in Fate."

" I do not wonder at it," George Henry groaned, helping himself to salad. " This is quite an amazing joint of lamb, Stephen. Pray do not neglect it."

" I will not," Stephen promised.

There was a brief and interesting silence. Stephen pursued the subject later.

" We support theatrical enterprises and they prosper," he pointed out. " We organize an Open Air Theatre in England and, if we had not been firm with Mr. Hiram Pluck, we should have made a large fortune instead of a small one. We pay away a matter of five hundred pounds for a golf cup and back it comes."

" It is extraordinary," George Henry confessed. " I

have been in the open air for over two hours. I shall take a little more lamb."

" I am bound to say," Stephen went on, a moment or two later, " that Harold took his natural disappointment extraordinarily well."

" I entirely agree with you," was the hearty assent. " It was all the more remarkable because he considered the competition over and the Cup his."

" I am very pleased with Harold," Stephen declared. " It is a great thing to have a nephew who is plus one at golf."

" It is something to be proud of," George Henry agreed.

" We have been inclined to lose our sense of proportion when too much immersed in business affairs," Stephen continued. " Harold has given proof to-day of what I believe would be called, ' good sportsmanship.' I shall ——"

" *We* will," George Henry intervened promptly, " seek a means of recompensing him."

Sir Philip Woodman came in, bluff and hearty. He had drunk a couple of glasses of champagne and felt better.

" Here you are! " he exclaimed, drawing up a chair. " I'll come and lunch at your table."

" With pleasure," Stephen assented.

" Delighted," George Henry echoed. " I should like to recommend the cold lamb."

" I'll eat anything," Sir Philip declared. " I'm ravenous. Nice club, this. Your little spec. I hear, Mr. Underwood. You keep these things very dark in the City."

" My brother and I own the debentures, that is all," Stephen explained.

" I know all about it," was the good-humoured comment. " I've been talking to Doll. I'll take half of them, if you like."

" You think it will be a good speculation, then? " Stephen observed, a little sadly.

" A dead snip," Sir Philip assured them. " You'll make a lot of money out of your golf, Mr. Underwood. What with thousand-pound pots, and owning prosperous links! — Why, it's almost as good as Basinghall Street! "

" Make money," Stephen repeated drearily.

" A lot of money," George Henry echoed.

" Not a shadow of a doubt about it," Sir Philip declared. " You're on a sure thing."

Stephen looked across at his brother.

" George Henry," he announced, " I shall take a large glass of port to-day."

" So shall I," George Henry agreed valiantly.

CHAPTER XXIX

GEORGE HENRY's deliberate and kindly essay at philanthropy seemed likely to turn out a complete success. From the little enclosed office which she occupied in solitary state, Miss Peggy Robinson compiled and copied the lists handed to her day by day, slowly, perhaps, but with undeviating accuracy. She was punctual and unobtrusive and, as the weeks went on, she recovered her health in a quite remarkable manner. Morning after morning George Henry opened the door of her office, bowed and wished her good morning. Morning after morning she looked up from her work, flashed back a cheerful response to his greeting and bent once more over her work. Very often he sought in vain for some excuse to linger. If ever one occurred to him, it eluded him at the critical moment. Gradually he arrived at the conviction that, for some reason or other, it was her wish to keep their relations entirely those of employer and employee. In course of time he ceased even to open the door as he passed. It seemed to him that the thrashing of the typewriter keys grew even more vigorous if he paused for a second outside the closed door.

Stephen alluded one morning to the success of his brother's experiment.

" George Henry," he said, " I am exceedingly pleased with Miss Robinson's typewriting. Her numerals are clear and distinct. She shows marked intelligence in the compilation of the lists submitted to her."

" I am glad," George Henry murmured.

"Her deportment, too, is admirable," Stephen continued. "As you know, we have steadily held out against girl clerks and feminine labour of every description. I yielded to your suggestion without demur but with considerable misgivings. I confess those misgivings were ill-founded."

"It is very pleasant to hear you say so, Stephen," George Henry sighed.

"It is time, I think," Stephen continued, "that she was consulted about her summer holiday. The other members of the staff are making their arrangements. You will not forget to mention our custom of paying double salary during vacation time. Miss Robinson has earned this recognition."

"I will speak to her this afternoon," George Henry promised.

It was an opportunity which he had greatly desired, yet, now that it had come, he was slow to avail himself of it. It was nearly five o'clock when, after a very considerable amount of hesitation, he knocked at the door of the small office and entered. Almost as he turned the handle, he was attracted by a sound which he had not heard for many months. Peggy was laughing, musically, wonderfully, in the fashion that had attracted him so much on that first visit to the " Milan." He stepped inside, pausing for a moment on the threshold. Harold was seated upon the desk with a cup of tea in his hand. Peggy was leaning back in her chair, her lips still parted, her eyes dancing.

"I beg your pardon," George Henry said, with involuntary stiffness.

The laugh faded away. Peggy looked at him with anxious, questioning eyes. Harold was in nowise discomposed.

"Tea interval," he explained pleasantly. "I've persuaded Miss Robinson to make the tea in the afternoons. That stuff old Peter brings in isn't fit to drink."

George Henry was aware that he had no cause for fault-finding. The quarter of an hour's interval for tea was a universally accepted custom in the warehouses and countinghouses. He turned away.

"There was something I had to say to Miss Robinson," he said. "It will do later or to-morrow morning."

"Please, no," Peggy declared, jumping to her feet. "The time is nearly up, Mr. Harold. Please take your tea outside."

Harold picked up his cup and departed, closing the door behind him. Peggy was still watching George Henry's expression anxiously.

"I haven't done wrong in making the tea, have I?" she asked timidly. "I wasn't really wasting time," she added, glancing at the clock.

"Of course not," George Henry assured her. "The tea interval is an established custom. My brother and I were discussing the subject of summer vacations, Miss Robinson," he continued. "You will be entitled to a fortnight. Can you give us any idea when you would like to have it?"

"Thank you," she replied, "I do not need any summer vacation. I should like to go on working."

"My brother and I will be away for the whole of August," George Henry went on. "It will be convenient for us if you will take either the first or the last fortnight in that month."

"But I don't want a holiday," Peggy repeated. "Am I to be driven out of the place?"

"You will need a change of air by the time August

arrives," George Henry declared. "Mr. Fenwick, the cashier, will explain our arrangements with regard to holiday salary."

"Have I done anything wrong, Mr. George Henry?" she asked, a little timidly.

All the laughter had gone out of her face now.

"Certainly not," he replied. "My brother has just expressed himself as exceedingly well satisfied with your work."

"I am so glad," she murmured. "But how about you? Of course I don't expect you to come and talk to me during office hours — although you always used to come and say good morning — but you seem, somehow, different — as though I had done something!"

"That is quite a mistake," he assured her.

"When there is no one else here," she persisted, "I think you might say 'Miss Peggy', if not 'Peggy.'"

"My dear Miss Peggy," he said, "we are entirely satisfied with your work and we hope that you are comfortable."

"Nothing else?" she asked softly.

He felt himself in the toils of an intolerable nervousness. For the life of him he could not be natural, could not put into words a tithe of his feelings, felt himself battling to keep the kindness from his tone.

"Nothing else," he answered, almost harshly.

She drooped her head and bent over the typewriter. George Henry went back to the private office.

"Well?" his brother inquired.

"Miss Robinson will take her holiday either the beginning or the end of August," George Henry announced.

"Good!" Stephen exclaimed. "The most suitable time."

"I see the car is here," George Henry remarked, looking out of the window.

Stephen smiled.

"I hope you will approve," he said. "It is a fine evening and I have already signed the letters. I thought we might run down and have a round of golf — say nine holes, at any rate. You look a little tired, George Henry. I think that it would do you good."

"It is very thoughtful of you," George Henry replied. "I shall enjoy it immensely."

George Henry was certainly not himself. He scarcely spoke during the long drive down, made the necessary changes to his toilet in silence, and proceeded to the tee without enthusiasm. He topped his first drive without complaint and holed a long putt on the green without exaltation. By the end of the round Stephen was beginning to get worried.

"George Henry," he said, "you were off your game."

"I was certainly playing badly," his brother admitted.

"You were playing without concentration," Stephen continued. "You swung at the ball as though you were indifferent in what direction it went. Golf cannot be approached in that spirit."

"You were playing well enough, anyway," George Henry remarked, making an effort to change the conversation.

"I did nine holes in forty-one," was the half-meditative, half-vainglorious admission.

"You are too good for your handicap," George Henry declared.

"My handicap is to be lowered," Stephen confessed proudly. "Mr. Doll thinks that eight would be a liberal allowance for me."

" I congratulate you," George Henry murmured.

" Golf," Stephen acknowledged, as they took their places in the car for the homeward journey, " has brought a wonderful new interest into our lives."

" Wonderful," George Henry echoed.

" In the old days," Stephen proceeded, " I was sometimes conscious, especially as the fine weather came, of a desire for something which did not seem to come in the ordinary routine of our lives. I was puzzled how to explain my discontent. The problem is now solved. I feel that golf has filled up that empty space."

George Henry sighed.

" It is curious," he admitted, " that I, too, have been conscious of some sensation of the sort — a restlessness even after the most satisfactory day's work and good night's rest. Golf, of course, is a great resource. I am not sure, however, that it is completely satisfying."

" If you would take the wrist matter a little more seriously," Stephen suggested, " and play your mashies off the right foot ——"

" I will try that," George Henry promised. " I have, perhaps, a slight attack of liver."

" Such an ailment at this time of the year is not uncommon," Stephen remarked. " It might be advisable to consult a physician."

George Henry shook his head.

" It is not serious enough for that," he declared.

" Perhaps a simple remedy would be effective," Stephen suggested. " The medicine chest is in your room."

" I will look through it," was the somewhat spiritless rejoinder.

George Henry leaned back in his place and closed his eyes. He was very well aware that, for the first time in his life, he was not being entirely frank with his

brother. His indisposition was of the mind and not of
the body. No visit to the physician or the application
of any of those carefully selected remedies with which
their joint medicine chest was stocked was likely to be
of any service to him. He was haunted with thoughts
which had first flitted dimly through his mind on that
day when he and his brother had broken through the
grey routine of their lives and migrated westwards for
their midday meal. He remembered turning his head
at the first sound of Peggy's laugh — a little peal of
music, it had seemed to him. The memory of that frank
and yet not forward smile remained with him all the
time. He was dizzy to think what might not have happened but for his own colossal folly, but for that ungenerous and miserable little plot, the memory of which
had many times been a torment to him. — He had found
her propinquity during the last few months strangely
disturbing. Incased though she was in that dull little
office, invisible sometimes for the whole day, still the feeling that she was close at hand seemed all the time to
have ministered to that growing sense of restlessness
and dissatisfaction. But it was only this afternoon that
the pain had come — a pain poignant but incompre-
hensible, commencing at the sound of her laugh, Harold's careless attitude, the sense of familiarity between
the two, justified entirely by their age and kindred
tastes, which had suddenly turned all his vague longings
into pain. It was a sharp medicine but a wholesome
one, he tried to tell himself. She belonged to a different
order of things. She might feel grateful to him, but it
was the law of nature that she should turn to youth.
The law of nature! It was a horrible, joy-destroying
phrase. It sounded in his ears like a knell, as they sped
through the blue and scented twilight. It sounded in

his ears again as, after some slight changes to their
toilet, Stephen led the way cheerfully into the grillroom
for their evening meal.

" A capital idea, this," the latter declared, as they
seated themselves. " That round of golf and the drive
have given me quite an appetite, George Henry. You
must recover your interest in the game. Wrist! That
is what you must fix your mind on. What do you say
to a grilled sole and a cutlet to follow? "

George Henry, at that moment, was not capable of
saying anything. He was looking across the room towards a table in a distant corner, where Harold and
Peggy, their heads very close, were dining together.

CHAPTER XXX

Summer progressed with all the glory of unclouded skies and burning sun. The heat seemed to radiate from the pavements of Basinghall Street and Mincing Lane, but the brothers Underwood zealously continued their task of money-getting. Towards the middle of July, however, Stephen began to show signs of uneasiness. He looked at the calendar one morning as he and his brother divested themselves of their grey Homburg hats and tucked their gloves neatly behind the pegs.

"George Henry," he confided, "I feel that any day now we may receive a visit from Mr. Duncan with the balance sheet."

"I saw him in the street yesterday," George Henry replied. "I was afraid that he was coming here."

"It is not our fault," Stephen continued, a little bitterly, "if the prices of rubber and indigo remain high, and if our venture in nitrate has turned out a success. We must trade to the best of our ability, and it would be absurd not to exercise our best judgment."

"Unfortunately," George Henry sighed, "we seem to have a sort of second sight in these matters."

"We are like the man whom our grandfather used to talk about," Stephen remarked, "who used always to know if there was going to be a drop in raw materials by a pain in his toe. Our instincts appear to be always well founded."

"Our private drawings," George Henry pointed out, "are larger by far than they have ever been."

"I doubt whether they are sufficiently large to satisfy Mr. Duncan," Stephen replied.

"We must not be bullied by Mr. Duncan," George Henry declared, with some spirit. "We do our best. We can't eat any more, we can't drink any more, we can't drive in more than one car at a time, we can't live in more than one flat at a time. Mr. Duncan is unreasonable."

"I am entirely with you," Stephen agreed. "All the same, I was wondering — the heat is very trying. Supposing we anticipate our annual holiday? Mr. Duncan will have cooled off a little by the time we get back."

George Henry looked thoughtfully out of the window. He had apparently recovered from his recent indisposition, but his mouth was a little stern and there seemed to be one or two additional lines round his eyes. The gap' of years between himself and his brother seemed to have become filled up.

"I should be glad to get away," he admitted, a little abruptly. "Where did you think of going, Stephen?"

"My inclinations would lie towards a quiet golfing holiday," his brother confessed. "As against that, of course, we should be spending no money."

"I suppose," George Henry ruminated dolefully, "that we ought to go abroad."

"Stop! Stop!" Stephen exclaimed, striking the table with his fist. "We must be firm, George Henry. We must not make ourselves slaves to this necessity of spending money. I will not go abroad. Neither you nor I can speak the language. We do not care about the food. We are strange to the mode of traffic. We will take our holiday where we enjoy it."

"Some of these Scotch hotels, I understand," George Henry said hopefully, "are quite expensive."

"Not if you stay *en pension*," Stephen replied. "They insist then upon reduced terms."

"Let us," George Henry suggested, "take the car and motor from place to place. They will charge us double prices if we stay for only a night or two and, in cases where they are full up, we shall have to pay a great deal extra for accommodation."

"It sounds reasonable," Stephen assented. "It is an idea."

"We can take Robert with us as well as Smithers," George Henry went on. "We should have to pay his board and wages if he remained here. Scotch hotel proprietors are a clever race of people. They will charge us more if we appear with two servants."

"Capital!" Stephen approved. "Let me see. Next Monday are the sales. On Tuesday I think that we might start. — Goodness gracious!"

Stephen had turned his head to answer the knock at the door. The visitor who was being introduced, however, had brushed past the confidential clerk. She was a middle-aged woman, fashionably but severely dressed. She wore eyeglasses, and, in some respects, she was ridiculously like her brothers.

"Amelia!" Stephen exclaimed. "My dear girl!"

"Amelia!" George Henry echoed. "Do sit down."

Amelia came and pecked both brothers on the forehead.

"You never come to see me, either of you," she declared, as she carefully dusted a chair with a newspaper and sat down.

"Our time is much occupied," Stephen explained hastily.

"We are very busy," George Henry assured her.

"Busy or not," Amelia said sternly, "you seem to have changed the fashion of your life very considerably."

"We have been compelled to launch out a little," Stephen acknowledged.

"Well, it isn't my business," she remarked. "We agreed to go our own ways years ago. You were different then, though. What I have come to see you about doesn't concern ourselves. It concerns Harold."

"Harold, my dear Amelia," Stephen told her, "is giving us far greater satisfaction."

"We have improved his position," George Henry declared.

"Some day or another we hope to invite him to join the firm," Stephen confided.

"I am glad to hear of this, of course," their sister admitted. "But what I want to know is, are you helping him in this folly? Are you with him or against him? I only want to know."

"What folly?" they both inquired, almost in unison.

She deliberately opened a pair of lorgnettes and looked at them each in turn.

"Do you mean to say that you don't know?" she demanded.

"We have no idea at all," Stephen assured her.

"None whatever," George Henry echoed, with a sinking heart.

"My son Harold," Amelia announced, "has actually had the presumption to tell me that he is thinking of marriage."

"Harold! Marriage!" Stephen exclaimed.

This time George Henry remained silent.

"The thing is, of course, ridiculous," his mother continued. "Still, the other night at the theatre, I saw him with a young person in the stalls. She was plainly dressed — quite shabbily, in fact — but she had an air of the stage. I remonstrated with Harold and he had the impertinence to tell me that he was thinking of getting engaged to the young person in question."

" Do you know who she was? " George Henry asked mournfully.

" Your typist," Amelia declared, shutting up her lorgnettes with a snap.

" It is the first we have heard of it," Stephen assured his sister fervently.

" Absolutely the first," George Henry agreed.

" Let her be brought in here," Amelia directed. " I should like an interview with her."

Stephen and George Henry exchanged glances. Their decision appeared to be unanimous.

" I do not think that that would be quite fair upon the young lady," Stephen said. " Harold is the person with whom we have to deal."

" Nonsense! " Amelia exclaimed. " The young woman must have led him on shamefully. It is as well for her to understand that nothing can come of it. Absolutely nothing! "

Stephen shook his head.

" The days have gone when that sort of attitude was admissible," he reminded his sister. " If Harold has made advances to the young lady, no one can possibly blame her for accepting them."

" A typist! " Amelia gasped.

" A young lady earning her living by typewriting," Stephen said coldly, " is, in our opinion, entitled to as much consideration as the young lady who sits at home in luxury, waiting for a husband. We can bring no pressure to bear upon Miss Robinson, nor can we allow her to be bullied."

" You won't dismiss her? " Amelia demanded.

" Certainly not," Stephen replied. " We will speak

to Harold, if you like. He is certainly too young to marry. We had no idea — no idea at all — that things had gone so far."

"Not the slightest idea," George Henry echoed.

Amelia was dissatisfied and furious.

"You are just the same as ever," she declared angrily. "No wonder we quarrelled, no wonder we left off seeing anything of one another! You are full of the ideas of a hundred years ago."

"On the contrary," Stephen retorted. "I think that we are in advance of the times, if anything, in this matter. However, we will not argue."

"You never would," Amelia snapped. "That's what always made you so irritating — both of you. You won't even let me see the young person?"

"Certainly not," was Stephen's decision. "We will talk to Harold, if you wish it. We have no right whatever to interfere with the young lady — neither have you."

"I could tell her what I think of her," Amelia muttered.

"She might retaliate," George Henry observed.

"I can't think what you employ such a creature for," Amelia persisted. "She's been on the stage, hasn't she? Harold couldn't deny it."

"We are satisfied with her character," Stephen pointed out. "Her antecedents are not our concern."

"And that's all I get for coming to see you!" Amelia grumbled, rising to her feet.

"We will speak to Harold with pleasure," Stephen promised. "He's too young to marry and we shall not hesitate to tell him so."

"A lot of good that will do," his sister scoffed. "I

am sorry I came. You're both just as pig-headed and difficult as ever. Good morning."

George Henry made a point of escorting his sister to her car. When he returned, he found Harold already installed in the private office.

"Saw the old dear coming in," he explained, " so I thought I might as well face the music, what!"

"Are we to understand, Harold," Stephen asked him point-blank, " that you wish to marry Miss Robinson?"

"Look here, nunks," Harold replied, " I am going to forget that this is Basinghall Street and talk to you as man to man — you understand? I am not going to have the mater down here bullying Miss Robinson."

"We have already declined to let your mother interview the young lady," Stephen told him.

"Do we understand," George Henry asked, without turning around, " that you are engaged to marry Miss Robinson?"

"I am going to be," Harold asserted, " and nobody is going to stop me."

"Steady, steady, my lad!" Stephen protested. " Sit down. Don't begin by looking for trouble. Neither your uncle nor I have a word to say against Miss Robinson."

"She's as straight as they make 'em," Harold declared, " and a good-plucked 'un, too."

"Your defence of the young lady is quite unnecessary," Stephen assured his nephew. " Both your Uncle George Henry and I have the highest opinion of her. The only question is whether your age and prospects justify your thinking of marriage?"

"May have to wait a bit," Harold admitted. " We don't mind that. What a man needs in life," he pointed out, " is something to sort of keep him steady. One soon gets tired of racketing about. I have done my share. Ready to settle down to-morrow."

" How old are you? " Stephen inquired politely.

" Twenty-three," Harold replied. " That is, you know, in actual years. I've knocked about a good deal, though. Seen quite enough of the gay life."

" And the young lady? " George Henry asked, still without turning his head.

" That's all right, as soon as I feel that I can say the word," Harold declared confidently. " I haven't dared to raise her hopes too high. You see, if you two and the mater were all unreasonable, we might have to put the thing off for a bit."

" I see," George Henry murmured.

" Very considerate of you," Stephen remarked.

" Is it my fancy," Harold inquired, with some return to his former manner, " or is there an undercurrent of sarcasm floating about? "

" It is possible," Stephen acknowledged, " that we may be finding it difficult to take you altogether seriously. Twenty-three is very young to think of marriage, Harold."

" Maybe," Harold acquiesced stolidly. " I'm thinking of it, all the same."

" Against your mother's wishes."

" Not too much of the paternal touch," Harold begged. " You know very well that even you two couldn't get on with the mater, especially since she took up Christian Science. She isn't human about these little things."

" The fact remains," Stephen insisted, " that she is your mother and entitled to a certain amount of consideration from you."

" That's all right," Harold remarked truculently,

" but she isn't going to have anything to say about the girl I marry."

" I think that Harold is right," George Henry observed. " That is a matter on which he must choose entirely for himself. I suggest," he continued, " that you leave us for a time, Harold. Your Uncle Stephen and I will talk this matter over and let you know our decision."

Harold left the room with much less than his usual jauntiness. Stephen watched him with a puzzled expression.

" Harold is distinctly changed," he observed.

" He seems to have lost a great deal of his flightiness," George Henry agreed.

The confidential clerk appeared with his arms full of papers.

" We will adjourn our discussion," Stephen suggested, " until after lunch, if agreeable to you, George Henry."

" It would be best," his brother agreed, already, apparently, immersed in one of the lists.

CHAPTER XXXI

STEPHEN and George Henry, about a fortnight later, very dusty after a long day's motoring, looked around them with interest as the car approached the front of a large and very handsome hotel, built on the extreme edge of the moor which they had been traversing, in the shadow of the hills. Only a few hundred yards distant was the sea and, stretching away from the grounds, what appeared to be a remarkably fine golf course.

"The place seems to be well kept and prosperous," Stephen announced.

"With such a situation and the golf links close at hand," George Henry said cheerfully, "it can scarcely fail to be expensive."

Stephen appeared dubious.

"So far," he remarked, "the accounts which we have heard of the rapacity of Scotch innkeepers seem to be somewhat exaggerated."

"If only, in our younger days," George Henry sighed, "we had had some little experience with the gun."

"Or the rod," Stephen put in.

"The rent of some of these moors with sporting lodges is most satisfactorily exorbitant," George Henry pointed out. "The gillies, too, have a gleam in their eyes which suggests extras. I could not understand the whole conversation of the keeper whom we talked to on the moor that day, but I gathered that it was the liberal-handed gentleman who saw the most sport."

"If we should hear of a moor with a golf links included," Stephen observed, "we might consider the matter for next year. Harold has had some experience in shooting and, if we could overcome our aversion to firearms, there are many schools round London where instruction is imparted."

They drew up at the front door of the hotel. The place had certainly a very superior and well-kept appearance. A hall porter in livery opened the door.

"Have you engaged rooms, gentlemen?" he inquired dubiously.

"Not yet," Stephen replied.

"We're verra full," he went on.

"Good!" Stephen declared. "We like to see plenty of people around."

"And we serve no meals except to residents — residents in the hotel. Tourists must go on to the village. It's four miles and there is a respectable inn there."

"An excellent arrangement," Stephen conceded, leading the way into the hall.

One or two superior-looking people, mostly in golfing attire of a pronounced character, glanced at them from behind their papers. A tall, dark young man, very pale and with smoothly brushed black hair, came forward to accost them.

"We are looking for rooms," Stephen explained.

The young man regarded them with a pitying smile.

"We are quite full up," he replied. "We do not take tourists."

"Capital!" Stephen approved. "We dislike hotels where people are always coming and going. We wish to take rooms for a month. We may not be able to stay so long, but we will pay for the rooms in advance if desired."

The young man glanced towards the entrance and

saw things which prompted him to modify his tone. The Rolls-Royce looked very handsome in the sunlight. A correct-looking manservant was standing discreetly in the background.

"I am not sure that anything could be arranged, sir," he said hesitatingly. "What accommodation did you desire?"

"Two large bedrooms overlooking the sea," Stephen replied, "each with a bathroom, if possible — if not, one bathroom between the two; a sitting room, and accommodation for a manservant and a chauffeur."

"If you will come this way I will show you the best I can offer," the young man promised politely.

They ascended in the lift and inspected with a disparaging air the apartments offered.

"Poky," Stephen declared. "Very poky."

"We are not looking for your least expensive rooms," George Henry explained. "My brother and I like air and space."

The young man turned away from the rooms which they had been inspecting.

"We have a suite here," he announced. "The best in the house. It will be occupied a little later on by the gentleman who owns the shooting. It happens to be vacant for a short time now, if you would care to see it."

The suite was instantly approved of.

"And the terms?" Stephen asked anxiously.

The young man named a figure — named it a little defiantly, as though he expected his prospective guests to shrink away. Stephen passed his arm through his brother's and led him into a corner.

"This is much better than anything we have come across yet, George Henry," he pointed out. "We have been obliged to leave three places because of the low prices. I think that we might settle down here for the rest of our holiday."

"There will, no doubt, be extras," George Henry remarked hopefully. "I feel that we should do well to leave that in the hands of the management."

"We will take the suite on the terms you mention," Stephen decided, turning back to their cicerone. "Please have our luggage sent up."

The young man was a little staggered, but he bore up.

"There are a few extras ——" he began.

"No doubt, no doubt," Stephen interrupted. "We can hear about those later."

"Meals served in the rooms," the young man persisted. "Service up here is so difficult that we are compelled to charge double price."

"Quite so," Stephen agreed.

"Very reasonable," George Henry acquiesced.

"We will dine in the sitting room to-night," Stephen decided. "And we will have our breakfast served here every morning. See that our things are sent up at once, if you please. My brother and I would like to inspect the golf course."

The young man bowed and left them. The brothers stepped out on to the balcony. Stephen, especially, was in excellent spirits.

"Delightful situation!" he exclaimed, looking around. "Beautiful air! We get the ozone here, too, George Henry, and a fine view of the golf links."

"A most desirable spot," George Henry agreed.

"And really expensive," Stephen declared. "One might almost call it exorbitant."

"We are most fortunate," George Henry murmured.

The brothers strolled down to the golf links an hour

later. They found the clubhouse small, owing to its proximity to the hotel, but there was a delightful lawn where many people were sitting about in wicker chairs, and the place generally had a well-kept and prosperous appearance. The secretary, who was installed in an exceedingly comfortable office, welcomed them genially but with some restraint. He was a slim, ruddy-complexioned man, wearing a single, unattached eyeglass, and attired in the largest checks and the fluffiest stockings either George Henry or Stephen had ever beheld.

" You wish to play golf, gentlemen? " he inquired, swinging around in his chair.

" We should like to very much," Stephen replied. " What are your terms by the week or month? "

The secretary named them. They were high, but not sensationally so.

" We will take two tickets for a month," Stephen announced.

The secretary drew a book towards him.

" You can start any morning after eleven," he said, " and in the afternoons after three, if playing with a member."

" Stop! " Stephen exclaimed. " I gather then that there are restrictions upon visitors' play."

" That is so," the secretary admitted. " We have a certain number of members whose interests must be considered."

" Quite so," Stephen agreed. " It will, perhaps, be better if my brother and I join the club."

The secretary smiled tolerantly.

" The entrance fee," he told them, " is a little high. It has just been raised to ten guineas. The subscription is five guineas a year."

Stephen nodded approvingly.

"We should both like to join," he announced.

The secretary permitted himself to show some surprise.

"You belong, I presume, to some recognized golf club?"

"I am the president of the Fursedown Hill Golf Club," Stephen told him modestly. "We are both acquainted with Sir Philip Woodman, who, I believe, is on the committee here."

The secretary became a human being.

"Is your name Underwood?" he inquired.

"It is," Stephen acknowledged.

"Are you the gentleman who gave the wonderful Cup for competition, and then won it?"

"That was entirely an accident," Stephen protested. "You must allow me to explain. My brother and I had only started golf a few months previously, we had never played in a competition and our entrance was simply intended as a compliment to the other competitors. Whilst I was finishing my round it was arranged between my brother and the secretary, bearing in mind the fact that my nephew's was the best score in, that the actual winner of the cup should take it, whoever he might be."

"It was a question of the sweep," George Henry explained. "Several of the competitors were in a hurry to get away and desired a decision."

"It was unfortunate in its way, but unavoidable," Stephen pointed out. "I am presenting another cup for the Autumn Meeting."

"We shall be delighted to have you join us," the secretary declared. "I will put up your proposal forms this evening. In the meantime, we shall be pleased to have you play as members."

" We very much appreciate your courtesy," Stephen assured him.

" We are very much obliged," George Henry echoed.

" I hope you are going to play a few holes now," the secretary continued. " The caddy shed is round to the left. If you would like the professional to show you the course, I fancy that he is at liberty. His charges are a little high, but he is an excellent fellow."

The brothers smiled.

" We are going to like this place," Stephen observed, as they crossed a little stretch of turf before the professional's shop.

" I like it already," George Henry declared.

" Silver Queens are four shillings," Stephen confided. " I heard that man on the lawn complaining."

" The place will suit us," George Henry decided with conviction.

CHAPTER XXXII

IT was almost like the commencement of a new adventure when Stephen and George Henry stepped into their car on the morning after their return to London and started for the City. They were both becomingly tanned, and Stephen, at any rate, was in excellent spirits. Their holiday had cost them quite a satisfactory amount. They had become life members of the Scottish golf club and they had taken a deer forest, moor and lodge for next season at a rent of two thousand pounds.

"I have been greatly surprised at Harold's silence," Stephen remarked, as they glided along the Embankment. "Although we were both opposed to any formal engagement between him and Miss Robinson, you suggested, and I think quite rightly, that there was no objection to his arriving at an understanding with the young lady. The absence of any news from him is rather remarkable."

"Harold was always a bad correspondent," George Henry reminded his brother.

"He should nevertheless have acquainted us with the progress of his suit," Stephen declared. "In sympathizing with him to the extent that we have done, we shall without doubt incur Amelia's resentment. He should have thought of that. He should, I think, have shown more gratitude."

"I have no doubt," George Henry said, looking out across the river, "that he finds the progress of his love affair with Miss Robinson entirely absorbing. Still, he should have written — he certainly should have written."

Everything seemed very familiar in Basinghall Street except that George Henry failed to detect the click of the typewriter as they passed the little enclosed office. Harold, however, was in his accustomed place and joined with the rest of the staff in their chorus of respectful greetings. For an hour or more the time of the brothers was fully occupied in receiving reports from various heads of departments, to all of which Stephen gave his undivided, and George Henry his feigned, attention. When a moment of respite arrived, Stephen leaned back in his chair.

" I think," he suggested, " that it would be interesting to have a word or two with Harold."

George Henry's fingers shook a little. He seemed to be still absorbed in the latest quotations for indigo.

" Certainly," he murmured. " By all means."

Harold promptly obeyed their summons. He entered with the air of a young man who has a grievance. Stephen pointed to a chair.

" Harold," he said, " we have been expecting to hear from you."

" I meant to write," Harold admitted. " Nothing to write about, though. Besides, I don't mind admitting," he went on, " since you have opened the subject, that I have had what you might call a facer. Been deucedly hard hit, you know."

George Henry slowly raised his head.

" We understood," Stephen continued, " that, although we were not prepared to sanction any formal engagement, you were to arrive at some sort of an understanding with Miss Robinson."

" I did," Harold replied gloomily. " Got the knock

of my life. Absolutely off my feed for a week. Nothing but Brighton pulled me round."

" Are we to understand ——" Stephen began incredulously.

" Wouldn't listen to me," Harold interrupted. " Wasn't having me at any price. Didn't matter about the mater, didn't matter whether you people were willing or not, didn't matter whether I had an income or was a pauper — she wasn't having any! "

Stephen was half sceptical, half amused at his nephew's discomfiture. George Henry, on the other hand, sat with clasped hands and a strange look in his face, from which the healthy colour seemed to have momentarily vanished.

" Do you mean to say that she refused you? " Stephen demanded, point-blank.

" Handed me the mit," Harold complained. " Began by laughing at me and, when I stuck at it like a Briton, I got what I asked for — no. Can you beat it? "

" Did she give any reason? " George Henry asked, speaking for the first time.

" All the old stuff," was the gloomy reply. " Didn't want to marry a man she didn't care for. Talked about me as if I were a baby in leading strings."

" She must be a remarkably sensible young woman," Stephen declared.

" Eh? " his nephew exclaimed.

" I mean," Stephen went on, " that if she felt like that it was exceedingly sensible of her not to mind saying so. Most girls are only too anxious to escape from a life of dependence."

" Where is she now? " George Henry demanded.

" Haven't an idea," Harold confessed. " She gave a week's notice here. I expect," he added, stroking his chin, " she didn't like the idea of meeting me every day. Quite natural."

George Henry turned round and faced his nephew.

" You let her give up her post here," he said, " entirely out of niceness of feeling on your account, and you have never even taken the trouble to find out what has become of her. Doesn't that strike you, Harold, as being remarkably selfish? "

" Hadn't looked upon it in that light," Harold admitted. " Of course I was feeling pretty raw for a day or two, but there was no need for her to clear out."

" And you have no idea of her address? " George Henry persisted.

" None whatever, unless she's still at Chenies Court," the young man replied.

George Henry rose to his feet. He crossed the floor deliberately, and took down his hat from the peg.

" I will join you at luncheon, Stephen," he announced.

They both stared after him — Harold, open-mouthed, Stephen with a new comprehension.

" My aunt! " Harold gasped.

" Prophetic," Stephen murmured.

Outside, George Henry picked up a taxi and drove at once to Chenies Court. The five flights of stone steps seemed to him interminable, but he mounted them at last. He knocked timidly at her door. As before he heard the click of a typewriter, a little faster this time. Then it stopped. She came and opened the door.

" You! " she exclaimed.

" Me," George Henry admitted.

She laughed a little nervously. Then she stood on one side.

" Please come in," she invited — " on one condition."

" Condition? " he repeated.

"That you don't talk about Harold."

George Henry became a man. Peggy was looking wonderfully desirable. She was a little pale, but her eyes were as blue as ever, her hair seemed to have recovered its burnish, her quivering lips were irresistible.

"I don't want to talk of Harold," he assured her. "I want to talk of myself."

"Then come in," she begged, closing the door behind him. "I sit here sometimes and dream of that first visit of yours. It was the most wonderful thing that ever happened to anybody. You're not cross with me for leaving Basinghall Street, are you?"

"Of course not," he replied.

"I had an odd feeling about it," she went on, nervously fingering the keys of her typewriter. "I can't quite explain it. Only, day by day you marched by my office without even glancing in. And if ever you did come, Harold was about, making an idiot of himself. And, at last — well, I simply couldn't bear it any longer. I should have had to come away, even if Harold hadn't been so foolish."

"You really don't care about Harold, then?"

She laughed genuinely — laughed in the old fashion, with a glint of real mirth in her eyes.

"Care about a conceited baby like that!" she exclaimed. "Why, he isn't anything yet. He's a child."

George Henry stood very close to the typewriter.

"Peggy," he said, "I behaved very badly once. I have never felt more ashamed of anything in my life. You shall know the whole story presently, if you want to. I beg you to believe now that I am in earnest. If Harold is too young for you, I am certainly a great deal too old; but I can at least give you a comfortable home, and even luxury. Will you marry me, Peggy?"

She held him by the arms and looked up at him steadfastly, almost imploringly.

"You haven't said what I want to hear yet," she
whispered.

"It comes strangely to my lips," he faltered, "because I have never said it to any woman. But — I
love you, Peggy."

Her arms were suddenly around his neck, her face
against his.

"Why ever couldn't you have told me so before?"
she sighed. "You must have been a perfect idiot not
to see that it was you I cared for all the time."

CHAPTER XXXIII

STEPHEN was waiting lunch for his brother when the latter arrived. His few words of welcome were never finished. He looked at the late arrival with amazement.

" Dear, dear! " he exclaimed. " I never realized how much good your holiday had done you. You are looking remarkably fit and well."

George Henry beamed and sat down in silence.

" Lay another place," he directed Louis.

" Miss Robinson is going to honour us? " Stephen inquired.

" She is going to honour me, also, by becoming my wife," George Henry announced, taking the plunge.

Stephen stretched out his hand.

" God bless my soul! " he cried. " Well, well! We have talked of this, but it seems incredible. She's a nice girl, George Henry, a very nice girl. There was nothing in that nonsense of Harold's, then? "

" She had not the least idea that he was in earnest," George Henry explained. " She just treated him as a boy and, I dare say, was glad to be taken out now and then. I must confess I thought otherwise at the time."

Stephen understood the whole situation now. He was tactful enough, however, not to pursue the subject.

" Peggy will be here in a moment," his brother continued — " in fact, she is waiting outside. She insisted upon it that I should break the news to you first."

" This," Stephen remarked a little anxiously, " will give you a great advantage over me, George Henry.

You will have an establishment to keep up. I shall find it difficult to keep pace with you."

"I do not think that you need trouble," George Henry replied. "I have my misgivings at times as to whether matrimony necessarily does lead to increased expenditure. The fact of it is that Peggy is an exceedingly sensible young woman who was very soundly brought up. I have always noticed that she never seemed inclined to waste her money. — Here she is."

Both brothers rose at once to their feet. Peggy looked very charming in a plain blue serge coat and skirt, and a quiet hat. She had entered the room unobserved, and was standing before their table with a deprecating little smile upon her lips. She held out her hand shyly to Stephen. An attentive waiter hurried up with a chair.

"My dear," Stephen said warmly, "this is a great pleasure, a very great pleasure indeed. Do sit down. Please, George Henry, see that Miss Peggy sits down at once. I have heard the news, dear, and I am delighted. I am sure that you will make my brother very happy."

"How sweet of you not to mind!" she exclaimed, sinking into the chair. "I was afraid you would think that, because I have been on the stage, I was just an empty-headed, frivolous sort of person. I really am very sedate, very domesticated indeed. I am longing for a home, and I am not at all extravagant."

"Not at all extravagant," Stephen repeated without enthusiasm.

"Not extravagant," George Henry echoed gloomily. "I told you so."

"Not a bit," she declared. "However much I get for housekeeping, I am going to save out of it. And the same with my dress allowance. You are both far too generous, but I do want you to realize, Mr. Stephen," she added, turning towards him, " that I am going to try and be a help to George Henry, and I don't think he'll find it any more expensive to have a house of his own, carefully looked after, than to live here."

" This — er " — the prospective bridegroom groaned — " is not exactly what we intended."

" There is not the slightest necessity, my dear," Stephen assured her anxiously, " for you to think about money matters. It would be wrong for you to attempt to save. My brother is an exceedingly wealthy man."

" Exceedingly wealthy," George Henry repeated. " Too much money altogether."

Peggy laughed in a puzzled manner.

" I am afraid that I can't realize the situation," she confessed.

Then Stephen, patting her hand gently, told her the whole story of their troubles, commencing with the discovery of their father's letter, and George Henry capped it by explaining the story of their cunningly planned but abortive attempt to be sued for breach of promise. She listened as though to a fairy tale. When it was finished she looked a little dazed.

" Then what you really want of me," she summed up at last, " is to be extravagant? "

" Precisely! Although that wasn't the only reason I asked you to marry me," George Henry hastened to assure her.

She smiled at him brilliantly.

" Thank you, dear," she whispered. " But you do want me — to spend money? "

" We do," the brothers echoed, almost simultaneously.

After that events marched. One morning, about two months later, Stephen and George Henry, the latter just returned from his honeymoon abroad and looking almost rakish, took their places once more at their accustomed luncheon table.

" It is exceedingly pleasant," the former remarked, " to think that your marriage will not interfere with our customary midday repast together. I should very much miss our luncheons, George Henry."

" And I," was the hearty response.

" I am in excellent spirits," Stephen continued. " You will remember that I gave four thousand pounds last week for a reputed Corot, to which I took a great fancy."

" I remember it quite well," his brother assented. " Some of the papers thought the price excessive."

Stephen beamed.

" I have been credibly assured," he went on, " that, if that picture were put up again, it would fetch no more than fifteen hundred pounds at the outside, and that, even at that price, it would be hard to find purchasers. I can, therefore, consider myself two thousand five hundred pounds to the bad upon that one picture. Promising, I think, George Henry."

" Excellent ! "

" And now tell me about your wife."

George Henry glanced towards the door, where the slight commotion which generally heralded the arrival of a distinguished client was apparent.

" She shall speak for herself," he whispered.

The head waiter, two *maîtres d'hôtel*, and the ordinary waiter for their table, bent almost double, were welcoming the brilliant apparition which had just appeared. Peggy, Parisienne of the Rue de la Paix, from the ospreys in her exquisite hat to the grey suède of her perfect shoes, wearing a wonderful smoke-coloured gown, and wrapped around with chinchilla, with a tiny Pekinese under her arm, came smiling towards them. Her cavalcade of followers fell back, their chief having provided her with a comfortable chair, and hung anxiously around until she had indicated her wishes as to luncheon. Stephen grasped her hands with genuine affection, and relieved her of the little cluster of gold trifles which hung from her finger.

"Caviare, I think you said, my dear," he remarked, after the first greetings, "some grilled salmon, some asparagus, and strawberries. An excellently chosen luncheon, I am sure."

"Madam shall be served," Louis replied reverently, as he turned away with one of his famous bows.

Peggy leaned over and patted George Henry's hand.

"You nice thing," she murmured. "I didn't mean to come in for lunch to-day, but I haven't a penny left in the world."

For a moment George Henry was taken aback.

"My dear, I gave you five hundred pounds this morning," he reminded her.

She leaned back with a laugh.

"Isn't he stingy!" she exclaimed, turning to Stephen. "Five hundred pounds, indeed! Why, I'd spent it all before twelve o'clock, and there are several places I am going to this afternoon where I haven't an account. I thought we should just have time, after luncheon, to go to the bank together, before it closes."

Stephen and George Henry exchanged one long, ecstatic glance.

"George Henry," his brother said solemnly, "I congratulate you!"

" On me? " Peggy asked artlessly.

" On you and the great solution," Stephen pronounced.

THE END

Lightning Source UK Ltd.
Milton Keynes UK
UKOW051016071011

179924UK00001B/112/P